But is he

But is he God?

A Fresh Look at the Identity of Jesus

David J. Lambourn

Paternoster:
thinking faith

20 19 18 17 16 15 14   7 6 5 4 3 2 1

First published 2014 by Paternoster
Paternoster is an imprint of Authentic Media Limited
52 Presley Way, Crownhill, Milton Keynes, MK8 0ES.
www.authenticmedia.co.uk

British Library Cataloguing in Publication Data

A catalogue record for this book is available from the British Library

ISBN 978-1-84227-833-8
978-1-78078-082-5 (e-book)

Cover Design by David McNeill (www.revocreative.co.uk)
Printed and bound by CPI Group (UK) Ltd., Croydon, CR0 4YY

Contents

Preface

Two thousand years after he walked the earth, the life of Jesus of Nazareth continues to challenge, fascinate and perplex us. No year seems to be complete without some new and controversial theory appearing about him. In the art, literature and theological reflection of every age he has appeared in a myriad of guises, eluding every attempt to pin him down.

But all too often today, the most provocative questions of all are pushed to one side, or dismissed out of hand. Is he, as Christians of many different traditions over the centuries have believed, the human face of God? Could the Creator and Sustainer of the entire universe really have come to earth as a human being? If so, what would be the implications for us today? These are questions which challenged me for many years, and they continue to challenge many today.

For Jews, Muslims, and even many who would call themselves 'Christian', such ideas are shocking ones. How can a real historical figure also be in charge of the universe? Why would God choose to reveal himself as a human being? If Jesus is God, how can the Father be 'God' as well? At best, such ideas seem foolish, and at worst, blasphemous.

The Bible itself, however, is not silent on these issues. Much of the evidence for Jesus' ultimate identity is not immediately obvious, and yet when considered as a whole it becomes more and more compelling. And the issue is clearly one of the utmost importance: Christ's question to his disciples, 'Who do you say I am?' (Matt. 16.15), is, I believe, addressed to every single one of us.

This book, then, is something of a detective story. I invite the reader to join me in sifting through a large body of evidence spanning many centuries of history, and to come to his or her own conclusions. In the first six chapters we will trace a series of clues scattered through the Old Testament that point towards a mysterious divine figure who seems to share all the characteristics of God himself, and yet who remains somehow distinct from him. In chapters seven to nine we will examine the amazing similarities between the descriptions of Jesus in the New Testament and those of Yahweh, the God of Israel, in the Old, and consider the central place of Christ in the worship of the early church. Finally, in chapters ten and eleven, we will discuss the main objections that have been raised to the idea of Christ as 'God', before seeing what conclusions we can draw. Chapter twelve ends with a personal challenge to the reader to follow through the implications of what we have discovered.

Countless volumes have been written down the centuries exploring some of these issues, but they have almost always been aimed at a narrow audience of trained theologians, using language beyond the grasp of many ordinary Christians. In just one small branch of theology, for example, the unsuspecting reader is likely to encounter such puzzling terms as *synoptic problem* (would I need to see a doctor?), *M* and *Q* (don't they appear in James Bond films?), or *redactor* and *pericope* (forgotten prehistoric animals, perhaps?). In this volume I have attempted to present the evidence in a clear and logical manner and in simple, non-technical language, without trying to dilute the content.

I have aimed the material in this book at several groups of readers. It will be particularly helpful for those wanting to discover the reasons behind the belief held firmly for centuries across the vast majority of Christian traditions that Christ is 'true God from true God', and to equip those wishing to explain such beliefs to others (such as Jehovah's Witnesses) who may think differently. But it might also be of help to those Witnesses and others of a similar persuasion who want to question the scriptural basis of their understanding of Christ, and, in particular, to those interested in exploring the issue from a Jewish perspective.

With a few exceptions, I have attempted to provide a broad overview of the issues involved, rather than examining individual passages under the microscope. For those who enjoy picking Bible verses apart in more detail, there is a dedicated website associated with this book at **www.but-is-he-God.org** which explores some of the most contentious verses about the deity of Christ in greater depth than would have been possible within the main body of the text. As a handy reference guide, I have included on the site a large number of side-by-side comparisons which enable the reader to see more directly how closely many descriptions of Jesus in the Bible (and statements made by him) resemble those of God himself. A selection of these verses also appears in summary form at the end of each chapter, together with a set of questions prompting the reader to reflect on what they have just read. These might also be useful for study and discussion in small groups.

I can in addition recommend three other books for those who would like to explore the subject in more depth. Of these, the most immediately approachable is *Putting Jesus in His Place: The Case for the Deity of Christ* by Robert Bowman and Ed Komoszewski (Grand Rapids, Michigan: Kregel, 2007). Another helpful study is Robert Reymond's *Jesus, Divine Messiah: The New and Old Testament Witness* (Tain: Christian Focus Publications, 2003) which takes a more detailed look at some of the critical passages in question. And a standard nineteenth-century volume on the subject, *The Divinity of Our Lord and Saviour Jesus Christ* by Henry J. Liddon, is available in various formats online. I refer to all of these works repeatedly in the latter half of this book.

Throughout this volume I have held to a traditional point of view with regard to the truth, inspiration and overall harmony of Scripture, and the authorship of its various books. Today, most scholars would call this into question, but I would argue that this was the perspective held by Jesus himself, by those who wrote about him, and by much of the early church. It is from their vantage point, first and foremost, that I wish to survey the evidence. Admittedly, it may not be fashionable to view the Bible as a connected whole, or to see it as expressing the authentic voice of God, but remarkable patterns begin to emerge when we are prepared to consider Scripture on its own terms. To those who find this approach naïve and ill-considered, I would ask simply that they suspend disbelief and read this book with an open mind.

I have also made considerable reference to literature outside the Bible, both Jewish and Christian, where it throws light on the issues being covered. A large collection of Jewish traditions was gradually brought together in written form in the centuries following the life of Jesus. Following standard practice, I have labelled quotations from these with the lower-case letters *m*, *t*, *j* or *b*, which refer to the Mishnah, Tosefta, Jerusalem Talmud and Babylonian Talmud respectively (as is clear from the list of sources which follows). All Bible quotations, unless otherwise indicated, are taken from the New International Version. I do, however, make frequent use of other translations (notably the Revised Standard Version), details of which appear in the Appendix.

At a number of points we will encounter the special Jewish name for God, 'YHWH'. Although probably pronounced originally as 'Yahweh', it came to be considered so sacred by the Jews that only the high priest dared to utter it, on a single day of the year. In a small number of English translations, most notably the American Standard Version and the New World Translation, this word is rendered consistently as 'Jehovah', but since such a version of the name has no sound historical basis, I have kept the name 'Yahweh' in most places, alongside the familiar alternative of 'LORD' (in capitals) commonly found in English Bibles.

I would like in conclusion to express my grateful thanks to my uncle, Ray Lambourn, for his considerable assistance in the various stages of this book, and also to my family and friends for their continual love and support. I would also like to thank David Pawson for his invaluable suggestions at an earlier phase of writing. I do believe that the issues covered here are as vital in importance for the church today as they were more than sixteen centuries ago, and it is my hope and prayer that many would be as blessed by reading this book as I have been in writing it.

List of Abbreviations

1QS	*Rule of the Community* (Dead Sea Scroll)
'Abot R. Nat.	*Avot of Rabbi Nathan*
Adv. Jud.	Tertullian, *Against the Jews*
Ann.	Tacitus, *Annales*
Ant.	Josephus, *Antiquities*
Apoc. Ab.	*Apocalypse of Abraham*
Apol.	Tertullian, *Apology*
1 Apol.	Justin Martyr, *First Apology*
Autol.	Theophilus of Antioch, *To Autolycus*
b. 'Abod. Zar.	Babylonian Talmud, *Avodah Zarah*
b. Ber.	Babylonian Talmud, *Berakot*
b. Git.	Babylonian Talmud, *Gittin*
b. Hag.	Babylonian Talmud, *Hagigah*
b. Meṣ.	Babylonian Talmud, *Baba Metzi'a*
b. Qidd.	Babylonian Talmud, *Qiddushin*
b. Sanh.	Babylonian Talmud, *Sanhedrin*
Barn.	*Barnabas*
C. Ap.	Josephus, *Against Apion*
Carn. Chr.	Tertullian, *The Flesh of Christ*
Cels.	Origen, *Against Celsus*
2 Clem.	*2 Clement*
Conf.	Philo, *On the Confusion of Tongues*
Decr.	Athanasius, *Defence of the Nicene Definition*
Dem. ev.	Eusebius, *Demonstration of the Gospel*
Deus	Philo, *That God Is Unchangeable*
Deit.	Gregory of Nyssa, *De deitate Filii et Spiritus Sancti*
Dial.	Justin Martyr, *Dialogue with Trypho*
Did.	*Didache*

Diogn.	*Diognetus*
1 En.	*1 Enoch*
2 En.	*2 Enoch*
3 En.	*3 Enoch*
Ep.	Pliny the Younger, *Letters*
Exod. Rab.	*Exodus Rabbah*
4 Ez.	*4 Ezra*
Fug.	Philo, *On Flight and Finding*
Her.	Philo, *Who Is the Heir?*
Herm. Sim.	*Shepherd of Hermas, Similitudes*
Hist.	Tacitus, *Histories*
Hist. eccl.	Eusebius, *Ecclesiastical History*
HTR	*Harvard Theological Review*
Ign. Eph.	Ignatius, *To the Ephesians*
Ign. Rom.	Ignatius, *To the Romans*
Ign. Smyrn.	Ignatius, *To the Smyrneans*
Ign. Pol.	Ignatius, *To Polycarp*
Inst.	Lactantius, *The Divine Institutes*
Gen. Rab.	*Genesis Rabbah*
Haer.	Irenaeus, *Against Heresies*
j. Roš Haš.	Jerusalem Talmud, *Rosh HaShanah*
j. Ta'an.	Jerusalem Talmud, *Ta'anit*
J.W.	Josephus, *Jewish War*
Jub.	*Jubilees*
Lam. Rab.	*Lamentations Rabbah*
Legat.	Philo, *On the Assembly to Gaius*
Leg.	Philo, *Allegorical Interpretation*
Marc.	Tertullian, *Against Marcion*
m. 'Abot	Mishnah, *Avot*
m. Yoma	Mishnah, *Yoma*
Mart. Ascen. Isa.	*Martyrdom and Ascension of Isaiah*
Mek.	*Mekilta*
Migr.	Philo, *On the Migration of Abraham*
Mos.	Philo, *On the Life of Moses*
Mut.	Philo, *On the Change of Names*
Odes Sol.	*Odes of Solomon*
Or. Bas.	Gregory of Nazianzus, *Oratio in laudem Basilii*
Orat. ad Graec.	Tatian, *Address to the Greeks*
p^{72}	Papyrus 72, *Papyrus Bodmer VII–IX*

Paed.	Clement of Alexandria, *Christ the Educator*
Pat.	Tertullian, *Patience*
Pesiq. Rab.	*Pesiqta Rabbati*
PG	Patrologia graeca (ed. Jacques-Paul Migne; 162 vols; Paris, 1863)
Post.	Philo, *On the Posterity of Cain*
Praem.	Philo, *On Rewards and Punishments*
Praep. ev.	Eusebius, *Preparation for the Gospel*
Prax.	Tertullian, *Against Praxeas*
QE	Philo, *Questions and Answers on Exodus*
QG	Philo, *Questions and Answers on Genesis*
Sir.	Sirach/Ecclesiasticus
Somn.	Philo, *On Dreams*
T. Ab.	*Testament of Abraham*
t. Hul.	Tosefta, *Hullin*
t. Sotah	Tosefta, *Sotah*
Tg. Ps.-J.	*Targum Pseudo-Jonathan*
Vesp.	Suetonius, *Vespasian*
Vit. Const.	Eusebius, *Life of Constantine*
Wis.	*Wisdom of Solomon*
Yal.	*Yalqut Shimoni*

Introduction

Behold, I stand at the door and knock; if anyone hears my voice and opens the door, I will come in to him and eat with him, and he with me (Rev. 3.20 RSV).

You are at home, struggling to prepare for a vital engagement, when the doorbell rings. Outside are two eager young women who want to talk to you about the kingdom of God. Do you invite them in? Do you tell them to come back another time? Or do you politely ask them to leave?

This book began with what seemed at the time to be a 'divine appointment'. Knocking on a row of doors to invite people to attend our church's forthcoming Alpha supper, I chanced to arrive on the doorstep of a lady named Pam, who was a Jehovah's Witness, and we started a long discussion. Within a week, as part of her regular evangelistic activity, she quite unknowingly knocked at the door of my house, a good six miles away. Since both of us seemed to regard this as a sign from God (or should I say 'Jehovah'?) we made arrangements to meet and talk on a regular basis. It soon became clear, however, that there were some very basic areas of disagreement between us, much of which centred on the Trinity, and, in particular, whether it was right to describe Jesus as 'God'.

This question is, of course, not merely an idle talking-point, but one that lies at the very heart of the Christian faith. Every Sunday hundreds of millions of Christians around the world recite, in an amazing plethora of languages, the words:

God from God,
Light from Light,

True God from True God,
Begotten, not made,
Of one being with the Father.

Nearly 1,700 years ago, the controversy about the issues behind these words was causing rioting on the streets. Nowadays, in those churches that still use the Nicene Creed, they barely produce any reaction at all, beyond a curious sense of detachment, more like the feelings one gets in reciting a multiplication table!

Given the importance that these words clearly possess, this apathy is a little disturbing. After all, the question of whether Jesus is 'God' is arguably the central one which divides Christians not only from Jehovah's Witnesses, but from virtually every other major world religion. So does the Bible really support such an idea?

Let us test this out for a moment. Suppose that we invite our imaginary Jehovah's Witnesses indoors. Sitting down over coffee, we discover that our visitors are frighteningly persuasive. With some trepidation we bring up the subject of the deity of Christ. This, however, proves to be a very big mistake! Before long, the Witnesses, brandishing their own New World Translation of the Bible, have been able to turn up verse after verse which seems to disprove that Jesus was in any sense 'God'.

Finding ourselves completely wrong-footed, we hunt desperately for a line of defence. What about the Nicene Creed? It was, after all, specifically written to correct such beliefs. On closer inspection, however, it proves completely useless for our purposes. The disconcerting truth is that none of the lines we quoted above actually appear in Scripture!

So we are left fumbling through the New Testament, trying rapidly to dig up any possible reference to Jesus as 'God'. How many will we unearth?

The strange answer is that it depends on which version of the Bible we are using. If we have a New International Version available, we will find no fewer than twelve. On the other hand, in an Authorized Version we might find seven, while in the New English Bible we see just four. And if our visitors consult their own New World Translation they will have just one explicit description of Jesus as 'God', John 20.28, which they can quickly explain away by a variety of means.

So have we been duped all along? Compared with the forthright declarations of the Nicene Creed, what we find instead is a rather meagre handful of references to Jesus as 'God', virtually all of which have a question mark over them: either the original Greek isn't completely clear, or the early manuscripts disagree – or both! The news, therefore, is not good. Our evidence is decidedly shaky. If this is all we have to stand on, we might as well enlist in the ranks at our local Kingdom Hall right away!

For a doctrine of such critical importance, the uncertainty here is extremely puzzling. It is like comparing maps of a major city centre, only to find half of the main streets obscured on many of the plans. So, are our visiting Jehovah's Witnesses right after all? Were the bishops who formulated the Nicene Creed simply caving in to pagan philosophical ideas? Or perhaps, as *The Da Vinci Code* would have us believe, it was all invented by the emperor Constantine! At this rate, our visitors will have us circling the neighbourhood with copies of *The Watchtower* in no time at all.

But might there be another reason? Could there be a hidden pattern in this apparently indecisive trail of clues? Might it be, in fact, that we are *meant* to read these verses from two different angles at once? Are we, in our desire for clear-cut certainties, demanding, like Thomas, to place our hands in the marks of the nails, when Jesus is asking us to make a leap of faith? Is it possible that, rather than providing us with a neatly worked-out theological package, he is positively *encouraging* us to dig more deeply into the Scriptures?

As Proverbs 25.2 points out:

> It is the glory of God to conceal a matter;
>> to search out a matter is the glory of kings.

Jesus put it another way when he said, 'The kingdom of heaven is like treasure hidden in a field. When a man found it, he hid it again, and then in his joy went and sold all he had and bought that field' (Matt. 13.44).

Let us begin to explore this question, therefore, with an open mind. A few isolated proof-texts here and there will hardly provide enough evidence to settle the question (although, as our website shows, the evidence for the divinity of Christ in many of the passages which seem to describe Jesus as 'God' is really fairly compelling). But the fact that it is possible to read them in a variety of ways shows that we need to spread our investigation much further. In order to draw firm conclusions, therefore, let us embark on a voyage of discovery through the many passages in the Bible which, in different ways, pose the question, 'Who do you say I am?'

Questions to consider:

(i) What do you believe about Jesus? Does it matter what others believe about him? Is it an issue that affects our eternal destiny? What aspects of Christian belief are essential for salvation, and what might be legitimate topics for disagreement?

(ii) If you belong to a church where the Nicene Creed is recited, do you feel that its statements tie up accurately with the words of Scripture? Is there anything that you would change if you could? What is the purpose of reciting the Creed over 1,600 years after it was written?

(iii) Jesus engaged with Samaritans even though they held different beliefs, had a different Bible, and were generally held in contempt by Jews at large. What is your reaction if Jehovah's Witnesses knock at your front door? Do you see it as a threat, or an opportunity? What do you think God's heart might be for these people?

1.

Jesus: More Than a Messiah?

Theirs are the patriarchs, and from them is traced the human ancestry of the Messiah, who is God over all, for ever praised! (Rom. 9.5)

Messiah – or Higher?

During the lifetime of Jesus, speculation about a coming Messiah seems to have been mounting steadily. In AD 6 a Roman procurator was installed to rule Judea, in place of the discredited Archelaus, and an intense expectation and longing for deliverance began to develop among certain segments of the population. Pinchas Lapide comments that at the time of Jesus 'no land in the world and no city under the sun awaited the Redeemer in such yearning fashion as did Jerusalem'.[1]

An important factor in this build-up of messianic expectation may well have been the 'seventy "sevens"' (generally understood as meaning 490 years) that the prophet Daniel was told would follow the decree to rebuild Jerusalem in the fifth century BC, 'to finish transgression, to put an end to sin, to atone for wickedness, to bring in everlasting righteousness, to seal up vision and prophecy and to anoint the Most Holy Place' (Dan. 9.24–25). According to different methods of calculation, the sixty-nine weeks mentioned in the prophecy after which 'the Messiah will be cut off and have nothing' (Dan. 9.26 NASB) come uncannily close to the ministry and death of Jesus.[2]

Clearly the prophecy gave rise to a great deal of speculation in Israel. Jesus himself, who refers prominently to a later part of the Daniel passage in Mark 13.14, makes the striking statement at the beginning of his ministry that '*the time is fulfilled*, and the kingdom of God has come near' (Mark 1.15 HCSB).[3] The same prophecy also appears to have influenced the first-century historian Josephus several decades later,[4] and even Roman writers seem to have been aware of it. Suetonius, for example, refers to 'an old and established belief' that 'had spread over all the Orient' later in the first century AD that 'at that time' a worldwide ruler would emerge from Judea, and a similar statement appears in the writings of Tacitus.[5]

Such an understanding may well lie behind John the Baptist's question in Luke 7.19, which seems to assume that, if Jesus himself was not the Messiah, someone else alive at the time must have been waiting in the wings. This state of heightened expectancy comes across clearly in the book of Acts, which refers to up to four potential 'Messiahs' other than Jesus himself.[6] It is not surprising that, to quote the New English Bible, the people were 'on the tiptoe of expectation' (Luke 3.15). So what kind of figure were they looking out for?

Jewish documents from this period provide us with some useful evidence. For instance, the Essene community at Qumran, drawing on a couple of prophecies in Zechariah (4.14 and 6.12–13), seems to have been expecting not one but two Messiahs, one an anointed priest and the other an anointed king. Others identify the figure with 'one like a son of man' who is described in Daniel 7.13–14, as we see in *4 Ezra* and the 'Similitudes' of *1 Enoch*. Still other groups seem to have been anticipating an end-time prophet, possibly identified with Elijah, who comes either as, or immediately before, the Messiah himself.[7]

But it is in the New Testament that the popular view of the Messiah comes into the sharpest focus. Setting aside Jesus' own comments on the matter, we can build up a fairly detailed picture of what the Jews were expecting from the statements of his disciples and contemporaries. What emerges are two somewhat contrasting images. On the one hand we see a series of beliefs about a human ruler who would re-establish the kingdom of David (Mark 11.10), embracing the idea that he would

- be born in Bethlehem (Matt. 2.4–6)
- be descended from David (Luke 1.69)

- restore the kingdom to Israel (Luke 24.21; Acts 1.6)
- reign as king of the Jews (Matt. 2.2; John 1.49; 18.33)
- bring deliverance from their enemies (Luke 1.71,74)
- bring revelation to the Gentiles (Luke 2.32)
- usher in a new era of peace (Luke 1.79).

Yet alongside these beliefs is the expectation of a more mysterious, supernatural figure, whose origin would be unknown (John 7.27), coming like the rising sun from heaven (Luke 1.78) as the unique Son of God (Matt. 16.16; John 1.49), an object of worship (Matt. 2.2,11), who would perform great miracles (John 7.31) and live for ever (John 12.34).

However, there is also evidence from Jewish writings around this time that some groups were expecting nothing less than a direct appearance of Yahweh himself on earth. A book entitled *Jubilees*, for example, talks of a time when God would 'appear to the eyes of all' and 'descend and dwell' as 'King on Mount Zion'.[8] And the New Testament itself quotes another source, *1 Enoch*, which describes the coming of God 'with ten thousands of His holy ones to execute judgement upon all'.[9]

Such expectations were by no means new. In fact, there are a number of passages in the Old Testament that seem to describe a future appearance of Yahweh to his people in a manner that would be clearly visible on earth. Among these the following are particularly noteworthy:

> I know that my redeemer lives,
>   and that in the end he will stand on the earth.
> And after my skin has been destroyed,
>   *yet in my flesh I will see God;*
> I myself will see him
>   with my own eyes – I, and not another (Job 19.25–27).

> The Lord may give you bread of adversity and water of affliction, but he who teaches you will *no longer keep himself out of sight*, but *with your own eyes you will see him* (Isa. 30.20 REB).

> A voice of one calling:
> 'In the wilderness prepare

the way for the LORD;
make straight in the desert
a highway for our God . . .
And the glory of the LORD will be revealed,
and all people will see it together' (Isa. 40.3,5).

When the LORD returns to Zion,
   they will see it with their own eyes (Isa. 52.8).

What is interesting here is that in the two books in the Old Testament, Isaiah and Zechariah, where these references to the 'coming' of Yahweh to earth are most apparent, there is *no clear distinction* between the *appearing* of God and the *coming* of the Messiah. We can demonstrate this by quoting a particularly well-known passage, Isaiah 9.6, where a 'son' will be born, who will carry 'the government . . . on his shoulders'. Yet he bears the titles 'Wonderful Counsellor, Mighty God, Everlasting Father', which are almost identical to descriptions of Yahweh elsewhere in the book.[10] Similarly, in Isaiah 61, famously quoted by Jesus as his manifesto of action in the synagogue in Nazareth in Luke 4.18–19, the one anointed by Yahweh (v. 1) later seems to speak out *as God in person* (vv. 7–8).

Another familiar example appears in Zechariah 9.9–10, in the description of the Messiah's arrival in Jerusalem on a donkey, as a king whose dominion will extend 'from sea to sea and from the River to the ends of the earth'. But the background to this is the promise that God himself would 'return to Zion and dwell in Jerusalem' (8.3). Later the prophet makes clear that it is Yahweh who will physically arrive on the Mount of Olives as 'king over the whole earth' (14.3–9). Yet this is the very place that in later Jewish thought was associated with the coming of the Messiah.[11] (As proof of this, the Mount of Olives is covered today with hundreds of graves of pious Jews who hope to be first to share in the resurrection!)

More intriguing still is the extraordinary declaration by Yahweh at Zechariah 12.10, where the description seems strangely to shift from God himself to someone else: 'They will look on *me*, the one they have pierced, and they will mourn for *him* as one mourns for an only child, and grieve bitterly for him as one grieves for a firstborn son.'[12] Put simply, if God is the 'me' in this passage, then who is the 'him'?

Questions like these also arise in some of the Psalms, particularly those that Jews and Christians have traditionally viewed as describing the rule of the Messiah. In Psalm 72, for example, prayer is made for the Anointed Ruler to 'judge your people in righteousness, your afflicted ones with justice' (v. 2). Yet we only have to look to Psalm 98 to see almost identical words used to describe the coming of Yahweh to earth as Judge (v. 9). Likewise, in Psalm 132, God promises to David, 'One of your own descendants I will place on your throne . . . for ever and ever' (vv. 11–12) but follows it almost immediately by declaring, 'This is *my* resting place for ever and ever; here *I* will sit enthroned' (v. 14).

We also find a number of places in the Psalms where the messianic ruler is given titles that are elsewhere reserved for Yahweh alone, such as 'God' (Ps. 45.6), 'Lord' (Ps. 110.1) and 'Most High' (Ps. 89.27, literally translated). In Jeremiah 23.6 he is even called *Yah·weh ṣiḏ·qê·nū* ('the LORD our righteousness' [NASB]) which led the Jewish rabbi Abba bar Kahana to argue that the Messiah's name was actually Yahweh itself.[13] And these are just a few of a whole series of parallels that appear in the Old Testament, as the accompanying chart makes clear:

Is the Messiah divine?	
Yahweh	**Messiah-King**
He is called 'God' (*'ĕ·lō·hîm*) (Ps. 118.27)	He is called 'God' (*'ĕ·lō·hîm*) (Ps. 45.6)
He is called 'Lord' (*'ă·dō·nāy*) (Isa. 6.1,3)	He is called 'Lord' (*'ă·dō·nāy*) (Ps. 110.1)
He is called 'the LORD' (*Yah·weh*) (Exod. 3.15)	He is 'The LORD our righteousness' (*Yah·weh ṣiḏ·qê·nū*) (Jer. 23.5–6 NASB)
He is called 'Most High' (*'el·yō·wn*) (Ps. 91.1)	He is called 'Most High' (*'el·yō·wn*) (Ps. 89.27 JB)
He is called 'Mighty God' (*'êl gib·bō·wr*) (Isa. 10.21)	He is called 'Mighty God' (*'êl gib·bō·wr*) (Isa. 9.6)
He will live for ever (Ps. 90.2)	He will live for ever (Pss 21.4; 110.4; Ezek. 37.25)
He is a wonderful counsellor (Isa. 28.29 RSV)	He is a wonderful counsellor (Isa. 9.6)
He receives worship (Exod. 34.14)	He receives worship (Isa. 49.7 NKJV; Dan. 7.14)

His name will endure for ever (Ps. 135.13)	His name will endure for ever (Ps. 72.17)
He is peace (Judg. 6.24)	He is peace (Mic. 5.5)
He is salvation (Pss 27.1; 35.3)	He is salvation (Isa. 49.6 NKJV)
He is the breath of our nostrils (Job 27.3)	He is the breath of our nostrils (Lam. 4.20 RSV)
He is called the 'Mighty One' (Isa. 49.26)	He is called the 'Mighty One' (Ps. 45.3)
He is the Stone of Israel (Gen. 49.24 NASB; Isa. 8.13–14)	He is the Cornerstone (Ps. 118.22; Isa. 28.16)
He is blessed for ever (Ps. 89.52 RSV)	He is blessed for ever (Pss 21.6; 45.2)
Blessed are those who take refuge in him (Ps. 34.8)	Blessed are those who take refuge in him (Ps. 2.12)
He will shepherd the flock of Israel (Ezek. 34.23; Mic. 5.4)	He will shepherd the flock of Israel (Ezek. 34.11–16)
He will lead them to quiet waters (Ps. 23.2)	He will lead them to springs of water (Isa. 49.10)
He will open the eyes of the blind (Isa. 35.3–5)	He will open the eyes of the blind (Isa. 42.7)
He will protect the poor and needy (Isa. 41.17)	He will protect the poor and needy (Ps. 72.12–13)
He is the light of Israel (Ps. 27.1; Isa. 60.19–20)	He is a light to the nations (Isa. 42.6; 49.6 RSV)
All nations will be blessed in him (Jer. 4.2 RSV)	All nations will be blessed in him (Ps. 72.17 NKJV)
He will bring everlasting righteousness (Isa. 51.6–8)	He will bring everlasting righteousness (Dan. 9.24)
He will bring worldwide peace (Isa. 2.3–4)	He will bring worldwide peace (Isa. 9.7; Zech. 9.10)
He redeems his people (Isa. 43.1)	He redeems his people (Ps. 72.14 RSV)
The death of his saints is precious in his sight (Ps.72.14)	The blood of the needy is precious in his sight (Ps. 116.15)
He loves righteousness and hates wickedness (Ps. 45.7)	He loves righteousness and hates wickedness (Pss 33.5; 5.4)
He will judge the world in righteousness and the peoples with equity (Ps. 98.9)	He will judge the poor with righteousness and the meek with equity (Isa. 11.4 RSV; Ps. 72.2,4)
He will bring justice to the nations (Isa. 2.4)	He will bring justice to the nations (Isa. 42.1)
All nations will rally to him (Isa. 2.2–4)	All nations will rally to him (Isa. 11.10)
Kings will bring him gifts (Ps. 68.29)	Kings will bring him gifts (Ps. 72.10)
He is enthroned for ever (Ps. 93.2; Lam. 5.19)	He is enthroned for ever (2 Sam. 7.13; Ps. 45.6)

He will be enthroned in Zion (Ps. 132.13–14; Mic. 4.7)	He will be enthroned in Zion (Ps. 2.6; Zech. 9.9)
He will be King over all the earth (Zech. 14.9)	He will be King over all the earth (Ps. 72.8; Zech. 9.10)
Nations will trust in his law (Isa. 2.3)	Coastlands will wait for his law (Isa. 42.4 RSV)
He has crushed the heads of the serpent (Ps. 74.14; cf. Isa. 27.1)	He will crush the head of the serpent (Gen. 3.15)
He will inherit the nations (Ps. 82.8)	He will inherit the nations (Ps. 2.8)
He slays the wicked with the breath of his mouth (Job 4.8–9; 15.30)	He will slay the wicked with the breath of his lips (Isa. 11.4)
His robes are stained with blood (Isa. 63.3)	His robes will be washed in blood (Gen. 49.11)
His name will be great (Gen, 12.2; Ps. 72.17)	His name will be great (2 Sam. 7.9)
He will rise like the sun (Isa. 60.2)	He will rise like the sun (Mal. 4.2; cf. Luke 1.78–79)
He will come like rain from heaven (Hos. 6.3)	He will be like rain from heaven (Ps. 72.6)

With so many close similarities we need to ask several important questions. What is the exact nature of the relationship between the Messiah and God? Does he merely 'represent' God like an ambassador? Or could he actually 'be' God in some mysterious way?

This issue comes to the fore in Luke chapter 7, where we are informed at one point that John the Baptist may have entertained some real doubts about whether Jesus was the Messiah. To discover more, he sends two of his disciples on a fact-finding mission, asking, 'Are you the one who is to come, or should we expect someone else?' (Luke 7.19).

Actually, there is more to this question than at first meets the eye. In Revelation 1.4 the one 'who is to come' is no less than God himself. So it is significant that, after responding with a breathtaking display of miracles and exorcisms, Jesus replies, 'Go back and report to John what you have seen and heard: *the blind receive sight, the lame walk*, those who have leprosy are cleansed, *the deaf hear*, the dead are raised, and the good news is proclaimed to the poor. Blessed is anyone who does not stumble on account of me' (Luke 7.22–23).

The significance of Jesus' answer to John lies in one of the Old Testament passages which he seems to use in his reply:

Then will *the eyes of the blind be opened*
   and the ears of the deaf unstopped.
Then will *the lame leap like a deer,*
   and the mute tongue shout for joy (Isa. 35.5–6).

What is striking about this passage in Isaiah is that it begins:

Be strong, do not fear;
your God will come,
   he will come with vengeance;
with divine retribution
   he will come to save you (Isa. 35.4).

Could it be, then, that the miraculous signs are proof, not merely that Jesus is the Messiah, but that, in his ministry, Yahweh himself has arrived on earth in person? Certainly, Jesus' subsequent remarks seem to point in this direction, where, in talking about John, he asks, 'But what did you go out to see? A prophet? Yes, I tell you, and more than a prophet. This is the one about whom it is written: "I will send my messenger ahead of you, who will *prepare your way before you*"' (Luke 7.26–27). But the verse Jesus is referring to in Malachi actually says, '"I will send my messenger, who will prepare the way *before me* . . ." says the LORD Almighty' (Mal. 3.1). Such a 'lifting' of verses about God and applying them to his own ministry, suggests Richard France, 'can hardly imply less than that the coming of Jesus is the coming of Yahweh for judgment'.[14]

There is a further clue to this earlier in the same gospel where Luke describes how John went ahead into the countryside to prepare for the arrival of Jesus (whose name means, literally, 'Yahweh is salvation') by using one of the verses about the 'coming' of God that we quoted earlier:

A voice of one calling:
'*In the wilderness prepare*
   the way for the LORD;
make straight in the desert
   a highway for our God . . .' (Isa. 40.3; cf. Luke 3.4–5)

Indeed, if we go back to look at this original prophecy from Isaiah more closely, we see this appearance of Yahweh himself presented in even more forthright terms:

> You who bring good news to Zion . . .
>> lift up your voice with a shout,
> lift it up, do not be afraid;
>> say to the towns of Judah,
>> *'Here is your God!'* (Isa. 40.9).

So it may be no coincidence that, immediately before Jesus' exchange with John the Baptist, Luke reports the onlookers as saying, 'A great prophet has appeared among us . . . *God has come* to help his people' (Luke 7.16).

It is not surprising, then, that when we look elsewhere in the New Testament, we find passages which had previously described the coming of Yahweh to earth now being applied directly to Christ himself. For example, where Isaiah 52 declares that 'every eye will see when the LORD returns to Zion' (v. 8 HCSB) we find in Revelation 1.7 that 'every eye' will now see Jesus when he comes again. In the same way, while Isaiah 66 says that Yahweh will 'come with fire' to 'punish all the people of the world whom he finds guilty' (vv. 15–16 GNB), Paul writes about Jesus being 'revealed from heaven in blazing fire' to 'punish those who do not know God and do not obey the gospel' (2 Thess. 1.7–8). And where Yahweh tells us in Isaiah 63.3 that he has 'trodden the winepress' of the nations 'in [his] wrath' and that their 'blood spattered [his] garments', we discover in Revelation 19 that it is now *Jesus* who is dressed 'in a robe dipped in blood' and who 'treads the winepress of the fury of the wrath of God Almighty' (vv. 13–15).

Similar echoes also ring out from Zechariah's graphic descriptions of the coming of God to reign as King in Jerusalem. For example, while (as we saw earlier) Zechariah 14.4 talks of Yahweh standing in the day of battle on the Mount of Olives, this is precisely the place to which (as Acts 1.11–12 seems to imply) many Christians expect Jesus will return at the end of history. And where the very next verse in Zechariah says, 'the LORD my God will come, and all the holy ones with him', we find this passage again altered in the New Testament to refer directly to the second coming of

Christ: 'May he strengthen your hearts so that you will be blame-less and holy in the presence of our God and Father when our *Lord Jesus comes with all his holy ones*' (1 Thess. 3.13).

It seems especially significant, then, that the two very prophe-cies which Jesus specifically chose to 'act out' in the last week of his life are directly linked to these descriptions of God's 'arrival' in the second half of Zechariah: the procession into Jerusalem on a donkey which we have already mentioned (Zech. 9.9) and the expulsion of the traders from the temple (Zech. 14.21 RSV). Tom Wright concludes from the background to these actions that 'he was not content to *announce* that YHWH was returning to Zion. He intended to enact, symbolize and personify that climactic event'.[15]

Wright's observations here are strongly backed up by the various gospel accounts of these events. To begin with, Jesus starts his journey from the Mount of Olives (Luke 19.29,37), the place, we noted earlier, of God's 'arrival' as King in Zechariah 14.5. Then, as he begins his descent into Jerusalem, he is challenged by the Phar-isees to silence the noisy chants of his followers. But he replies that 'if they keep quiet, the stones will cry out' (Luke 19.40). The point here is that while in the Old Testament human beings are capable of worshipping whomsoever they choose, mountains, hills and other inanimate objects *only ever* give praise to God (see Ps. 148.3–9).

John's account of Jesus' journey into Jerusalem (John 12.12–19) adds further important details. Here, to introduce Zechariah's description of the Messiah's entrance to the city on a donkey, John uses the words, 'Do not be afraid, Daughter Zion', which echo the writings of another Old Testament prophet, Zephaniah, who is describing the presence of Yahweh with his people. So there is an added significance when the crowd hail Jesus as 'King of Israel' (John 12.12–13 RSV), since in Zephaniah's prophecy this is a name for Yahweh himself:

> Sing, Daughter Zion;
> > shout aloud, Israel! . . .
> *The* LORD, *the King of Israel, is with you* . . .
> 'Do not fear, Zion;
> > do not let your hands hang limp.
> *The* LORD *your God is with you,*
> > the Mighty Warrior who saves' (Zeph. 3.14–17).

This impression that Jesus was coming as God in person is even clearer in the description of the cleansing of the temple which follows immediately after this in Matthew and Luke. In Malachi 3.1 we read how, in response to the question, 'Where is the God of justice?' (Mal. 2.17), Yahweh suddenly appears in his temple, promising to restore 'acceptable' sacrificial offerings (3.4) and to bring judgment 'against those who defraud labourers of their wages' (Mal. 3.5). Against this background, Jesus' action is not just an attack on rampant commercialism and injustice, but also serves as a forthright declaration of who he is.

Matthew adds an extra detail here when he mentions a further rebuke from the Pharisees about the children who were crying out 'Hosanna to the Son of David' in the temple courts. Jesus, in a manner which the religious authorities would have found doubly shocking, responds by applying to himself words from Psalm 8 that in the Old Testament refer to the worship of God alone. 'Do you hear what these children are saying?' they asked him. 'Yes,' replied Jesus, 'have you never read, "From the lips of children and infants you, Lord, have called forth your praise"?' (Matt. 21.16).

If we still have any doubt as to what Jesus meant here, we might do well to consider his rebuke to Jerusalem, made immediately before his cleansing of the temple: 'you did not recognise *the time of God's coming to you*' (Luke 19.44, as translated in several versions). Even though his literal words were 'you did not know the time of your *visitation*', the implied meaning in Old Testament terms is exactly the same: with his arrival in Jerusalem, God's long-standing promise to visit his people has at last found its fulfilment.

The volume of evidence from just one or two days in Jesus' life is remarkable enough in itself. There is, however, one further event which in the gospels of Matthew and Mark is closely linked in with this sequence of prophetic actions. On the way to Jerusalem Jesus tries unsuccessfully to find fruit on a fig tree. Discovering only leaves, he curses the tree so that it withers. The event becomes the basis of one of his greatest teachings on faith (Matt. 21.18–22 and Mark 11.12–14,20–24).

Again, the significance of this action becomes much clearer when we consider the Old Testament background. Once more Jesus seems to be deliberately 'acting out' a prophecy which appears to identify him with Yahweh in the Old Testament. In Micah 7.1–4, for example, the absence of early figs is a sign pointing to the day when God visits his people, while in Ezekiel, God declares forthrightly that 'I, Yahweh, am the one . . . who withers green trees and makes the withered green' (Ezek. 17.24 JB).

The withered leaves also recall Yahweh's warning given in Jeremiah 8.13:

> I will take away their harvest, declares the LORD . . .
> There will be *no figs* on the tree,
>   and their *leaves will wither.*
> *What I have given them*
>   *will be taken from them.*

Again, the outward 'sign' provides a thinly veiled declaration of who Jesus is claiming to be. Indeed, we can have little doubt that Jesus had this passage from Jeremiah in mind, since the event comes shortly before the parable of the tenants in the vineyard (Matt. 21.33–44) which ends with very similar words: 'Therefore I tell you that the kingdom of God *will be taken away from you* and *given* to a people who will produce its fruit' (Matt. 21.43).

There does seem, therefore, to be a clear pattern in these events, which, as we shall see later, appears to run as a consistent theme throughout Christ's ministry. Moreover, we should note that even where the Old Testament uses what might seem to be rather fanciful poetic descriptions of God treading on the waves of the sea (Job 9.8), or striding on the mountaintops (Amos 4.13; Mic. 1.3) or ascending to his throne (Ps. 47.5,8) or riding on the clouds (Ps. 104.3), the gospels suggest Christ fulfilling them as *literal* actions (Mark 6.48; 9.2; 10.37; 13.26). The message could not be clearer: Jesus is showing that Yahweh's promise to visit the earth is being fulfilled – *in him*!

Conclusion: Does It Make Sense?

We are left, therefore, with something of a puzzle. How could Yahweh come to earth and still be God? How could Jesus be God and still be a man? If Jesus is God, why is he so completely dependent on and submitted to his Father, who is also 'God'?

Questions like these are bound to arise as we begin to examine the evidence for the divinity of Christ, and we will attempt to tackle them more fully in later chapters. All we need point out at this stage is that the curious change of pronoun that we saw earlier in Zechariah 12.10 ('They will look on *me*, the one they have pierced, and they will mourn for *him* as one mourns for an only child') seems to point to an enigma at the very heart of the Bible, the mystery of someone who is both 'God' and yet also 'other than God'. I call this mystery the 'Divine Paradox', and it finds its fullest expression in chapter 1, verse 1 of John's gospel: 'In the beginning was the Word, and the Word was *with* God, and the Word *was* God.'

At first sight, this passage, like the one in Zechariah, seems to defy common sense. How can the Word be 'God' and yet also be 'with God'? Yet this statement is by no means unique. Looking back elsewhere over Isaiah and Zechariah, which we noted earlier are particularly rich in descriptions of the 'coming' of God to earth, we find on several occasions that a similar problem emerges, with two beings apparently described as 'God', as the following examples suggest:

> Listen to Me, O Jacob, even Israel whom I called;
> I am He, I am the first, I am also the last . . .
> From the first I have not spoken in secret,
> From the time it took place, I was there.
> And now the LORD GOD has sent Me, and His Spirit' (Isa. 48.12,16 NASB).

> For the LORD of Hosts says this: 'He has sent Me for His glory against the nations who are plundering you . . . Then you will know that the Lord of Hosts has sent Me' (Zech. 2.8–9 HCSB).[16]

Are such expressions merely figures of speech? Are they actually mistakes in the text? Or do they, in fact, lend support for the later Christian doctrine of the Trinity? These are questions which we will attempt to answer later. But however baffling we may find such passages, we should note that it is on a very similar kind of verse, the opening of Psalm 110, that Jesus chose to stake one of his boldest declarations of identity, when he had the following exchange with the Pharisees:

Jesus asked them, 'What do you think about the Messiah? Whose son is he?'

'The son of David,' they replied.

He said to them, 'How is it then that David, speaking by the Spirit, calls him "Lord"? For he says,

"The Lord said to my Lord:
   'Sit at my right hand
until I put your enemies
      under your feet'"'* (Matt. 22.42–44).[17]

Can we really be surprised that, from that day on, 'no one dared to ask him any more questions' (Matt. 22.46)?

Ten key statements about the coming of Yahweh	Ten key statements about the return of Jesus
• He is coming with his holy ones (Zech. 14.5)	• He is coming with his holy ones (1 Thess. 3.13)
• He is coming with fire (Isa. 66.15)	• He is coming with fire (2 Thess. 1.7)
• He is coming on the clouds (Isa. 19.1)	• He is coming on the clouds (Matt. 24.30)
• He is coming in glory (Ps. 102.16)	• He is coming in glory (Matt. 25.31)
• He is coming with vengeance (Isa. 35.4)	• He is coming with vengeance (2 Thess. 1.8)
• He is coming to conquer (Zech. 14.3)	• He is coming to conquer (Rev. 19.15)
• He is coming to judge the earth (Ps. 96.13)	• He is coming to judge the earth (Isa. 11.4)
• He is coming to reign (Zech. 14.9)	• He is coming to reign (Matt. 25.31)
• He is coming to gather his people (Ezek. 34.11–13)	• He is coming to gather his people (Matt. 24.31)
• He is coming to reward them (Isa. 40.10)	• He is coming to reward them (Rev. 22.12)

Questions to consider:

(i) Generally speaking, Jews since the time of Jesus have not accepted him as their Messiah because they feel that very few of the signs promised in the Old Testament were fulfilled in his lifetime. Christians believe that many of these will be completed at his second coming. Is there any evidence for two separate comings of Christ in the Old Testament? If so, where? If not, why not?

(ii) Jesus says that he was sent to the 'lost sheep of Israel' (Matt. 15.24). Have Christians lost the right to witness to Jews about Jesus through centuries of persecution in his name? Is there any need to share Christ with our Jewish friends, or do they already have their own covenant relationship with God? Does Romans 11.11–32 tell us about a future purpose for Israel, and if so, how might we (as the church) fit into that plan? What bearing might Jeremiah 31.35–37 have on this question?

(iii) The lives of Simeon and Anna (Luke 2.25–38) show a daily sense of anticipation for the coming of the Messiah. How much, if at all, are we expecting the return of Jesus? Could it happen tonight? If so, would we be ready to meet him?

2.

Jesus and the Divine Paradox

'To whom will you compare me? Or who is my equal?' says the Holy One (Isa. 40.25).

Testing the 'Divine Paradox'

The eleventh-century theologian Anselm once famously defined God as a being greater than any other which can be conceived. With a clever philosophical 'sleight of hand' he then went on to prove (or attempt to prove) that such a being must, by definition, possess a real existence.

Whatever one thinks of Anselm's 'proof', it does appear that the book of Job drives a coach and horses – if not an articulated lorry – through his definition of God! The problem is that Job, while on the one hand appearing to regard the Almighty as his principal accuser and opponent (see, for example, Job 16.7–14; 19.6–12; 30.20–21; 31.35), seems on the other hand to conceive of a being of equal or greater power who could 'arbitrate between us and impose his authority on us both' (Job 9.33 REB).

Without overturning the very foundations of the biblical belief in the uniqueness of God, it is extremely difficult to see how Job's requirement could be fulfilled. Yet it is clear from the passage in Job 19, which we quoted in the last chapter, that the mediator to which Job refers is none other than God himself, a God, moreover, who will stand visibly on the earth in Job's presence:

I know that my redeemer lives,
    and that in the end he will stand on the earth.

And after my skin has been destroyed,
> *yet in my flesh I will see God;*
I myself will see him
> with my own eyes – I, and not another (Job 19.25–27).

A similar issue arises in passages like Micah 7.9:

Because I have sinned against him,
> I will bear the LORD's wrath
until he pleads my case
> and upholds my cause.

Here the words inevitably beg the question, 'Plead to *whom*?'[1]

On the face of it, passages such as this might seem to provide an important clue to the 'Divine Paradox' which we met at the end of the last chapter. Even in the heart of the Old Testament, the mechanics of human salvation seem to require a real distinction within God's being, so that he can be at once both judge and jury, prosecutor and defence attorney. If this conclusion is true, it has significant implications for Judaism, Islam, and other forms of monotheistic belief that stress the inseparable nature of the one unique God.

But it is a big 'if'. Our notion of God, after all, comes ultimately from Judaism, where the undivided 'oneness' of God takes centre stage. John, who presents the Paradox in its most direct form, was himself a Jew. As we have already seen, there are a few precedents he could have found in Isaiah, Zechariah and some of the Psalms. But can we really trace such an idea consistently throughout the Old Testament?

In the next four chapters we will begin to address this question in more detail, by examining various descriptions that were applied to Jesus at different times: as the 'Image of God', as the 'Son of Man', as the 'Wisdom' or 'Word' of God, and as 'Immanuel', to see what background they have in the Old Testament. But we will begin by trying to solve an intriguing puzzle.

A Case of Double Vision?

One of the distinguishing thumbprints of the film producer Alfred Hitchcock was that he included a walk-on part for himself in many of his own movies. The result is a miniature version of our paradox: the creator appearing within his own creation, disguised as a character within the plot!

In Jewish thought, the idea of God appearing as a human being is often regarded as nonsensical. Numbers 23.19 states categorically that God is not a human being, while Deuteronomy 4.12–18 seems to suggest that he cannot be represented in any external form.

Yet we only have to turn back a few pages into Genesis to see this apparently 'unbreakable' rule already appearing to fall apart! In chapter 18, for example, a mysterious visitor pays a call on Abraham. As the chapter proceeds, his identity unfolds through a series of tantalizing clues. To begin with, he is described as a man, who sits down, has his feet washed and shares in a meal with his two companions who, as we later find out, are angels. Yet Abraham's response is to address him as 'Lord' (*'ă·dō·nāy*) and to offer what appears to be worship (18.2).

This passage is by no means an isolated one. Throughout the first half of the Old Testament the same enigmatic being seems to reappear like Hitchcock in a 'cameo role', turning up unexpectedly at various times to discharge a variety of functions. But his identity is shrouded in mystery. He is often described as 'the angel of the LORD', or, in later Jewish thinking, 'the angel of the presence' (see Isa. 63.9).[2] But is he an angel? Is he a man? Is he God himself?

About halfway through the Genesis 18 account, things seem to become a little clearer. In verse 13 we are clearly told that the mysterious stranger is no less than Yahweh in person. But then something rather unexpected happens. In verses 17–19, we seem to have *two* beings, both described as 'Yahweh', one of whom appears to talk about the other: 'Then the LORD [referring to one of the men described in Gen. 18.2] said . . . "I have chosen him, so that he will direct his children and his household after him to keep *the way of the LORD* by doing what is right and just, so that *the LORD* will bring about for Abraham what he has promised him"' (Gen. 18.17–19).

In the following chapter the situation develops further. Having announced his intention to go down to Sodom and Gomorrah (18.20–21), 'Yahweh' seems, on his arrival, to be in need of some heavenly assistance: 'Then the LORD [again apparently referring to the man described in Gen. 18.2] rained down burning sulphur on Sodom and Gomorrah – *from the LORD* out of the heavens' (Gen. 19.24).

Clearly, if two beings are called 'Yahweh' here, we have a problem, since Isaiah 45.5 states emphatically that 'apart from me there is no God'. Yet the difficulty here is far from unique. On closer inspection, verses of the kind we have considered above appear throughout the Old Testament, from the very first chapter of Genesis to the last chapter of Malachi. We included some striking examples of these at the end of the last chapter, and a further selection appears in the accompanying chart. Such passages, if we were to take them at face value, might naturally lead us to assume that there were *two* divine powers at work!

Yahweh and Yahweh: Examples of circular *or* twinned statements about God in the Bible

- Then *God* said to Jacob, 'Go up to Bethel and settle there, and build an altar there to *God*, who appeared to you when you were fleeing from your brother Esau' (Gen. 35.1).
- *The LORD* answered Moses, 'Is *the LORD's* arm too short?' (Num. 11.23)
- *The LORD* declares to you that *the LORD* himself will establish a house for you (2 Sam. 7.11)
- *The LORD* said, 'Go out and stand on the mountain in the presence of *the LORD*, for *the LORD* is about to pass by' (1 Kgs 19.11).
- *the LORD* will march at your head, your rearguard will be Israel's *God* (Isa. 52.12 NEB).
- Therefore, *our God*, hear the prayer and the petitions of Your servant. Show Your favour to Your desolate sanctuary for *the Lord's* sake (Dan. 9.17 HCSB).
- And *the LORD* said to him, '. . . I will have pity on the house of Judah, and I will deliver them by *the LORD* their God' (Hos. 1.6–7 RSV)
- 'I will strengthen them in *the LORD* and in his name they will live securely,' declares *the LORD* (Zech. 10.12).

- No one has ever seen *God*; the only *God*, who is *at the Father's side*, he has made him known (John 1.18 ESV).
- Now *the Lord* is the Spirit, and where the Spirit of *the Lord* is, there is freedom (2 Cor. 3.17).
- May *the Lord* grant that he will find mercy from *the Lord* on that day! (2 Tim. 1.18)
- But about the Son he says, 'Your throne, O *God*, will last for ever and ever; a sceptre of justice will be the sceptre of your kingdom. You have loved righteousness and hated wickedness; therefore *God*, your *God*, has set you above your companions' (Heb. 1.8–9; cf. Ps. 45.6–7).

In fact, this idea that Yahweh has a 'mirror image' is precisely the conclusion reached by the Jewish writer Philo of Alexandria around the time of Christ. Commenting on Genesis 9.6, where God says that he created humankind 'in the *image of God*' (so that *'ĕ·lō·hîm*, the Hebrew word for God, appears *twice*, as both subject and object of the sentence), he goes on to ask why Yahweh should appear to talk about himself here 'as if of some other god'. Philo's conclusion, extraordinary for a Jew, does indeed appear to be that a second divine power is involved in the process of creation.[3]

So was Philo right? Are verses of this kind arranged in the way they are for purely poetic reasons? Are they simply figures of speech? Or do they point us to a more profound truth?

Certainly, the original context of the verse that Philo uses, which first appears in Genesis 1.27, may well be significant, and was clearly understood to be so by many early Christian writers.[4] In the previous verse, God (*'ĕ·lō·hîm*, itself a *plural* noun in Hebrew, though it takes a *singular* verb), appears to speak out as *more than one* ('Let *us* make mankind in *our* image').[5] Philo himself makes the remarkable statement that the words 'let us make' are 'implying a number of creators'.[6] Does the *repetition* of *'ĕ·lō·hîm* in verse 27, therefore, direct us to a significant deeper truth about Yahweh?

The question arises again in connection with passages describing the 'angel of the LORD'. In chapter 3 of Zechariah, for example, the angel speaks out as Yahweh and yet appears to refer to *another* being called 'Yahweh': 'Then he showed me Joshua the high priest standing before the angel of the LORD, and Satan standing at his right side to accuse him. The LORD said to Satan, "*The* LORD *rebuke you, Satan! The* LORD, *who has chosen Jerusalem, rebuke you!*"' (Zech. 3.1–2).

A similar puzzle arises in the description of the 'burning bush' in Exodus 3. On the one hand, this is presented as an 'appearance' of the 'angel of the LORD' (v. 2) and on the other, as God himself 'coming down' to rescue his people from Egypt (vv. 7–8). Yet there is no hint in the passage that these two descriptions are in conflict with one another. Strange as it may seem, it is as if this angel were somehow a mirror image of Yahweh himself.

What, then, is the difference between Yahweh and his angel? Certainly, if we turn to Exodus 33.2–3, the angel of the LORD seems to be clearly set apart from God: '*I will send an angel before you* and drive out the Canaanites, Amorites, Hittites, Perizzites, Hivites and Jebusites . . . *But I will not go with you*, because you are a stiff-necked people and I might destroy you on the way.' However, if we then turn forward to Judges 2.1–2, we find that the very same 'angel' so carefully *distinguished* from God in the previous passage seems to speak out as Yahweh himself in the first person:

> The angel of the LORD went up from Gilgal to Bokim and said, 'I brought you up out of Egypt and led you into the land that I swore to give to your ancestors. I said, "I will never break my covenant with you, and you shall not make a covenant with the people of this land, but you shall break down their altars." Yet you have disobeyed me . . .'[7]

This unresolved question becomes particularly challenging in Judges 6, where the angel of the LORD pays a call on Gideon. Here the dialogue swings back and forth in such a way that it is impossible to tell whether it is really God or an angel who is speaking, since two distinct beings again appear to be described as 'LORD':

> When the angel of the LORD appeared to Gideon, he said, 'The LORD is with you, mighty warrior.'

'Pardon me, my lord,' Gideon replied, 'but if the Lord is with us, why has all this happened to us?' . . .

The Lord turned to him and said, 'Go in the strength you have and save Israel out of Midian's hand' . . .

Gideon replied, 'If now I have found favour in your eyes, give me a sign that it is really you talking to me. Please do not go away until I come back and bring my offering and set it before you.'

And the Lord said, 'I will wait until you return' . . .

The angel of God said to him, 'Take the meat and the unleavened bread, place them on this rock, and pour out the broth.' . . . And the angel of the Lord disappeared. When Gideon realised that it was the angel of the Lord, he exclaimed, 'Alas, Sovereign Lord! I have seen the angel of the Lord face to face!'

But the Lord said to him, 'Peace! Do not be afraid. You are not going to die' (Judg. 6.12–23).

Equally confusing, also, is Jacob's blessing on Ephraim and Manasseh in Genesis 48.15–16:

May the God before whom my fathers
    Abraham and Isaac walked faithfully,
the God who has been my shepherd
    all my life to this day,
the Angel who has delivered me from all harm
    – may he bless these boys.[8]

Did Jacob really believe that God was an angel? Or is this some kind of early description of the Trinity?[9]

In fact, if we pull together all the descriptions of the angel of the Lord in the Old Testament, we seem to arrive at two completely opposite sets of statements (see inset). How, then, are we to make sense of these apparent contradictions? Is there, in fact, any way of reconciling them, or are we left with an impossible riddle? Before giving up in bafflement, there is one possible place to which we might turn for a solution.

Who is the angel of the LORD?

Option 1: He is God
- He describes himself as 'God' (Gen. 31.11–13; Exod. 3.2,6)
- He describes himself as 'LORD' (Exod. 3.2,15)
- He claims the title 'I AM' (Exod. 3.2,14; Judg. 13.11[?])
- He is addressed as 'Lord' (*'ădō·nāy*) (Gen. 18.3,27–32; Exod. 3.2/4.10)
- His presence equals God's presence (compare Exod. 32.34 and 33.14)
- The name 'angel' is used interchangeably with that of 'God' (Gen. 48.15–16; Hos. 12.3–4; Zech. 12.8) and 'Lord' (Judg. 6.11–23; Zech. 3.1–2)
- He is worshipped (Josh. 5.14; Judg. 13.20)
- He receives intercession (Gen. 18.23–33)
- He receives sacrifice (Judg. 6.19–21; 13.19–20)
- He has authority to bless (Gen. 21.17–18) or curse (Judg. 5.23)
- He has authority to forgive sins (Zech. 3.4) or to withhold forgiveness (Exod. 23.21)
- He executes judgement (2 Kgs 19.35)
- He performs miracles (Judg. 6.11–21)
- He can speak through human lips (1 Chr. 21.18–19)
- He talks of 'my Spirit' (Zech. 6.4,8)
- He brings salvation and redemption (Isa. 63.9)
- He surrounds his people (Ps. 34.7; cf. Zech. 2.5)
- He can take on different physical forms (Exod. 3.2; 14.19)

Option 2: He is someone other than God
- He refers to God as someone else (Gen. 21.17; 22.11–12)
- He can address God (Zech. 1.12)
- He can be addressed by God (2 Sam. 24.16)
- He is sent by God (Exod. 23.20; 33.2; Num. 20.16; 1 Chr. 21.15)
- He does not act on his own authority (2 Sam. 24.16; 1 Chr. 21.15)
- He is God's military commander-in-chief (Josh. 5.13–15)
- He can speak prophetically: 'Thus says the Lord' (Zech. 3.6–7 RSV)
- He intercedes on behalf of Israel (Zech. 1.12)

> - He mediates between human beings and God (hinted at in Job 16.19–21; 33.23–26)
> - He stands between heaven and earth (1 Chr. 21.16)
> - He pronounces judgement on God's behalf (Zech. 3.1–2)
> - He acts as God's agent, bearing his name and authority (Exod. 23.20–21)

The Mysterious Stranger

To begin our search for an answer to the enigma of the angel of the LORD, we need to travel backwards in time once more into the book of Genesis. At one point in the story we find ourselves at a well between Israel and Egypt, a symbol of life and hope in a dry place (Gen. 16.7, 14). Here we meet a woman who has been drawn into a relationship with a married man, and is running away from the rejection and ill-treatment she has experienced as a result. At the well she encounters a mysterious stranger who seems to know a great deal about her life, gives her hope for the future, and persuades her to return to where she came from.

Jumping forward two thousand years, the scene seems to repeat itself. Once more we find ourselves at a well (possibly nearly as old as the one in the Genesis account[10]) with a woman who has been involved with a man who is not her husband. She also seems to have experienced rejection as a result of her situation, since she is escaping from contact with her fellow townsfolk.[11] Yet after she meets a mysterious stranger who seems to know everything about her life, she returns in excitement to tell everyone about him.

In the first case the woman is Hagar, Abraham's maidservant, and the stranger is the angel of the LORD, whom she recognizes to be Yahweh in person (Gen. 16.13). In the second case the woman is an unnamed inhabitant of Samaria, while the stranger turns out to be Jesus of Nazareth, who reveals his identity in John 4.26 using the divine name 'I AM' (*ego eimi*: more on this in chapter seven).

For both of the women, it is a life-changing encounter, as they come face to face with the divine love that sees directly into their lives. In the first example Hagar comes out of the exchange saying,

'I have now seen *the One who sees me*'; in the second, the woman says, 'Come, see a man who told me *everything I've ever done.*'[12]

Another intriguing glimpse into the future appears in the book of Judges. In chapter 13 we are introduced to Manoah and his wife, later to be the parents of Samson, who have lost all hope of having a child. One day they meet a man of God who builds their hopes up once more, and as a result they urge him strongly to stay and eat with them. All this time his identity is concealed from them. It is only when they sacrifice a food offering to Yahweh and the stranger disappears from their midst that they realize that they have met with God in person (v. 22).

Jumping forward many centuries again brings us an uncanny sense of *déjà vu*. Two disciples (again, possibly a married couple)[13] are walking to a village called Emmaus from Jerusalem, utterly downcast after the crucifixion of Jesus. On the way, they meet a man of God who builds up their hopes once more that their leader is alive, and as a result they urge him strongly to stay and share a meal with them. All this time his identity is concealed from them, and only when they break bread and the stranger disappears from their sight do they realize that they have been with Jesus himself (Luke 24.13–35).

Is there a pattern emerging here? Certainly, as we suggested earlier, the theme of the 'mysterious stranger' seems to play a powerful role throughout both the Old and New Testaments. For example, Abraham, after winning a crucial military operation to rescue his brother, is blessed by a 'priest of God Most High', who promptly disappears from the story (Gen. 14.18–20); Jacob, terrified of meeting the brother he has deceived, wrestles all night with a man he has never seen before (Gen. 32.24–32); Joshua, about to embark on a critical battle for Jericho, comes face to face with 'the commander of the army of the Lord' who tells him to take off his shoes (Josh. 5.13–15); Elijah is running for his life from the evil Queen Jezebel, but is fed by an angelic visitor in the middle of the desert (1 Kgs 19.1–8); Shadrach, Meshach and Abednego are about to be burnt alive, but a fourth figure is seen in the furnace facing the ordeal with them (Dan. 3.19–28). No sooner does the enigmatic stranger appear than he is gone again, yet in each case he appears to perform a vital role in the course of events.

This same puzzle over identity seems to hang over many of the appearances of Jesus in John's gospel. Unlike the detailed background information given him by Matthew and Luke in their gospels, he seems to arrive on the scene from nowhere (1.36); he appears to the Samaritan woman in the story we read earlier as a stranger asking for a drink (4.7); he heals a lame man by a pool who has no idea who he is (5.12–13); he arrives in secret in Jerusalem and preaches to the crowds in the temple, unannounced (7.10–15).

These question marks seem to increase after Jesus rises from the dead, where the doubt about his identity injects a dramatic irony which gives each story a powerful twist: Mary Magdalene thinks he is the gardener (20.15); the disciples glimpse him as an unknown figure by the Sea of Galilee who offers advice about fishing (21.5–6); and in Luke's gospel he appears on the road to Emmaus, as we have seen, as a traveller who seems at first sight to know nothing about the crucifixion, only to reveal that he actually knows a great deal more about it than his distraught companions (24.13–27).

The puzzle over identity is a key feature in each of these stories. Generally speaking, those involved only recognize the visitor *afterwards*, with their attitude changing from intense curiosity to awe. In the case of the angel of the LORD the witnesses discover that they have actually *seen God*; in the case of Jesus the revelation moves through progressive stages as we travel through John's gospel, but also culminates in him being called 'God' by Thomas in a moment of profound insight.

The apparent contradiction here, of course, is that the Old Testament states that it is impossible to see God and live (Exod. 33.20; Judg. 13.22). The New Testament is equally emphatic that no one has seen God (John 1.18; 6.46; 1 Tim. 6.16; 1 John 4.12) apart from Christ himself (Matt. 11.27; Luke 10.22). Yet Jesus made the astonishing claim that to see him was to see the Father (John 14.9). Writers such as Paul and the author of the book of Hebrews attempted to grapple with this idea by describing Jesus on different occasions as 'the image of God' (2 Cor. 4.4; Col. 1.15), 'the form of God' (Phil. 2.6 RSV) and 'the exact representation of his being' (Heb. 1.3).

So is it legitimate to view the descriptions of the angel of the LORD as appearances of Christ before his life on earth? And what consequences would this have for our understanding of his ultimate identity? We will begin to explore these questions in more detail in the next chapter.

Conclusion: Wrestling with the Mysterious Stranger

The examples we have discussed in this chapter have revealed two important facts. Firstly, they are a salutary reminder to us that not everything we encounter in life is quite what it first appears to be. Viewed through a different set of eyes, our perspective on something can change drastically. Like the disciples on the road to Emmaus, our estimation of who Jesus is will depend on the set of assumptions that we start with.

Secondly, they have shown us that the *either/or* logic which we use in everyday life is quite inadequate when we investigate the identity of such figures as the 'angel of the LORD', or, as we shall see later, when we consider Christ as the 'Son of Man' or the 'Wisdom of God'. However satisfying it may be for us to place things in neat categories, the Bible is not always so accommodating. Just as Jesus very often answered a question by asking another question (and the angel of the LORD does this occasionally too),[14] so Scripture sometimes does the same. On occasions we are left, to quote Churchill's famous description of Russia, with 'a riddle wrapped in a mystery inside an enigma'.[15]

Bearing in mind both these observations, it is striking to note that the questions we raised earlier about the identity of the angel of the LORD (is he God – or isn't he?) are very similar to the ones in the introduction to this volume concerning those verses in the New Testament which seem to provide direct evidence for the deity of Christ. When read one way, they appear to suggest that Jesus is 'God', but then, viewed differently, they seem to say something quite different.

A classic example is Romans 9.5. Here, Paul, discussing the burden he feels for his fellow Jews, suddenly appears to describe Jesus as 'God over all'. There is no obvious reason why he should do so at this point in his letter, and he does not go on to develop the idea. Instead, the thought melts away and we are left wondering what he meant.

In her fascinating little book *Eats, Shoots and Leaves*, Lynne Truss mentions an old English rhyme which runs:

Every Lady in this Land
Hath 20 Nails on each Hand;
Five and twenty on Hands and Feet;
And this is true, without deceit.[16]

At first sight, the poem appears to make no sense at all. Only when we shift the main breaks in the sentence so that they follow 'Nails' and 'five' do the pieces of the jigsaw fit together.

The problem in Romans 9.5 is very similar. Depending on where we place the full stops and commas, the verse could be read in several possible ways:

> from their race, according to the flesh, is the Christ *who is God* over all, blessed for ever (ESV)

> of their race, according to the flesh, is the Christ. *God* who is over all *be* blessed for ever (RSV)

> from whom is the Christ according to the flesh, who is over all, *God blessed* forever (NASB)

Of these, the first describes Christ as 'God'; the second *distinguishes* him from God, while the third simply hovers between the two opposites. As punctuation marks in the earliest Greek versions we have of the verse are scant and sometimes non-existent, there is no means of being absolutely certain which one sums up most accurately what Paul had in mind.

The curious thing is that every other time Paul seems to describe Jesus as 'God' the same question marks start appearing. In Acts 20.28, for example, the various texts and commentators disagree; in Philippians 2.6 the precise meaning of the words is hotly debated; in 1 Timothy 3.16 the description of Christ as 'God' is absent from the earliest surviving manuscripts; while in 2 Thessalonians 1.12 and Titus 2.13 the sentence can be read in two or more possible ways.

The same is true elsewhere in the New Testament, if we look at the chart on the next page (or, for a more detailed examination, at our website **www.but-is-he-God.org**). John, for example, seems to refer to Jesus directly as 'God' on several different occasions, and these seem to be arranged in a much more deliberate pattern than the apparently random occurrences in Paul. However, in John 1.18 the manuscript sources disagree, while in 1 John 5.20 it is by no means clear to whom the word 'God' is referring. Even in John 1.1 there are several ways in which we could interpret the grammar.

The Divine Paradox: Some unanswered questions

- In Matthew 1.23, is Jesus himself described as 'God with us' (NIV) or does his name 'Immanuel' mean 'God *is* with us' (REB), suggesting simply that God is on our side?
- In John 1.1, is the Word presented as 'God' (NJB) or 'a god' (NWT)?
- In John 1.18, is Christ described as 'the only Son' (JB) or 'the only God' (ESV)?
- In John 10.33, is Jesus claiming to be 'God' (NASB) or 'a god' (NEB)?
- In Acts 20.28, was Paul describing Jesus' blood as the blood of God (Living Bible) or the blood of 'the Lord' (REB)?
- In Romans 9.5, who is 'God over all': the Father (GNB) or Jesus (NIV)?
- In Philippians 2.6, is Christ 'truly God' (CEV) or less than God (CJB)?
- In 2 Thessalonians 1.12, is Paul talking about 'the grace of *our God and Lord*, Jesus Christ' (NLT) or 'the grace of *our God* **and** *the Lord* Jesus Christ' (NASB)?
- Does Titus 2.13 describe 'our great *God and Saviour*, Jesus Christ' (NRSV) or '*the great God* **and** *our Saviour* Jesus Christ' (KJV)?
- Is Hebrews 1.8 saying of Jesus, 'God, your throne shall last for ever' (JB) or 'God *is* your throne forever' (NWT)?
- Does the beginning of 2 Peter describe 'the righteousness of our *God and Saviour* Jesus Christ' (HCSB) or 'the righteousness of *our God* **and** *the Saviour* Jesus Christ' (ASV)?
- Do the words 'true God' in 1 John 5.20 apply to the Father (CEV) or to the Son (*The Message*)?

We are left, then, in something of a quandary. The fact is that, of the thirty translations surveyed in the appendix to this volume, *no two* are in total agreement as to which verses in the Bible describe Jesus as 'God'.[17] At first sight, it almost appears as if we are looking at the Tower of Babel in miniature!

However, if the Divine Paradox of John 1.1 is true, it might provide a novel explanation for this problem. The solution is, quite simply, that *the nature of the paradox itself prevents these passages from being too explicit.* Like the 'mysterious stranger' who engages with Jacob at Peniel and who talks to the disciples on the road to Emmaus, verses which seem to describe Jesus as 'God' pose a challenge to us as to their ultimate nature and meaning. Sometimes, as is the case with Romans 9.5, they seem to appear as if from nowhere, and then disappear again without trace! As with Jacob, we must choose to wrestle with them and press into them to extract their full significance. Could they, like the puzzling identity of the 'angel of the LORD', be telling us two different things at the same time?

As human beings, we may feel uncomfortable with such apparent 'contradictions', which elude our tidy patterns of thought. But the more we look, the clearer it becomes that these 'contradictions' actually form part of a much larger pattern, a pattern that ultimately points to something profound at the very heart of God's nature. As we continue considering the relationship between Jesus and the angel of the LORD in the next chapter, we will begin to unravel this pattern a little further, giving us a deeper insight into Jesus' extraordinary statement: 'I am in the Father and the Father is in me' (John 14.11).

Ten key statements about Yahweh	Ten key statements about Jesus
• There is no other LORD (Isa. 45.18)	• He is the LORD (Jer. 23.5–6)
• There is no other God (Deut. 32.39)	• He is God (John 20.28)
• There is no other Creator (Isa. 44.24)	• He is the Creator (Heb. 1.10–12)
• There is no other Saviour (Isa. 43.11)	• He is the Saviour (Luke 2.11)
• There is no other Rock (Isa. 44.8)	• He is the Rock (1 Cor. 10.4)
• There is none other equal (Isa. 46.5)	• He is God's equal (John 5.18)
• There is none other righteous (Isa. 45.24 RSV)	• He is the righteous one (Acts 3.14)
• There is none other holy (Rev. 15.4)	• He is the holy one (John 6.69)
• No other name is exalted (Ps. 148.13)	• His name is exalted (Phil. 2.9)
• No one else can share his glory (Isa. 48.11)	• He shares the Father's glory (John 17.5)

Questions to consider:

(i) The Old Testament contains several stories where people avoid recognition by adopting a disguise. Would it be consistent with God's character to do this as well? What would be the purpose? Are there times when God has intervened directly in your life, but you only realized it afterwards?

(ii) Many of the encounters in this chapter are with people whose emotions have reached their lowest ebb. Have you ever met with God in a special way in these circumstances? What was the result?

(iii) Can two opposing statements ever be true at the same time? How do you react if one passage of Scripture appears to contradict another? Is it possible for a verse to deliberately convey several different (and perhaps opposite) meanings at once?

3.

Jesus as the Image of God

Jesus answered: 'Don't you know me, Philip, even after I have been among you such a long time? Anyone who has seen me has seen the Father' (John 14.9).

A Case of Mistaken Identity?

In the Vatican Library in Rome is what is probably the earliest surviving manuscript of the entire Bible in existence, dating from about the fourth century AD. Because of its great age, it has exerted a strong influence on many modern translations of the New Testament. However, in the letter of Jude it contains a version of verse 5 so extraordinary that most recent translations have scrupulously avoided it: 'Now I want to remind you, although you once fully knew it, that *Jesus*, who saved a people out of the land of Egypt, afterwards destroyed those who did not believe' (Jude 5 ESV).

'Difficult to the point of impossibility' is how one leading scholar described his committee's opinion of this reading of the verse, despite its appearance in a number of other early manuscripts.[1] In some ways, the reaction is understandable. After all, if church tradition is correct, the remark was made by *Jesus' own brother*!

However, an even earlier manuscript (dated controversially by one expert as early as AD 80[2]) appears to make the same claim. It reports Paul as saying in 1 Corinthians 10.9 that it was *Christ* who was being put to the test when the Israelites complained against God in the wilderness.[3] This is clearly apparent if we compare the following passages:

But the people grew impatient on the way; *they spoke against God* and against Moses, and said, 'Why have you brought us up out of Egypt to die in the wilderness?' . . . Then the LORD sent venomous snakes among them; they bit the people and many Israelites died (Num. 21.4–6).

How often they rebelled against him in the wilderness
	and grieved him in the wasteland!
Again and again they put God to the test;
	they vexed the Holy One of Israel (Ps. 78.40–41).

We must not put Christ to the test, as some of them did and were destroyed by serpents; nor grumble, as some of them did and were destroyed by the Destroyer (1 Cor. 10.9–10 ESV).

Before dismissing the evidence of these two ancient versions out of hand, it is worth remembering that, in the story of Israel's escape from Egypt and return to the promised land, the activity of God is inextricably tied up with that of the angel of the LORD, who sometimes speaks and acts as Yahweh in person (as we saw in Exod. 3.2 – 4.17 and Judg. 2.1–3). On the face of it, this seems to have much in common with the overlap of identity between God and his Messiah that we noticed in chapter one. So could there be a connection between the two things? Could, in fact, the angel's visits be understood as *additional* appearances of Christ before his life on earth? Do they, once more, suggest that Jesus might be the human face of Yahweh himself?

This idea is not a new one. It was advocated by early Christian writers such as Justin Martyr as long ago as AD 150.[4] And, if we look at the Old Testament, there are a number of similarities between the angel of the LORD and the promised Messiah that seem to support it. For instance, in Numbers 24.17, the coming ruler is described as a 'star', a word that often refers to an angelic being (see Job 38.7), while in another passage sometimes seen as referring to the Messiah, Malachi 3.1, the 'messenger' who arrives suddenly in the temple as 'the Lord you are seeking', is, literally translated, the '*angel* of the covenant' (NJB).

Stronger connections appear in Isaiah 9.6, where the Messiah's name is described as 'Wonderful', the name that is used by the angel of the LORD in Judges 13.18 (RSV), and as '*Prince* of Peace', the same Hebrew word used for the heavenly 'commander of the army of the LORD' in Joshua 5.14, and employed seven times in the book of Daniel to refer to angelic beings. There is an even closer link in the Greek Septuagint translation of Isaiah 9.6, where the child to be born is actually described as 'angel of great counsel'.

There is also a clear similarity between the 'angel of the LORD' of Exodus 23.20–21 and the 'new Moses' promised in Deuteronomy 18.18–19:

> *See, I am sending an angel ahead of you* to guard you along the way and to bring you to the place I have prepared. Pay attention to him and *listen to what he says. Do not rebel against him*; he will not forgive your rebellion, since *my Name is in him.*

> *I will raise up for them a prophet* like you from among their fellow Israelites, and I will put my words in his mouth . . . *I myself will call to account* anyone who does not *listen to my words* that the prophet speaks *in my name.*

These links are heightened by Micah 5.2, which describes the coming Messiah as one whose '*goings forth* are from long ago' (NASB), strongly suggesting repeated earlier visits. (The same Hebrew word is used in Psalm 19.6 to describe the regular circuit of the sun across the sky from east to west!)

When we consider the ministry of Jesus we discover some further thought-provoking parallels with the angel of God. For instance, both stand in God's presence (Isa. 63.9; Heb. 9.24) as mediators (Job 33.23; 1 Tim. 2.5) and intercessors (Zech. 1.12; Heb. 7.25). They are sent by God (1 Chr. 21.15; Gal. 4.4) to bring salvation (Isa. 63.9; Matt. 1.21) but also to deliver judgement (2 Kgs 19.35; 2 Thess. 1.7–10). They share God's Spirit (Zech. 6.5–8; Rom. 8.9) and possess his name 'Yahweh' (Exod. 23.21; John 17.11), which they reveal to his people (Exod. 3.2,14–15; John 17.6).

It is also worth noting that the very place where Jesus triumphs over the powers of evil on the cross (Col. 2.15) is on part of the same ridge where the angel of the LORD saved the life of Isaac two thousand years earlier (Gen. 22.11–12) and where, a thousand years after this, Yahweh acts through his angel to stop the plague against Jerusalem (1 Chr. 21.5–18,27).[5]

As we have already noted in the last chapter, however, the most striking similarities between the ministry of Jesus and that of the angel of the LORD occur in relation to the appearances of Christ after his resurrection, and it is here that we can uncover some of the most intriguing evidence of all.

Clearer Than a Talking Donkey?

A casual glance at the first chapter of Acts might lead one to believe that the various resurrection appearances of Jesus were confined to the forty days leading up to his ascension. The angels' message to the apostles in verses 10 and 11 certainly seems to suggest that he will not be seen in the same way until he returns in glory.

But Paul records an *extra* appearance of Jesus to him on the road to Damascus several years later. Writing to the Corinthians, he points out that 'he *appeared* to Cephas, and then to the Twelve. After that, he *appeared* to more than five hundred of the brothers . . . Then he *appeared* to James, then to all the apostles, and last of all he *appeared* to me also, as to one abnormally born' (1 Cor. 15.5–8). The Greek word Paul uses for 'appeared', *ōphthē*, has a distinctive background. It is the *same* word that is used in the Septuagint, the Greek translation of the Old Testament that he used on many occasions, to describe a number of the appearances of the angel of the LORD from Genesis onwards.

This is significant because there are some fascinating parallels between Paul's dramatic first encounter with the risen Christ on the road to Damascus (Acts 9.1–9) and two Old Testament stories involving the angel of the LORD. One of these is Jacob's meeting with the angel of God in Genesis 32. In this story we see that he, like Paul, is on a journey; and, also like Paul, that he has a violent *physical* encounter which leaves him permanently marked (Jacob leaves the experience with a limp, just as Paul, temporarily blinded, may have developed a chronic eye condition).[6] After this, however, as we see again in the 'road to Damascus' account, he has his life set on a radical new course, receiving a new name and a new destiny (Gen. 32.28; cf. Acts 26.16–18).[7]

There is, however, a very significant contrast between the two stories. When Jacob asks for the angel's name, he gets no answer, though he concludes that he has seen God 'face to face' (Gen. 32.30). On the other hand, when Paul asks, 'Who are you?' (the question that, according to John 21.12, none of the original disciples dared ask the risen Christ), he is told straight away, using the divine name 'I AM' that Jesus has previously used with the woman at the well in Samaria.[8] We get the distinct impression that the wraps are being taken off what in the Old Testament was a closely guarded secret.

There are also remarkable links between Paul's vision and Balaam's encounter with the angel of the LORD in Numbers 22.21–35. The background to the two stories has much in common. Paul is travelling with the authority of the high priest in Jerusalem to wreak havoc on the Christian converts in Damascus. With a similar sense of urgency, Balaam has been hired by Balak, the king of Moab, to place a curse on the Israelites, who he fears will take over his land (Num. 22.1–6).

In each case, however, the plan goes disastrously wrong. Both men are interrupted mid-course by a surprise encounter with a heavenly visitor which causes them to fall to the ground. As a result, freshly armed with a new set of instructions, they end up confounding their hearers when they reach their destination, suitably chastened, by preaching a message completely opposite to the one intended! The moral in both stories is that God can turn curses into blessings by the unlikeliest of means. (All that seems to be missing in Paul's case is the talking donkey!)

Paul's experience is one of a number of examples of the intriguing parallels between the visits of the angel of the LORD in the Old Testament and the appearances of Jesus after his resurrection (see inset). Once more, they seem to hint that the identity of the 'mysterious stranger' of the Old Testament is now being revealed for all to see.

These similarities, however, are not confined to the gospels and Acts. We notice them also in the descriptions of the risen, glorified Christ that appear in the book of Revelation. For example, the portrayal of the returning Christ in Revelation 19.11–16 as the commander of God's armies, bearing the sword of his judgement recalls the 'commander of the army of the LORD' in Joshua 5.13–15 who, like the angel of the LORD in Numbers 22.31 and 1 Chronicles

---

The risen Christ and the angel of the LORD: Some parallels

- Jesus' first recorded appearance after his resurrection is to a woman (John 20.14); the same is true of the angel of the LORD in Genesis 16.7.
- Jesus is able to penetrate through walls and locked doors (John 20.19,26); the same is true of the angel of God in Daniel 3.25,28 and 6.17,22.
- Jesus is sometimes accompanied by two angelic figures (Luke 24.4; John 20.10–14; Acts 1.10); the same is true of the divine visitor in Genesis 18.2 / 19.1.
- Jesus' true identity is revealed in the offering of food (Luke 24.30–31,41–43; John 21.12); the same is true of the angel of the LORD in Judges 6.19–22 and 13.19–22.
- Jesus is recognized as 'God' by Thomas in a spontaneous outburst of awe and wonder (John 20.28); the same is true of the reactions of Hagar, Jacob, and Manoah (Gen. 16.13; 32.30; Judg. 13.22) and particularly of Gideon who, like Thomas, *demands* physical proof (Judg. 6.17–24).
- Jesus repeatedly commissions and sends out his followers as his witnesses and servants (see Matt. 28.18–20; Luke 24.45–51; John 20.21–23; 21.15–17; Acts 1.8; 26.16–18); the same is true of the angel of the LORD in Exodus 3.2–10, Judges 6.11–16, and Zechariah 3.6–7.
- Jesus gives a final set of instructions and then ascends into heaven in front of his astonished disciples (Acts 1.4–9); the same is true of the angel of the LORD in Judges 13.13–14,20.

21.16, carries a drawn sword. (The irony here is that Joshua, who has the same basic name as Jesus in Hebrew and Greek, is the commander of God's *earthly* army. Was he meeting his heavenly double?)

More striking is the uncanny resemblance between the dazzling appearance of Christ in the opening chapter of Revelation and that of the mysterious figure in Daniel 10, who may well be the angel of the LORD. Indeed, the match is so close here that it becomes difficult to believe that we are not, in fact, reading two descriptions of the same person:

I looked up and there before me was a man *dressed in linen*, with a *belt of fine gold from Uphaz round his waist*. His body was like topaz, his *face like lightning*, his *eyes like flaming torches*, his *arms and legs like the gleam of burnished bronze*, and his *voice like the sound of a multitude* . . . Then I heard him speaking, and as I listened to him, *I fell into a deep sleep*, my face to the ground.

A *hand touched me* and set me trembling on my hands on knees . . . Then he continued, '*Do not be afraid*, Daniel' (Dan. 10.5–12).

And when I turned I saw seven golden lampstands, and among the lampstands was someone like a son of man, *dressed in a robe* reaching down to his feet and with a *golden sash round his chest*. The hair on his head was white like wool, as white as snow, and his *eyes were like blazing fire*. His *feet were like bronze glowing in a furnace*, and his *voice was like the sound of rushing waters* . . . His *face was like the sun* shining in all its brilliance.

When I saw him, *I fell at his feet* as though dead. Then *he placed his right hand on me* and said: '*Do not be afraid*' (Rev. 1.12–17).

Against this background, it is interesting to see that the idea of a glorified figure alongside Yahweh in heaven is not only confined to the New Testament. For instance, the Babylonian Talmud, a major body of Jewish rabbinical teaching dating from about AD 500, relates the story from the early second century of four rabbis who, like Paul in 2 Corinthians 12.2–4, are said to have been taken up to paradise. Of these, one dies, one goes mad, and one (Elisha ben Abuyah) lapses into heresy, leaving only one (the famous Rabbi Akiba) who returns unscathed.[9] What was it that had this extraordinary effect on them? A subsequent account hints at what they saw when it tells of how the third rabbi, Abuyah, abandoned 'correct' Jewish doctrine by concluding that there were two divine powers in heaven.[10] Did he, like Paul on the Damascus road or John in Revelation, have a vision of the Messiah in glory? Did he secretly become a Christian? Certainly, one of his best-known sayings bears a striking similarity to a parable of Jesus.[11] (It is interesting to note that, according to the Talmud, he had on one occasion secretly hidden 'forbidden' writings in his clothes while teaching in the Torah academy, which tumbled out as he got up to leave![12])

Other Jewish writings from around the time that Jesus lived also talk of a glorified heavenly figure alongside God himself, with a variety of names suggested.[13] The Dead Sea Scrolls, for example, include some interesting speculation about Melchizedek, the king who, as we saw, mysteriously appears in Genesis 14.18–20 to bring Abraham bread and wine, and to whom Abraham pays a tenth of all his possessions (which, according to later Old Testament practice, should be set aside rightfully for Yahweh himself). In one of the scrolls, 11QMelchizedek, he is given the title 'God' and 'Prince of Light' who at the end of time will execute judgement and destroy Satan. The writer of the book of Hebrews, perhaps aware of such traditions, likens Melchizedek directly to Christ: 'Without father or mother, without genealogy, without beginning of days or end of life, resembling the Son of God, he remains a priest for ever' (Heb. 7.3).

In later Jewish thought these different ideas came together in discussion about a figure called Metatron, the heavenly representative of humankind, God's mediator and judge, and the guardian of heavenly secrets.[14] It is interesting to note that Metatron is elsewhere described as the 'lesser Yahweh' and as one who stands face to face with God in heaven.[15] This provides an interesting point of contact with John 1.1, which might literally be translated, 'the Word was *facing towards* God, and the Word was God.'

It appears, then, that some Jewish writers were also conscious of a 'Divine Paradox', even if they approached the problem in a somewhat different manner. We should note, however, that Metatron was still usually understood to be a created being,[16] whereas, as we shall see, John's view of Christ here goes far beyond this. But the similarity here between the New Testament and certain lines of Jewish thought is nevertheless an intriguing one.

The Face of God Revealed?

Can we, on the basis of all the passages we have considered so far, definitely identify Jesus with the angel of the LORD? For all the remarkable similarities, there is, apart from the reference to Melchizedek in Hebrews 7.3, little in these verses that proves an *indisputable* link with the New Testament. True, the hint in

John 8.56–58 that Jesus had seen Abraham might just possibly be a reference to Abraham's 'mystery guest' in Genesis chapter 18, while Paul seems to make an apparent connection between Jesus and the angel of God in Galatians 4.14, and talks of Christ descending 'with the voice of the archangel' in 1 Thessalonians 4.16. But it hardly looks like evidence that would stand up in a court of law!

However, the parallels seem too numerous and too widespread to dismiss outright. What, then, should we conclude? Was Jesus merely an angel, as the Jehovah's Witnesses believe? Since the first chapter of Hebrews very definitely *rules out* the idea of Jesus as a created angelic being, we do not need to entertain such an idea seriously. As we have seen, the descriptions of the 'angel of the LORD' in the Old Testament clearly point to a figure who is in some sense actually God himself.[17]

Another possible conclusion is the one reached by second-century writers such as Justin Martyr. Not only do they identify Jesus directly with the angel of the LORD, but they also seem to view *any* visible appearance of God in the Old Testament from the Garden of Eden onwards as a visit from Christ before his human life on earth.[18]

Despite the questions this idea raises, it is not hard to understand why they might have arrived at such a belief. There is, after all, no *clear* distinction in the Old Testament between the appearances of the angel of the LORD and direct visions of Yahweh himself (the technical term for these being a 'theophany'). For instance, Abraham's encounter in Genesis 18 is described in very similar terms to Adam's exchange with God in the Garden of Eden; although both the LORD's companions in Genesis 18 are later described as angels (19.1), no such description is applied to the main visitor. As we have seen, he is simply a man (18.2) who seems also to be God (18.10–14).

The same can be said about the previous chapter, in which the LORD also 'appeared' to Abraham without any further explanation of the circumstances; the fact that he 'went up' at the end of the encounter (v. 22) may hint that he was being revealed in the form of an angel (as in Judg. 13.20), but we are not clearly told.[19] In the Septuagint the same Greek word *ōphthē* is used to describe both these appearances, just as it is used elsewhere for those of the angel of the LORD.

In fact, even in the most dramatic descriptions of God appearing in glory on his heavenly throne (in chapters such as Exod. 19; 24; Isa. 6; Ezek. 1; Dan. 7), there is not always a clear-cut distinction between Yahweh and his angel. In Exodus, for example, the fact that the angel of the LORD speaks as God (3.2,4), acts as God (14.19,24) and bears God's name within him (23.20–21) might provide a possible explanation for why Yahweh, in the accounts of his 'arrival' on Mount Sinai, speaks about 'the LORD' almost as someone else, in the manner we discussed in the last chapter:[20]

> And the LORD said to Moses, 'Go to the people and consecrate them . . . and be ready by the third day, because on that day the LORD will come down on Mount Sinai in the sight of all the people' (Exod. 19.10–11).

> The LORD descended to the top of Mount Sinai and called Moses to the top of the mountain. So Moses went up and the LORD said to him, 'Go down and warn the people so they do not force their way through to see the LORD and many of them perish' (Exod. 19.20–21).

> Then the LORD said to Moses, 'Come up to the LORD, you and Aaron, Nadab and Abihu, and seventy of the elders of Israel. You are to worship at a distance, but Moses alone is to approach the LORD; the others must not come near' (Exod. 24.1–2).

What is interesting here is how the signs that accompany the descent of Yahweh in these passages – the lightning, the clouds, the trumpet, and the gathering of God's people (Exod. 19.16–17) – are *precisely* the signs, mentioned in the *same* order, that we are told to expect at the second coming of Christ (Matt. 24.27–31).

The same thing can be said about the first chapter of Ezekiel, where the LORD who appears above the winged creatures on a sapphire throne is described in exactly the same terms as the (unnamed) man-like figure who stretches out a hand towards Ezekiel in chapter 8:

> Above the vault over their heads was what looked like a throne of lapis lazuli, and high above on the throne was *a figure like that of a man*. I saw that *from what appeared to be his waist up he looked like glowing metal, as if full of fire, and that from there down he looked like fire;* and brilliant

light surrounded him. Like the appearance of a rainbow in the clouds on a rainy day, so was the radiance around him.

This was the appearance of the likeness of the glory of the LORD (Ezek. 1.26–28).

I looked, and I saw *a figure like that of a man. From what appeared to be his waist down he was like fire, and from there up his appearance was as bright as glowing metal.* He stretched out what looked like a hand and took me by the hair of my head (Ezek. 8.2–3).

It is particularly striking in this case that the figure portrayed at first in such infinite remoteness shows, as Christopher Rowland points out, a remarkable willingness to step off the throne and become entangled in the affairs of human beings.[21]

Once more there are remarkable parallels here with Christ, if we consider the events of Easter Week and its aftermath. For example, this same figure, described here as 'like that of a man' but addressed by Ezekiel as 'Sovereign LORD' (9.8), visits the temple to pass judgement on idolatry (Ezek. 8.15–18; cf. Mark 11.15–17); marks out a chosen group for salvation (Ezek. 9.4; see John 17.11–12); announces an outpouring of wrath on Jerusalem (Ezek. 9.5–8; see Luke 21.20–23); promises to gather Jews from the nations to receive the Spirit (Ezek. 11.17–20; cf. Acts 1.4–8; 2.1–12) before finally ascending from Jerusalem on the Mount of Olives (Ezek. 11.23–24; see Acts 1.9–12).

Remarkable though these links are, probably the strongest echoes of both these accounts occur in the story of Jesus' transfiguration, where his appearance changes to a dazzling white before three of his disciples at the top of a mountain (Matt. 17.1–8; Mark 9.2–8; Luke 9.28–36). The same basic features that we see in the passages from Exodus and Ezekiel (clouds, brightness, a heavenly voice, fear and prostration) feature prominently in the gospel descriptions of the event. And, as with Moses, the mountaintop location is significant: Micah 1.3 reminds us that it is Yahweh who 'treads on the heights of the earth'.

Undoubtedly, the effect of this event on the three disciples present must have been staggering. When Peter writes that 'we were eye-witnesses of his *majesty*' (2 Pet. 1.16),[22] he uses a Greek word which, as Robert Reymond points out, is only used elsewhere in the New Testament to describe divine beings.[23] John writes similarly that 'we have seen his *glory*' (John 1.14), a word which, for John, is almost equivalent to deity itself.[24] The impact of what happened on both men can be judged by the fact that shortly before these statements they quite openly describe Jesus as 'God' (2 Pet. 1.1; John 1.1).

Given this experience, it is perhaps hardly surprising that John forges a link which Larry Hurtado calls 'mind-boggling'[25] when he views the description of 'the LORD Almighty' in Isaiah 6.1–5 as an appearance of Christ himself: 'Isaiah said this because he saw *Jesus'* glory and spoke about him' (John 12.41).[26] Similarly, when John writes in Revelation 1.14–15 of the glorified Christ that 'the hair on his head was white like wool, as white as snow . . . and his voice was like the sound of rushing waters,' he is merging together two descriptions of Yahweh enthroned in heaven drawn from Daniel 7.9 and Ezekiel 43.2. Such references can hardly be accidental: on the contrary, they again point us back directly to the question John has raised in the verse which opens his gospel.

It is particularly interesting, therefore, to note that the much more intimate revelation of Yahweh that is given to Moses in Exodus 34 also has strong links with the first chapter of John's gospel. When God came and 'proclaimed his name' to him (in Hebrew thought, the reflection of his innermost being) it was not just as 'Yahweh' but as '**Yahweh Yahweh**' ('*the LORD, the LORD*': vv. 5–6).[27] Moses in turn responds, 'Lord … if I have found favour in your eyes . . . then let *the Lord* go with us' (v. 9). And the LORD then replies, 'all the people among whom you are shall see the work of *the LORD*' (v. 10 RSV).

There are strong echoes of this double use of the divine name in John 1.1 and John 1.18 ('No one has ever seen **God**; the **only God**, who is **at the Father's side**, he has made him known' [ESV]). Indeed, the words 'no-one has ever seen God' may well refer back to the warning God gives to Moses before the vision that '*no one may see me and live*' (33.20). In the same way, when John writes that 'We have seen [Jesus'] glory . . . full of grace and truth' (John 1.14), he recalls Moses' request to see the glory of God (Exod. 33.18) who then reveals himself as 'abounding in lovingkindness and truth' (34.6 NASB).

Here then, from the perspective of John's gospel, is a possible interpretation of the *second Yahweh* in God's name in Exodus

34.6. For Moses the vision is powerful but partial; with Jesus it is complete. Moses only gets to see God's back (Exod. 33.23); in Jesus, however, the *face* of God is finally revealed. In him, the disciples are seeing not merely a portrait, but the real thing: 'Anyone who has seen me has seen the Father' (John 14.9).

Conclusion: Two for the Price of One?

The apparent overlap we have noticed between Yahweh and the angel of the LORD brings with it a strange sense of irony. Throughout the Old Testament, God zealously guards his uniqueness against any comparison with other beings. In Isaiah 48.11, for example, he declares, 'I will not yield my glory to another.' At the same time, Deuteronomy 6.4 seems to rule out the idea that God would 'split' himself into separate parts. Yet, as we have seen, this is *precisely* what seems to be taking place in the examples we have considered.

We should remember here that the belief in a supreme and unique God, undivided, unchanging and unequalled, was the central principle that set apart the Jewish faith from the cultures around it. It was a claim that was both logical and attractive. Yet we find that the two books that most enshrine the core values of Judaism, Genesis and Exodus, are the very ones which challenge this 'tidy' and 'uncluttered' view of God's nature at the most basic level.

It is, of course, not the only instance of a simple, straightforward understanding of truth being apparently undermined from within. Much of the way we instinctively look at the world around us stems from figures such as Isaac Newton (1642–1727), who thought of the universe as governed by a set of laws as predictable as a clock. Theologically, Newton was a Unitarian. His calculations led him to believe that this single set of laws required a single God to hold them in place. Therefore, he reasoned, Jesus could not be fully divine.

In the early twentieth century, however, it was shown that, at the level of the very large and the very small, Newton's laws do not hold rigidly. Relativity shows us, for example, that two things happening at the same time for one observer could happen at different times for another observer travelling at high speed. Time, in other words, is not the absolute, unchanging property that Newton considered it to be. Quantum mechanics, meanwhile, tells us that the more precisely we measure the speed of a particle, the less we can know about its position. One consequence of the theory is that the tiniest building blocks of matter can appear to exist in two places at once. In an elaboration called 'entanglement theory', one recent study suggests that particles seem to 'communicate' with each other at more than 10,000 times the speed of light.[28]

The universe, in other words, is much stranger than we originally thought, and the very act of observation seems to change it. It as if the 'Divine Paradox' is woven into the very fabric of reality itself! But if the world around us does not fit into our nice, tidy patterns of human thought, the same is surely true to an even greater degree in the realm of the spirit. As Jesus himself said, 'The wind blows wherever it pleases. You hear its sound, but you cannot tell where it comes from or where it is going' (John 3.8). We need to bear this in mind before laying down too many preconditions about what God *should* or *should not* be like.

A helpful parallel can be found in the writings of Lewis Carroll. When Alice, in her journey through the looking-glass world, goes into a shop whose shelves are stocked full of goods, she is somewhat perplexed to find the contents mysteriously disappear when inspected more closely. We noticed a rather similar situation in the last chapter: when the two disciples in Emmaus finally discover the identity of the stranger who has befriended them, he vanishes at that very moment from before their eyes. In other words, we need to be prepared for an 'answer' that simply throws up more questions.

And questions there certainly are! In particular, why, given the Old Testament's insistence on the existence of only one true God, do we find, the more we dig below the surface, that a *second* Yahweh keeps emerging into view? What light does that throw on our understanding of Jesus? In particular, could he still be fully *human* in every sense of the word? These are issues that we will continue to explore in the chapters which follow.

It seems increasingly clear, however, that the Divine Paradox runs as a fault line through the entire Bible, from the opening pages of Genesis right through to the end of Revelation. From the puzzling appearances of the 'angel of the LORD' in Genesis and

Exodus to the curiously indecisive references to Jesus as 'God' in the New Testament, the same question seems to reappear in a variety of different forms. How does God intervene in the world and yet remain God? Clearly we need to investigate further.

Ten key statements about Yahweh	Ten key statements about Jesus
• He is a unique God (Isa. 46.9)	• He is a unique God (John 1.18 ESV)
• He is a great God (Neh. 9.32)	• He is a great God (Titus 2.13)
• He is a mighty God (Jer. 32.18 RSV)	• He is a mighty God (Isa. 9.6)
• He is the true God (John 17.3)	• He is the true God (1 John 5.20)
• He is God with us (Hag. 2.4)	• He is God with us (Matt. 1.23)
• He is God over all (Eph. 4.6)	• He is God over all (Rom. 9.5)
• He is our God and Saviour (Isa. 45.21)	• He is our God and Saviour (2 Pet. 1.1)
• He is *my* God and *my* Lord (Ps. 35.23 RSV)	• He is *my* Lord and *my* God (John 20.28)
• He was God from everlasting (Ps. 90.2)	• He was God from everlasting (John 1.1)
• He is God enthroned for ever (Lam. 5.19)	• He is God enthroned for ever (Heb. 1.8)

Questions to consider:

(i)   Jesus said, 'Anyone who has seen me has seen the Father' (John 14.9). What do we understand by this statement? Would those listening have been shocked by it? What does Jesus show us about the Father that we do not already know from the Old Testament?

(ii) Many of the encounters described in the last two chapters take place in the context of journeys. Where are you in your journey with God at present? Have there been any surprises or discouragements on the way? What might threaten to throw you off course?

(iii) 'As the heavens are higher than the earth, so are my ways higher than your ways and my thoughts than your thoughts' (Isa. 55.9). Do our attempts to understand who God is diminish our sense of awe and wonder? What role, if any, should human reasoning have in our attempts to explore his character and nature?

4.

Jesus as the Son of Man

No one has ever gone into heaven except the one who came from heaven – the Son of Man (John 3.13).

A Puzzling Expression?

In the early years of the twentieth century, the French composer Claude Debussy (1862–1918) wrote two sets of piano pieces called *Preludes*. Of these the second piece in Book 1 is particularly interesting in that, for the first time, it dispenses completely with the seven-note scales that had dominated Western classical music over many centuries, relying to a large degree instead on an 'artificial' scale made up of six equal steps. The title of the piece (if it is a title, since it appears, rather intriguingly, in brackets at the end of the piece) is *Voiles*, which means 'Sails'.

Or does it? In Debussy's mysterious, shadowy world, nothing is ever quite as it seems. Although in French *la voile* means 'sail', *le voile*, in the masculine, means 'veil'. In the plural, there is no way of knowing which one Debussy means, or whether he means both at the same time!

As we have already seen, such problems of interpretation are not uncommon in Scripture. In John 1.5, for example, the Greek could be translated, 'the darkness has not overcome it' but it might also mean, 'the darkness has not *understood* it'. Likewise, John 3.7 might mean 'you must be born again,' but it could also be translated, 'you must be born *from above*.' The solution may be, as we saw at the end of chapter two, that we are meant to take *both* meanings on board at once.

The same issues seem to surround the title 'Son of Man', which Jesus applies to himself with great frequency in the gospels. Far from making his identity clear, it seems only to produce great puzzlement from his listeners. 'Who is this "Son of Man"?' they ask him in John 12.34 (and do not get a straight-forward reply)!

Part of the reason for the confusion seems to be that, in Hebrew and Aramaic, the phrase usually means no more than 'human being'. This is clearly the case, for example, in Psalm 146.3 (RSV):

> Put not your trust in princes,
>> in a *son of man*, in whom there is no help.

Elsewhere in the Old Testament, in the parallel couplets so characteristic of Hebrew verse, it is simply used as an alternative for the word 'man', as we read in Numbers 23.19:

> God is not a man, that he should lie,
>> or a *son of man*, that he should change his mind (ESV).

There are, however, three occasions in the Old Testament where the phrase 'son of man' is associated with a much more exalted being, who also in some ways embodies the entire nation.

One of these is particularly interesting in this regard:

> You transplanted a vine from Egypt;
>> you drove out the nations and planted it.
> You cleared the ground for it,
>> and it took root and filled the land . . .
> **Watch over this vine,**
>> **the root your right hand has planted,**
>> **the son you have raised up for yourself.**
> Your vine is cut down, it is burned with fire;
>> at your rebuke your people perish.
> Let your hand rest on *the man at your right hand,*
>> *the son of man you have raised up for yourself.*
> Then we will not turn away from you;
>> revive us, and we will call on your name (Ps. 80.8–9,14–18)

Here, in the first passage highlighted in bold type, the 'son you have raised up for yourself' is clearly the same as the 'vine' (the nation of Israel itself). But the same description is then applied to 'the man at your right hand', identified in the Targums (free translations of the Old Testament into Aramaic possibly similar to those in use at the time of Jesus) as 'King Messiah'.[1] This image reminds us of how the Messiah is said to reign at God's right hand in Psalm 110.1, and is clearly echoed in Christ's description in Mark 14.62 of the Son of Man 'sitting at the right hand of the Mighty One'.

The words 'son of man' also appear in Psalm 8, and the writer of the letter to the Hebrews applies them directly to Jesus (Heb. 2.6–8). On this occasion, however, the 'son of man' picture seems to represent not just Israel, but the entire human race:

> What is man that you are mindful of him,
>   *and the son of man* that you care for him?
> Yet you have made him a little lower than the heavenly beings
>   and crowned him with glory and honour.
> You have given him dominion over the works of your hands;
>   you have put all things under his feet (Ps. 8.4–6 ESV).

If the psalmist has in mind God's commission to Adam to rule over creation (Gen. 1.26–28), the writer to the Hebrews appears here, like Paul, to see Jesus as the second Adam, willing to 'taste death for everyone' in order to restore the dominion that humankind had lost (Heb. 2.8–15).

The words 'son of man' in the Old Testament seem, therefore, to describe humanity at a variety of different levels. But there is one book in the Old Testament which appears to take the expression to an altogether higher level of meaning. Can it throw any light on what Jesus meant when he used the title for himself?

Daniel's Vision in Babylon

The book of Daniel occupies a unique place in the Old Testament because of the way it offers snapshots of the entire span of human history and the role of Israel within it. As we saw in chapter one, it figured significantly in the teaching of Jesus and in the thinking of many of his contemporaries. But hidden within this rich treasure-house of stories, visions and prophecies is also a vital clue in our search for Jesus' true identity.

Exiled in Babylon, far from his homeland, the prophet Daniel one day receives an extraordinary vision:

> In my vision at night I looked, and there before me were the four winds of heaven churning up the great sea. Four great beasts, each different from the others, came up out of the sea . . .

> As I looked,
>   thrones were set in place,
>   and the Ancient of Days took his seat.
> His clothing was as white as snow;
>   the hair of his head was white like wool.
> His throne was flaming with fire,
>   and its wheels were all ablaze.
> A river of fire was flowing,
>   coming out from before him.
> Thousands upon thousands attended him;
>   ten thousand times ten thousand stood before him.
> The court was seated,
>   and the books were opened . . .

> In my vision at night I looked, and there before me was *one like a son of man*, coming with the clouds of heaven. He approached the Ancient of Days and was led into his presence. He was given authority, glory and sovereign power; all nations and peoples of every language worshipped him. His dominion is an everlasting dominion that will not pass away, and his kingdom is one that will never be destroyed (Dan. 7.2–3,9–10,13–14).

There are three obvious elements to this amazing scene. Firstly, we see the four great beasts, depicting four great world empires which were to dominate the course of history. Then we see the image of a courtroom with Yahweh (described as 'the Ancient of Days') enthroned in glory as the heavenly Judge. Finally, we see the power of the earthly kingdoms broken and the figure described as a 'son of man' receiving authority to rule in their place.

So what do the words 'son of man' mean here? Certainly, the expression does suggest a human being, given that Daniel himself is addressed as 'son of man' in the following chapter. But clearly the meaning here is bigger than that. There are suggestions in the vision that, as we saw in the Psalms, the 'son of man' may represent all of God's people (vv. 18,27) or even act as a ruler and figurehead for humanity itself (v. 14).

We can, however, also approach this question from a different angle. We are only told here that he is 'one *like* a son of man'. On two other occasions in the book of Daniel an unnamed heavenly being is described in similar terms. In chapter two we pointed out that when Shadrach, Meshach and Abednego are thrown into the fiery furnace in Daniel 3.21–25 a fourth person is seen walking around in there with them, described as '*like* a son of the gods' and later as God's 'angel' (v. 28).[2] And in chapter three we noticed that when Daniel fasts and prays in 10.2–3 he is visited by a glorious angelic being (who, as we saw, may well be the angel of the LORD) described as 'one *in the likeness* of the sons of men' (10.16 RSV).

So are we looking at the *same* figure in each of these cases? It is worth stepping back a moment here to look at the bigger picture. All of the apparently unrelated episodes in the book of Daniel seem to share the same underlying storyline, with the humbling of a series of rulers of world superpowers who seek to take for themselves the authority which rightly belongs to Yahweh alone. On each occasion a significant role is played by a heavenly redeemer, standing with the suffering of God's people, who comes to rescue and vindicate them. Like the 'mysterious stranger' that we first met in chapter two, this redeemer seems to keep reappearing in a variety of guises, whether as a supernatural 'rock' (2.34–35), as an angel of God (3.28; 6.22), as a 'holy one' (4.23), as a disembodied hand (5.5), as the 'Prince of Princes' (8.25) or as an apparently defeated but ultimately victorious Messiah (9.24–26).

In other words, we have a picture of someone in Daniel 7.13–14 who is certainly human but seems to be much more than that: his origin, like the 'angel of the LORD', is shrouded in mystery. On the one hand he seems to be clearly distinguished from Yahweh, enthroned in the vision as 'the Ancient of Days'. Yet in contrast with the four *earthly* beasts that come up out of the sea, representing four world empires, he comes from heaven on the clouds, an image normally restricted to God alone (see Pss 18.10–11; 104.3; Isa. 19.1; Nah. 1.3). Furthermore, he is the only person in the Old Testament to be *given* glory apart from Yahweh himself, who consistently *refuses* to share it with anyone else (Isa. 42.8; 48.11).

The impression is heightened by several other factors. Firstly, he is 'worshipped' (at least, according to the NIV – the Aramaic verb *pelach*, though often translated 'serve', is only ever used elsewhere in the book to describe the worship of Yahweh or other gods). And the description '*like* a son of man' strongly recalls the figure '*like* that of a man' that Ezekiel sees in a similar vision 'high above on the throne' (Ezek. 1.26) who is clearly none other than Yahweh himself. Seyoon Kim rightly observes that the figure Daniel sees is 'a deity appearing in human form and likeness'.[3]

With this in mind we should see how closely the description of the 'son of man' in Daniel 7.13–14 ties in with what is said about Yahweh himself earlier in the book. In a letter addressed to his subjects in chapter 4 the king of Babylon, Nebuchadnezzar, writes that 'It is my pleasure to tell you about the miraculous signs and wonders that the Most High God has performed for me . . . *His kingdom is an eternal kingdom; his dominion endures from generation to generation*' (Dan. 4.2–3). These words bear a strong resemblance to the way Daniel describes the 'son of man' in his vision:

'*His dominion is an everlasting dominion that will not pass away, and his kingdom is one that will never be destroyed*' (Dan. 7.14).

It might seem ludicrously far-fetched to assume from this that the 'son of man' and 'the Most High God' are one and the same. However, this is *precisely* the conclusion one might reach from the interpretation of Daniel's vision which appears later in chapter 7. Here the 'son of man' drops from view and appears to be *replaced* by the 'Most High', who is now described in almost identical language (cf. vv. 14 and 27 in the NIV). What is more, if one reads verses 21 and 22 at face value, the 'Ancient of Days' and the 'Most High' now seem to be *distinguished* from one another, in the manner we have seen many times in the last two chapters.

'As I watched, this horn was waging war against the holy people and defeating them, until the *Ancient of Days* came and pronounced judgment

in favour of the holy people of the *Most High,* and the time came when
they possessed the kingdom.'

The idea that Daniel should have a vision of two figures, *both* of
whom seem to be 'God', is quite extraordinary, even compared
with what we have read so far about the angel of the LORD. Yet
important evidence to support this idea appears elsewhere in the
book. For this we need to turn back a few chapters.

The reason why Daniel gains such high status in Babylon in the
first place is because King Nebuchadnezzar has had a terrifying
dream (Dan. 2.1). Summoning all his magicians and astrologers, he
threatens them with imminent execution unless they can relate to
him the contents of the dream (a pretty tall order!). In desperation
they turn to the Hebrew servant Daniel, who, doubtless to their
enormous relief, is able to explain the nightmare in its entirety.

What the king has seen is a great statue made up of four metals
of increasing strength but decreasing value. These four sections of
the statue represent four earthly kingdoms, which most scholars
agree are the *same* four kingdoms represented in Daniel 7 (traditionally identified in church history as Babylon, Persia, Greece
and Rome). In the end the statue is struck by a rock ('stone' in
most translations) that is 'cut out of a mountain, *but not by human
hands*' (Dan. 2.45), causing it to be broken into fragments and
scattered across the earth. The phrase 'not by human hands' is
extremely significant: it draws a clear distinction between the four
kingdoms, representing the summit of human achievement, and
the stone which, by contrast, is *definitely not* of human origin; the
image is used elsewhere to describe Yahweh himself (Gen. 49.24
ESV; Isa. 8.14).

The important question for us is, if the four kingdoms are the
same as those in chapter 7, do the mountain and the stone play
the *same* role as the 'Ancient of Days' and the 'son of man'? The
reason for asking this question is that, by definition, *the stone must
be composed of the same material as the mountain from which it is cut.*
Could the 'son of man' and the 'Ancient of Days', in other words,
represent two different aspects of Yahweh's being?

The question is heightened by the obvious link in both these
accounts with the description of the Tower of Babel in Genesis
11, where it is *God* who causes Babylon, the original pinnacle

of human achievement, and the first of the empires portrayed in the two Daniel stories, to be scattered across the earth. Here Yahweh describes his action in demolishing a counter-kingdom set up against him *in the plural: 'Let us go down* and confuse their language' (v. 7). While it is fashionable to regard this as the 'plural of majesty' (rather like the royal 'we'), I would like to suggest that it tells us something more profound about the nature of God (careful comparison of vv. 7 and 9 shows that Yahweh is talking to himself here, not to another angelic being). Does Daniel's vision, happening in the very place of Yahweh's 'descent' to earth in Genesis 11, offer the same kind of insight into who God is?[4]

An even stronger parallel with Daniel's vision appears in Zechariah chapter 3. Here, like Daniel 7, we see a courtroom scene in which two divine figures, Yahweh and his angel, seem to portray different aspects of one supreme being. In Zechariah the angel of the LORD pronounces judgement on behalf of Yahweh in favour of Joshua the high priest, representing God's people, defeating the accusations made against him by Satan. In Daniel 7 the 'Ancient of Days' comes and pronounces judgement in favour of the 'saints of the Most High' against the attacks of the 'fourth beast' who has been prevailing over them. If Zechariah presents Yahweh in two different guises, performing two different courtroom roles, could we make the same case for the 'Ancient of Days' and the 'son of man' in Daniel 7?

It is perhaps significant here that a later Jewish tradition does indeed associate *both* figures in Daniel's vision with two different aspects of the same God. Such speculation resulted partly from the fact that Daniel 7.9 mentions *thrones* (plural) that are set in place when the Ancient of Days (singular) takes his seat. The Babylonian Talmud, for example, talks of two seats for the Ancient of Days, reflecting his contrasting attributes: one is for justice, and one is for mercy.[5] And in older versions of the Septuagint, the distinction between the two figures seems to have disappeared even further: here the 'son of man' comes *as* the Ancient of Days. Christopher Rowland concludes from this that the human figure possesses 'the form and character of God himself'.[6]

It is striking, therefore, to see the *same* thing happening in Revelation 1.12–16. Here we are presented with 'someone like a son of man', a description clearly drawn from Daniel 7.13, yet with images of 'blazing fire' and hair that is 'white like wool' that obviously relate to the portrayal of the Ancient of Days in Daniel 7.9. As David Capes observes, 'the merging . . . modifies the story in Daniel 7 and appears to identify Jesus with God'.[7] Given the obvious implications here, it is hardly surprising that John fell at the feet of Christ 'as though dead' (Rev. 1.17).

What Did Jesus Mean?

It is clear from what we have read so far that Jesus had a very rich background to draw upon when he used the expression 'Son of Man'. As we have seen, it might refer to him as simply a man; it might suggest that he is somehow representing all of God's people or the entire human race; it might imply an exalted heavenly being; it might suggest an aspect of God himself. It might, indeed, suggest all of these things together.

In the first two categories we find that many of the times Jesus uses the phrase 'Son of Man', it is associated with his betrayal, rejection and death (see later inset). This recalls the way it was often applied (on almost a hundred occasions!) to the prophet Ezekiel, rejected for speaking in parables (Ezek. 20.49), who at one point symbolically bears the sins of the entire nation in his own body (Ezek. 4.4–8). For instance, when Jesus says, 'the Son of Man did not come to be served, but to serve, and to give his life as a ransom for many' (Matt. 20.28) he seems to be referring to himself both as a distinct individual *and* as representing the whole of humanity. A similar idea occurs in another 'Son of Man' passage, where he says that 'whatever you did for one of the least of these brothers and sisters of mine, *you did for me*' (Matt. 25.40).

At the same time we find many statements which Jesus made about the 'Son of Man' pointing to a glorified heavenly being, like the one described in Daniel 7 and in later books such as *1 Enoch*.[8] His origin is in heaven (John 3.13); he comes as a sign to his generation, greater than the kings or the prophets (Luke 11.30–32); and from there he will return to his heavenly home (John 6.62) to sit at God's right hand (Mark 14.62). Subsequently he is to return in glory on the clouds of heaven (Matt. 24.30) at a moment when he is least expected (Matt. 24.44), like lightning flashing from one end of the sky to another (Luke 17.24).

Yet there are clearly occasions where the 'Son of Man' seems to point towards a figure who is nothing less than God himself. Here the divine significance of the 'Son of Man' title often becomes clearer when we consider the Old Testament background. For instance, when Jesus says 'the Son of Man . . . *will reward each person according to what they have done*' (Matt. 16.27) he is directly recalling the psalmist's address to Yahweh, 'You *reward everyone according to what they have done*' (Psalm 62.12).

The same appears to be true in Luke's 'Sermon on the Plain', when Jesus says, 'Blessed are you when people **hate you**, when they **exclude you** . . . **because of the Son of Man**. *Rejoice* in that day and leap for joy, because great is your reward in heaven' (Luke 6.22–23). Here his words seem to echo Isaiah 66, where Yahweh declares, 'Your own people . . . **hate you**, and **exclude you because of my name** . . . *Rejoice* with Jerusalem and be glad for her . . . For you will feed and be satisfied at her comforting breasts' (66.5,10–11).

Similarly, when Jesus says in Luke 19.10 that 'the Son of Man came to *seek and to save the lost*' he appears to recall the words of Yahweh in Ezekiel 34: 'I myself will search for my sheep and look after them . . . I will *search for the lost* and bring back the strays' (vv. 11,16).

Perhaps nowhere is the full significance of the title 'Son of Man' clearer, however, than in the parable of the sheep and the goats in Matthew 25.31–46:

> When the Son of Man *comes in his glory*, and *all the angels with him*, he will *sit on his glorious throne. All the nations will be gathered* before him, and he will separate the people one from another as a shepherd separates the sheep from the goats. *He will put the sheep on his right and the goats on his left.*[9]

Here, not only do we see the Son of Man on his throne, in command of angelic forces (v. 31) as Judge (v. 32) and King (v. 34), all roles that previously were considered to belong to God himself, but the specific details of the parable recall no fewer than five descriptions of Yahweh in the Old Testament:

For the LORD will rebuild Zion
> *and appear in his glory* (Ps. 102.16).

I saw the LORD *sitting on his throne* with all the multitudes of heaven standing round him *on his right and on his left* (1 Kgs 22.19).

As for you, my flock, this is what the Sovereign LORD says: *I will judge between one sheep and another, and between rams and goats* (Ezek. 34.17).

I will gather all nations
> and bring them down to the Valley of Jehoshaphat . . .
for there I will sit
> *to judge all the nations on every side* (Joel 3.2,12).

Then the LORD my God *will come, and all the holy ones with him* (Zech. 14.5).

However, although the Son of Man is presented with all the attributes of God here, we find these qualities bound up with the frailty of the human condition, in that, as we have seen, whatever is done to his followers is also said to be done directly to the Son of Man himself (Matt. 25.40,45).[10]

Even so, as Robert Reymond comments, 'The portrait he draws of himself in this final judgement scene is so awesome and majestic that it is simply moral perversity that prevents one from viewing him here in terms of his full divine character as God.'[11]

This same tension between the 'human' and 'divine' qualities of the 'Son of Man' appears in John chapter 5, where the voice of Jesus as 'Son of Man' causes graves to open and the dead to rise and face his judgement (John 5.27–29). On the one hand this seems to be a clear reference back to Ezekiel, who as a human 'son of man' speaks to the dry bones of Israel so that life enters into them and lifts them up from their graves (Ezek. 37.4–14). Yet they also reveal a divine fingerprint: only Yahweh in the Old Testament, as heavenly Judge, exercises true authority over life and death. Once more Jesus seems to display the perfect face of humanity and divinity at the same time.

Ten pointers to a human 'Son of Man'

- He has nowhere to lay his head (Matt. 8.20)
- He comes 'eating and drinking' (Matt. 11.19)
- He will suffer like John the Baptist (Matt. 17.12–13)
- He will be delivered into the hands of men (Matt. 17.22)
- He will give his life as a ransom for many (Matt. 20.28)
- He will be handed over to be crucified (Matt. 26.2)
- He will suffer many things and be rejected (Luke 9.22)
- He will be mocked, insulted, spat upon, flogged and killed (Luke 18.31–32)
- He will be 'lifted up' on the cross (John 3.14)
- He offers us his flesh to eat and his blood to drink (John 6.53)

Ten pointers to a divine 'Son of Man'

- He can take away sins (Matt. 9.6; cf. Yahweh in Ps. 103.3)
- He is 'Lord of the Sabbath' (Matt. 12.8; cf. Yahweh in Exod. 20.10)
- He is the 'divine sower' (Matt. 13.37; cf. Yahweh in Jer. 31.27–28)
- He is in command of angels (Matt. 13.41; cf. Yahweh in Ps. 148.2)
- He is also the Son of God (Matt. 16.13,16; Mark 9.7/9; Luke 22.69–70; John 1.49–51 and 5.26–27)
- He rules the coming kingdom (Matt. 16.28; cf. God the Father in Luke 9.27)
- He is coming on the clouds with glory (Matt. 24.30; cf. Yahweh in Exod. 24.15–16 and Ps. 18.9–12)
- He is the divine 'I AM' (Mark 14.62; John 8.28; cf. Yahweh in Exod. 3.14–15)
- He is 'lifted up' (John 3.14; cf. Yahweh as 'high and lifted up' in Isa. 6.1 RSV)
- He brings healing and is worshipped (John 9.35–38; cf. Yahweh in Exod. 23.25)

A similar comment could be made about John 1.51, perhaps the most striking 'Son of Man' reference in the gospels. Here we find that each of the different aspects of 'Son of Man' that we have discussed so far – as single individual, as ideal representative of the human race, as heavenly mediator and as God himself – are brought together in a single image. In this verse Jesus is echoing the story in Genesis 28.12–19 in which Jacob sees angels ascending and descending upon a ladder which stretches between heaven and earth, with God standing at the top of the ladder, and himself at the bottom: 'Very truly, I tell you, you will see heaven opened and the angels of God ascending and descending upon the Son of Man' (NRSV).

Here Jesus presents himself as bridging the gulf between heaven and earth, between God and humankind, creating an open doorway into heaven itself.[12] As a result, just as Jacob can say *this is* the gate of heaven (Gen. 28.17), Jesus is now able to say *I am* the gate (John 10.7). The diverse range of meanings contained in the term 'Son of Man' here takes on a central importance: Jesus needed to be *completely* divine to span the gulf between God and humankind, and *completely* human to lift us up with him to the heights of God. We are therefore reminded of the necessity of keeping both these truths firmly in place: if the ladder is not completely secure at either end, our salvation is at risk.

As this chapter has shown, the term 'Son of Man' raises many questions. What, exactly, did Jesus intend us to understand from it? Why, given the extensive use he makes of it, is it ignored almost completely by the other writers of the New Testament?[13] And why, two thousand years later, are we further than ever from agreeing what it means? As Joseph Ratzinger points out (better known to us as the recent Pope Benedict XVI), the many attempts to explain the expression have led to 'a graveyard of mutually contradictory hypotheses'.[14] But, as he later comments, 'The enigmatic term . . . presents us in concentrated form with all that is most original and distinctive about the figure of Jesus, his mission, and his being. He comes from God and he is God. But that is precisely what makes him – having assumed human nature – the bringer of true humanity.'[15]

In other words, the richness of the expression 'Son of Man' lies in the way it embraces so many different layers of meaning, and we should avoid trying to pin it down to a single idea: it resonates at a variety of different levels. Like the shadowy figure of the 'angel of the LORD', it expresses in a powerful way the mystery of the Divine Paradox that we considered in the last three chapters. Yet it is this very tension within the idea that enables it to express so beautifully the mystery of God becoming man in Christ, and heaven and earth meeting within a single human body.

Ten key statements about Yahweh as Judge	Ten key statements about Jesus as Judge
• He will gather the nations for judgement (Joel 3.2)	• He will gather the nations for judgement (Matt. 25.31–32)
• He will gather them like wheat (Mic. 4.11–12)	• He will gather them like wheat (Luke 3.17)
• All will appear before him (Rom. 14.10)	• All will appear before him (2 Cor. 5.10)
• He divides the sheep from the goats (Ezek. 34.17)	• He will divide the sheep from the goats (Matt. 25.32–33)
• He knows what lies within us (1 Kgs 8.39)	• He knows what lies within us (John 2.25)
• He will bring every hidden deed to judgement (Eccl. 12.14)	• He will bring every hidden deed to judgement (1 Cor. 4.5)
• He searches hearts and repays according to our deeds (Jer. 17.10)	• He searches hearts and repays according to our deeds (Rev. 2.23)
• He can blot us out of the book of life (Exod. 32.33)	• He can blot us out of the book of life (Rev. 3.5)
• He can burn with unquenchable fire (Jer. 4.4)	• He can burn with unquenchable fire (Luke 3.17)
• He disciplines those that he loves (Prov. 3.12)	• He disciplines those that he loves (Rev. 3.19)

Questions to consider:

(i) Read chapters 1 – 3 of Revelation. How much does the picture of Jesus as the glorified 'Son of Man' differ from the one we have in the gospels? Which of his seven letters to the churches challenges us most in our personal walk with God? Are we hot, cold or lukewarm (Rev. 3.16)?

(ii) In the parable of the sheep and the goats (Matt. 25.31–46) the Son of Man appears to determine our eternal destiny on the basis of actions performed. Is this a correct understanding of the parable? If so, how does it relate to Paul's teaching that we are saved by God's grace alone (Eph. 2.8–9)?

(iii) How much time do we spend thinking about the final judgement? Why is the subject avoided so much in our churches today? Are we afraid of it? Why might it be important for us that the Son of Man as Judge is completely divine, but also completely human?

5.

Jesus as the Wisdom of God

We preach Christ crucified: a stumbling-block to Jews and foolishness to Gentiles, but to those whom God has called, both Jews and Greeks, Christ the power of God and the wisdom of God (1 Cor. 1.23–24).

God's Partner in Creation?

Anyone who has compared a Catholic Bible with the one used by most Protestants will have noticed a number of extra books scattered throughout the Old Testament. These books are called the 'Apocrypha': they appeared in the Septuagint, the version of the Old Testament used by the Greek-speaking Jews and by much of the early church, but never in the Hebrew Bible. Catholics regard them as Scripture whereas Protestants do not. While there may be a strong case against placing them in the Bible on an equal basis with other books of Scripture, they do provide a fascinating insight into the period between the Old and New Testaments.

Of these books, two are particularly worth reading. One is called 'The Wisdom of Jesus son of Sirach' (commonly known as 'Ecclesiasticus') and is similar in style to the book of Proverbs, but with a few statements remarkably close to some we find later in the gospels.[1] The other is entitled 'The Wisdom of Solomon' and has no real parallel anywhere in the Old Testament, though its turns of phrase are clearly echoed in the writings of Paul.[2] Such correspondences may go some way to explaining why one of the earliest lists of Christian literature, the Muratorian Canon, actually includes the book as part of the *New* Testament.

What is interesting about both books for our discussion here is the extensive reference they make to a figure described in the feminine as 'Wisdom', which we first encounter in chapters 1 to 8 of the book of Proverbs. Here we find that 'Wisdom' shares the role of creator and teacher with God himself, being present 'at the first, before the beginning of the earth' and 'rejoicing before him always' (Prov. 8.23,30 ESV).

The possibility that such a being could have a real existence seems to conflict with the clear message of the Old Testament that God created the world unaided, with wisdom simply an essential part of his character. If we compare the following two passages, for example, there seems on the surface to be a direct contradiction of thought:

I, the LORD, am the maker of all things,
Stretching out the heavens by Myself,
And spreading out the earth *all alone* (Isa. 44.24 NASB).

I was there when he established the heavens,
     when he drew the horizon on the oceans.
I was there when he set the clouds above,
     when he established springs deep in the earth.
I was there when he set the limits of the seas,
     so they would not spread beyond their boundaries.
And when he marked off the earth's foundations,
I was the architect at his side.
I was his constant delight,
     rejoicing always in his presence (Prov. 8.27–30 NLT).

The explanation usually given is that this personalized description of Wisdom is simply a figure of speech, bringing out one particular aspect of God's character in a more poetically engaging way. Such an answer would help explain why, in some versions of the Bible, such as the NIV, Luke 11.49 is translated 'Because of this, *God in his wisdom said*, "I will send them prophets and apostles, some of whom they will kill and others they will persecute"' where the original Greek says, 'Therefore also the *Wisdom of God* said, "I will send them prophets and apostles, some of whom they will kill and persecute"' (RSV).

It is interesting, therefore, that in the version of this verse which appears in Matthew 23.34, Jesus makes *himself* the author of the statement: 'Therefore *I am sending you* prophets and sages and

teachers: Some of them you will kill and crucify; others you will flog
in your synagogues and pursue from town to town' (Matt. 23.34).
Is Jesus perhaps implying that this mysterious figure of Wisdom
does really exist – that he, in fact, is that figure? It is striking how,
immediately after saying this, Jesus clearly addresses Jerusalem
using the *feminine* imagery of Wisdom in Proverbs ('how often I
have longed to gather your children together, *as a hen gathers her
chicks under her wings'* [Matt. 23.37]).[3]

There are other occasions, too, when he seems to apply to
himself the images of Wisdom from Proverbs and Sirach (see inset
on the next page). Paul also seems to come to the same conclusion,
describing Jesus as 'the wisdom of God' (1 Cor. 1.24), in whom
are hidden 'all the treasures of wisdom and knowledge' (Col. 2.3).
His thinking, however, appears not just to reflect the first section
of Proverbs, but also some of the passages in Wisdom of Solomon,
where we find statements such as the following:

For wisdom is a kindly spirit . . . which *holds all things together* . . .
(1.6–7 NRSV)

For she is a breath of the power of God,
    and *a pure emanation of the glory of the Almighty;*
. . . she is a reflection of eternal light,
    a spotless mirror of the working of God,
    and *an image* of his goodness (7.25–26 NRSV).

She reaches mightily from one end of the earth to the other,
    and she *orders all things well.*
. . . what is richer than wisdom,
the *active cause of all things*? (8.1,5 NRSV)

Using very similar language Paul goes on to write to the Colossians
that: 'The Son is the *image of the invisible God*, the firstborn over all
creation . . . *all things have been created through him* and for him. He
is before all things, and *in him all things hold together*' (Col. 1.15–17).

The letter to the Hebrews also seems to reflect some of the same
turns of phrase when it states that: 'The Son is the *radiance of God's
glory* and the *exact representation* of his being, sustaining *all things*
by his powerful word' (Heb. 1.3).

Jesus and Wisdom
compared

'*Come to me*, all you who are weary and burdened, and *I will give you rest* . . . For *my yoke is easy* and my burden is light' (Matt. 11.28,30).

> *Come to her* with all your soul . . .
> For at last *you will find the rest she gives* . . .
> *Her yoke is a golden ornament* . . . (Sir. 6.26–30 RSV).

Then Jesus declared, 'I am the bread of life. *Whoever comes to me will never go hungry, and whoever believes in me will never be thirsty*' (John 6.35).

> *Come to me*, you who desire me,
>   and eat your fill of my fruits . . .
> *Whoever feeds on me will be hungry for more,*
>   *and whoever drinks from me will thirst for more*
> (Sir. 24.19,21 NEB).

Then Jesus, still teaching in the temple courts, *cried out* . . . '*You will look for me, but you will not find me*; and where I am, you cannot come' (John 7.28,34).

> Out in the open wisdom *calls aloud*,
>   she raises her voice in the public square . . .
> 'Then they will call to me but I will not answer;
>   *they will look for me but will not find me*' (Prov. 1.20,27).

On the last and greatest day of the festival Jesus stood [on the Temple Mount] and *cried aloud*, 'If anyone is thirsty let him *come to me*; whoever believes in me, *let him drink*.' As Scripture says, 'Streams of *living water* shall flow out from within him' (John 7.37–38 NEB).

> Wisdom has built her house . . . and *she calls*
>   *from the highest point* in the city . . .
> '*Come*, eat my food
>   and *drink the wine I have mixed*.
> Leave your simple ways and *you will live*' (Prov. 9.1,3,5–6).

Are these descriptions of Wisdom, then, simply a figure of speech? Do they, perhaps, point to a distinct, created being, as Sirach appears to imply? Or do they, as Wisdom of Solomon seems to suggest, describe what seems to be God's own *alter ego*, filling all things (7.24), creating all things (8.5) and knowing all things (9.11)? Here again we find ourselves wrestling with the idea of something which at one level appears to be an aspect of God himself but at another level seems to exist independently in its own right.

The Word that Walked the Earth

The passages we have been considering from Proverbs, Sirach and Wisdom are particularly useful in helping us to understand the background for the picture of the divine Christ at the Father's side, through whom the entire universe came into being, that we see at the beginning of John's gospel. To begin with, all three state that Wisdom was present before the world began;[4] and each one declares that Wisdom played a key role in the process of creation (Prov. 8.30; Sir. 1.9; Wis. 9.2). Wisdom of Solomon also tells us that those who accept and receive Wisdom can alone become God's friends (7.27–28; cf. John 1.12), while Proverbs 8.30 stresses the loving and joyful relationship between God and 'Wisdom' at his side (see John 1.18).

We should also note that, just as God tells Wisdom to 'make your dwelling' in Israel (Sir. 24.8 NRSV), so John says that 'the Word became flesh and *made his dwelling* among us' (1.14). In both cases the Greek word means 'to pitch one's tent', a clear reference to Yahweh dwelling with the Israelites in the wilderness in the tabernacle. Here they would meet with him and encounter his glory.

Despite these similarities, it is significant that John does not actually use the expression 'Wisdom' for Jesus in these passages. Instead, he uses the related idea of the 'Word' of God (*logos* in Greek) to describe who Jesus was. This link reflects the close similarity between 'Wisdom' and the 'Word' throughout the Old Testament. On the one hand, as with Wisdom, the Word simply expresses the inner nature of God himself: in the first chapter of Genesis, for instance, God *speaks out*, and instantly things come into being.

On the other hand, like Wisdom, the Word also appears to have a separate existence of its own: it is sent down from heaven to act on God's behalf (Ps. 107.20), and, like the various references to wisdom in the Old Testament which imply the principle of 'intelligent design' (see Job 39.26; Ps. 104.24; Prov. 3.19; Jer. 10.12), it is also presented as the binding force which holds together the whole of creation:

> Your word, O LORD, is eternal;
>   it stands firm in the heavens.
> Your faithfulness continues through all generations;
>   you established the earth, and it endures.
> Your laws endure to this day,
>   for all things serve you (Ps. 119.89–91).

Describing Jesus as the 'Word' of God, therefore, goes way beyond the idea of him simply acting as God's channel of communication to humankind: it connects him with the very ordering principle of the universe itself![5]

Just occasionally, the Old Testament seems to present the Word with almost human characteristics.[6] Particularly intriguing is the description of the Word in Isaiah 55.10–11 which 'goes out' from God and then 'returns' to him, to accomplish 'the purpose for which [he] sent it'. There is an interesting echo here in John's gospel where Jesus says that he 'came from the Father' and is 'going back to the Father' (John 16.28) in order 'to do the will of him who sent me' (John 6.38).

In Proverbs 30.2–6 the same combination of ideas appears in connection with both 'Wisdom' (v. 3) and the 'Word' (vv. 5–6) but in much more personal terms: '*Who* has gone up to heaven and come down?' (v. 4). The direct answer again seems to point towards Christ, as we read in John 3.13: '*No one* has ever gone into heaven except the one who came from heaven – the Son of Man.'[7]

More remarkable still is Zechariah 6, where the Word of Yahweh 'comes' to Zechariah and seems to speak as a personal envoy of God: 'Then the word of the LORD came to me, saying, "Receive the gift from the captives . . . Then *you shall know* that the LORD of hosts has *sent Me to you*"' (Zech. 6.9,15 NKJV). Once more there are clear echoes in John's gospel, where Jesus describes the disciples as those who '*know* that you have *sent me*' (John 17.25). The same form of words has already been used twice in Zechariah 2 in a passage in which the angel of the LORD has a significant role, suggesting a close link between the 'Word' of Yahweh and his angel (as is apparent in Zech. 1.7–9).

This connection between the Word and the angel of God is developed further in later Jewish writings.[8] In Wisdom of Solomon, for instance, God's dispatching of his Word to slay the firstborn in Egypt is described in particularly graphic language:

> Your *all-powerful word* from heaven's royal throne bounded, a fierce warrior, into the doomed land, bearing the *sharp sword* of your inexorable decree. And as he alighted, he filled every place with death; he still reached to heaven, while he stood upon the earth (Wis. 18.15–16 NAB).[9]

Yet again, we find echoes of this in the New Testament, where in Revelation 19.11–16 Jesus comes as 'the Word of God' bearing a 'sharp sword' to strike the nations.

Even stronger parallels with the New Testament appear in the Targums, expanded translations of the Hebrew Scriptures into Aramaic containing elements possibly originating from fairly close to the time of Jesus, where the Word often acts *in the place of God himself*. In the Targum of Onkelos, for example, we find at Genesis 3.8 that it is the *Word of God* that Adam and Eve hear walking in the garden; and it is the *Word of God* that Jacob declares will be his God at Genesis 28.20–21. The Jerusalem Targum, meanwhile, tells us that it is the *Word of God* which created humankind at Genesis 1.27, and even includes an example of a prayer *addressed* to the Word of God at Deuteronomy 33.7.

More striking is the Targum Neofiti to Genesis 1.1, which declares that, '*From the beginning* with wisdom the *Word of the Lord created* and perfected the heavens and the earth.' This bears an intriguing similarity to John 1.1–3: '*In the beginning* was *the Word* . . . Through him *all things were made*; without him nothing was made that has been made.'[10]

But if the Word presented *as* God, we also find, as with John 1.1, that the Word is *with* God. Not only do the Targums occasionally identify the Word with the angel of the LORD,[11] but they sometimes also show Yahweh *and* his Word acting together in distinct roles. For example, where Genesis 19.24 says, 'Then the LORD rained down burning sulphur on Sodom and Gomorrah – from the LORD out of the heavens,' the Jerusalem Targum tells us that it is the *Word of God* who sends down destruction from Yahweh.[12]

Of particular interest in this respect is one passage which appears to link the Word of God to the Messiah. The nineteenth-century writer Joseph Gurney refers to a statement made by the Italian scholar Petrus Galatinus (1460–1540) that, in a (now lost) Targum on the Psalms, the words of Psalm 110.1 ('the Lord said to my Lord') are represented as 'the Lord said to *his Word*':

> Galatinus quotes, as his authority, the following passage of a certain Jewish book entitled the Sepher Kibucim, or 'the book of collections of the sentences of the holy wise men;' – 'Rabbi Jodan, in the name of Rabbi Hama, said, In the future time, the holy and blessed God will cause the King Messiah to sit down on his right hand; as it is said in Psalm 110, "Jehovah said unto my Lord, sit thou on my right hand"; which the Targum of Jonathan Ben Uzziel thus explains: *God said to his Word*, Sit thou on my right hand.'[13]

Finally we should note that, in later Jewish thinking, these ideas developed into speculation about the *Torah*, the 'law' of God embodied in the first five books of the Old Testament. In a commentary on the first book of the Bible entitled *Genesis Rabbah* we read that, while heaven and earth are finite, the Torah is infinite (10.1); that the Torah existed for thousands of years before the world began (8.2); that God consulted the Torah before creating the world (1.1); and that the world was created *through* the Torah (1.1) and *for* the Torah (1.4). Although these statements date from centuries after the lifetime of Jesus, they carry remarkable echoes of what the New Testament says about Christ (see Mark 13.31; John 1.1; John 17.24; Col. 1.16).

Holding It All Together

So far we have shown how John's description of Jesus as the 'Word' of God springs from a clear background in the Old Testament and later Jewish writings. However, there is a significant extra dimension to John's use of the idea that relates to the realm of Greek philosophy. In Stoic thought at this time the term *logos* was used to describe the active principle of reason which was believed to uphold the entire universe. Indeed, Paul may well have been quoting the Stoic philosopher Epimenides in his sermon at the Areopagus in Athens when he says of God that 'in him we live and move and have our being' (Acts 17.28).

An important background for this combination of Jewish and Greek ideas can be found in the writings of the Jewish thinker Philo of Alexandria (c.20 BC – AD 50). Philo's understanding of the Old Testament, like many Greek-speaking Jews of his time, was strongly coloured by Greek thought. On the one hand he carried over from philosophers such as Plato a belief that God was too far removed from the material world to be actively involved with it. But by drawing, on the other hand, on the Stoic idea of the *logos* he was able to suggest something to bridge the gap: a principle of order, filling the whole universe, that could act as a link between finite human beings and an apparently remote, unchangeable God. As a result, he saw the *logos* not only as the means by which God made the universe, but also as the force that actively holds it together, and the channel through which God reveals himself to humanity.

Summarizing Philo's beliefs about the *logos*, James Dunn argues that for Philo:

> the Logos is what is knowable of God, the Logos is God insofar as he may be apprehended and experienced . . . It is only in and through the Logos and the powers that God even begins to enter within the range of man's perception. Or to use Philo's favourite sun and light symbolism, the Logos is to God as the corona is to the sun, the sun's halo which man can look upon when he cannot look directly on the sun itself. That is not to say that the Logos is God as such, any more than the corona is the sun as such, but the Logos is that alone which may be seen of God.[14]

The relevance of Philo for us today lies in the way he thought deeply about his faith and tried to relate it to the world of ideas around him. Some of his thoughts about the *logos* are far-sighted by today's standards: he even foresaw a time when, through the action of the *logos*, democracy would come to the whole world![15]

But Philo also helps us make sense of some of the material we have looked at earlier. Not only did he identify the *logos* with the angel of the LORD, with an ideal figurehead of humanity similar to the Messiah or the Son of Man, and with the Wisdom of God,[16] drawing together all the themes we have considered in the last four chapters, but he also gave it titles that anticipate many of those later given to Christ. Although Philo's understanding of the *logos* differs in some important ways from that of the early church, the sheer number of these matches is quite remarkable, given that he almost certainly arrived at them before any of the New Testament books had been written:

Descriptions of Jesus matching Philo's logos	
He is the solid foundation	Matt. 7:24–25 / *Somn.* 1.241
He is the divine physician	Luke 5.31 / *QG* 3.28
He is the Word before creation	John 1.1 / *Migr.* 6
He is God alongside Yahweh	John 1.1 / *QE* 2.62
He is God's gift to humankind	John 3.16 / *Praem.* 163
He is sent into the world	John 3.17 / *Her.* 205
He is the fountain of eternal life	John 4.14 / *Fug.* 97
He is the son, copying the Father's deeds	John 5.19 / *Conf.* 63
He is the bread of God	John 6.30–35 / *Leg.* 3.173
He is light	John 8.12 / *Somn.* 1.75
He is the shepherd	John 10.11 / *Mut.* 116
He is the way	John 14.6 / *Post.* 102
He is the truth	John 14.6 / *Her.* 143
He is the life	John 14.6 / *Fug.* 97
He is the source of salvation	Acts 4.12 / *Fug.* 186
He is the means of creation	1 Cor. 8.6 / *Leg.* 3.96
He is the rock in the wilderness	1 Cor. 10.4 / *Leg.* 2.86
He is the image of God	2 Cor. 4.4 / *Conf.* 147
He is the judge	2 Cor. 5.10 / *QE* 2.13
He brings unlimited blessing	Eph. 1.3 / *Mos.* 2.134
He brings the forgiveness of sins	Eph. 1.7 / *Mos.* 2.134

He brings peace, reconciling opposites	Eph. 2.14–16 / QE 2.68
He is raised on high to fill the universe	Eph. 4.10 / *Somn*. 2.245
He is the firstborn	Col. 1.15 / *Agr*, 51
He is the bond that holds all things together	Col. 1.17 / *Fug*. 112
He is the head of all things	Col. 1.18 / QE 2.117
He is the beginning	Col. 1.18 / QG 1.4
He is revealed in fire from heaven	2 Thess. 1.7 / QG 3.15
He overthrows and destroys God's enemies	2 Thess. 2.8 / *Fug*. 186
He is the mediator between humanity and God	1 Tim. 2.5 / QE 2.13
He is the radiance of God	Heb. 1.3 / *Deus*. 78
He is the exact representation of God's being	Heb. 1.3 / *Plant*. 18
He is the sustainer of all things	Heb. 1.3 / QE 2.13
He is the ruler of angels	Heb. 1.6 / *Conf*. 146
He is the sharp sword that divdes and separates	Heb. 4.12 / *Her*. 130
He is the Word that sees all things	Heb. 4.12–13 RSV / *Leg*. 3.171
He is Melchizedek	Heb. 7.3 / *Leg*. 3.82
He is our intercessor	Heb. 7.25 / *Her*. 205
He is a perfect high priest	Heb. 7.26 / *Fug*. 108
He is the veil separating the visible and invisible worlds	Heb. 10.20 / QE 2.94
He is eternally unchanging	Heb. 13.8 / *Fug*. 13
He is our advocate	1 John 2.1 / *Mos*. 2.134
He is without sin	1 John 3.5 / *Fug*. 117
He is the ruler of creation	Rev. 3.14 / QG 4.111
He exposes the nakedness of unworthy deeds	Rev. 3.15–18 / QE 2.101

The fact that a quarter of these echoes appear in the book of Hebrews may point to something significant. No one knows for certain who wrote the letter, but one possible candidate is Apollos,[17] a native of Alexandria in Egypt, where Philo had risen to great prominence.[18] Given that, in Acts, Apollos *already* has a basic grasp of the principles of the gospel (18.24–26), even before he has encountered other Christians, might suggest that he had adopted from Philo the principle of a divine *logos* who acts as a heavenly high priest.

This may be significant, as chapter 1 of Hebrews provides one of the most powerful arguments for the deity of Christ in the entire New Testament.

Another striking measure of overlap with Philo appears in John's gospel, where the deity of Christ is also a central theme, with some important common ground between the two writers in their thinking.[19] Again, this story has a fascinating twist. An intriguing legend that circulated at a later date relates that Philo met John and invited him back to his home, where the apostle healed Philo's wife of leprosy, received Philo into the church, and afterwards baptized him himself![20] Sadly, there is no hard evidence whatsoever to back up such a tale, nor the similar one that Philo met Peter in Rome.[21] It is, however, almost certain that Philo's output exerted a profound influence on several early Christian writers such as Justin Martyr, Clement of Alexandria and Origen. In particular, he clearly sets a precedent for the description of the 'Word' in John's gospel, who was with God in the beginning, through whom all things came into existence, and who is himself described as 'God' (John 1.1–3).

Completing the Jigsaw

To round off this survey, there is one further element we should add to the picture of Jesus' divine identity. Alongside the accounts of Wisdom and the Word of God in the Old Testament are important descriptions of the activity of the Spirit of Yahweh, and these provide a vital extra clue as to the nature of Christ and his relationship to God himself.

Throughout the Old Testament we see a close relationship between the Spirit and the Word – both, for example, are 'sent down' from heaven (Pss 104.30/107.20); both are involved in creation (Ps. 33.6);[22] and both often appear together elsewhere in close association (see, for example, 2 Sam. 23.2–3; Isa. 40.7–8; 59.21; Ezek. 11.5,14; Zech. 7.12). The same close links can also be seen with Wisdom: in the book of Wisdom, for example, the person of Wisdom appears to be *identified* with the Spirit (1.6–7; 7.7,22–25).

Moreover, as with the Old Testament picture of Wisdom, the Spirit is clearly described as having an independent existence. Indeed, far from being merely God's 'active force', as the Jehovah's

Witnesses believe, we see evidence of a distinctly personal nature,[23] a fact highlighted in the two opening and closing verses of the Bible. At the start of the Old Testament, in Genesis 1.2, the Spirit is said to be 'hovering over the waters', the Hebrew word implying the image of a mother bird fluttering over its brood, or, as a later Jewish commentary describes, 'like a dove which hovers over her young without touching them' (b. Hag. 15a: an intriguing link with the descent of the Spirit as a dove at Jesus' baptism). And at the other end of the Bible, in Revelation 22.17, the Spirit is said to be praying *alongside* the church (a prayer, note, to Jesus)!

At various points between these two extremes, the personal nature of the Spirit is strongly emphasized.[24] Twice in Acts (10.19–20 and 13.2) the Holy Spirit speaks in the first person, as he does to Ezekiel (see Ezek. 2.2 – 3.11), where extensive instructions are given. There is even an example in Ezekiel that might conceivably be understood as prayer *to* the Spirit (37.9).[25]

At the same time, we also find, as with 'Wisdom' and the Word, that there are a number of passages in Scripture where the descriptions of the Spirit seem to be another way of talking about Yahweh himself. For example, when the Spirit

- creates (Job 33.4), God creates (Job 10.8)
- gives us birth (John 3.5–8), God gives us birth (1 John 3.9; 5.18)
- speaks (2 Sam. 23.2), God speaks (23.3)
- utters Scripture (Heb. 3.7–11), God has spoken it (Heb. 4.3,7)
- is among us (Hag. 2.5), God is among us (Hag. 2.4)
- is present (Ps. 139.7), God is present (Ps. 139.8)
- departs (1 Sam. 16.14), God departs (1 Sam. 18.12)
- lives in us (1 Cor. 6.19), God lives in us (2 Cor. 6.16; cf. Eph. 2.22)
- is cheated (Acts 5.3), God is cheated (Acts 5.4)

Moreover, the Spirit is described on various occasions (e.g. Job 33.4) as the breath of the LORD, while the phrase 'Thus saith the Holy Ghost' (Acts 21.11 KJV) is the exact equivalent of the familiar Old Testament saying 'Thus saith the LORD'.

It is striking, therefore, to find this *same* overlap of identity between the Spirit and Christ. This is less obvious in the Old Testament, despite the clear link between the two themes in Isaiah 11.1–2, although, according to Jewish rabbinical tradition, the Spirit hovering over the waters in Genesis 1.2 is 'the spirit of King Messiah'.[26] However, in the New Testament, the connection becomes much clearer; for example, Christ and the Holy Spirit often perform the same tasks, which include:

- declaring us righteous (Rom. 4.25; 1 Cor. 6.11)
- making us holy (Heb. 2.11; 1 Pet. 1.2)
- living inside us (Col. 1.27; 1 Cor. 3.16 RSV)
- giving us life (John 6.33,63)
- embodying truth (John 14.6; 1 John 5.6)
- bearing testimony about Jesus (John 8.14; 15.26)
- teaching us (Acts 1.1; John 14.26)
- interceding for us (Rom. 8.26,34)
- acting as our advocate [Greek *paraklētos*] (1 John 2.1; John 14.16–17)
- distributing gifts (Eph. 4.8; 1 Cor. 12.7–11)
- appointing roles within the church (Eph. 4.11; Acts 20.28)
- bringing unity (Eph. 2.14; 4.3–4)

There are also connections in the life of believers in the way that, for example, we

- share in Christ (Heb. 3.14) just as we share in the Spirit (Heb. 6.4)
- have fellowship with Christ (1 Cor. 1.9) just as we have fellowship with the Spirit (2 Cor. 13.14)
- rejoice in Christ (Phil. 4.4) just as we rejoice in the Spirit (Rom. 14.17).

Moreover, as we pointed out earlier, the Spirit, so often called 'the Spirit of the LORD' in the Old Testament, is now also described as 'the Spirit of *Jesus*' (Acts 16.7). It is the Spirit of *Christ* who calls out within us 'Abba, Father' (Gal. 4.6); who assists us in times of trial (Phil. 1.19); and who even spoke to and through the Old Testament prophets (1 Pet. 1.11). In addition, despite a number of verses that present a clear distinction between Christ and the Spirit,[27] there are several New Testament passages which seem to present the Spirit and the risen Christ as being virtually interchangeable:

'And I will ask the Father, and he will give you another advocate to help you and be with you for ever – *the Spirit of truth* . . . I will not leave you as orphans; *I will come to you'* (John 14.16–18).

I pray that out of his glorious riches he may strengthen you with power through *his Spirit in your inner being,* so that *Christ may dwell in your hearts through faith* (Eph. 3.16–17).

'These are *the words of the Son of God,* whose eyes are like blazing fire and whose feet are like burnished bronze . . . Whoever has ears, *let them hear what the Spirit says to the churches'* (Rev. 2.18,29).[28]

Most intriguing of all are passages where the Spirit could be directly identified with *either* the Father *or* with Christ (or maybe with both at the same time!). In Romans 8.9–11 Paul writes:

You, however, are not in the realm of the flesh but are in the realm of the Spirit, if indeed the *Spirit of God lives in you.* And if anyone does not have *the Spirit of Christ,* they do not belong to Christ. But if *Christ is in you,* then even though your body is subject to death because of sin, the Spirit gives life because of righteousness. And if *the Spirit of him who raised Jesus from the dead is living in you,* he who raised Christ from the dead will also give life to your mortal bodies because of *his Spirit who lives in you.*

The same is true in 2 Corinthians 3.16–18, where the choice depends on whether the term 'Lord' here refers back either to Yahweh of the Old Testament (cf. Exod. 34.29–35), or, following the clear example in verse 14 (and with Paul's normal usage) to Christ himself:

But whenever anyone turns to the *Lord,* the veil is taken away. Now the *Lord* is the *Spirit,* and where the *Spirit of the Lord* is, there is freedom. And we all, who with unveiled faces contemplate the *Lord's* glory, are being transformed into his image with ever-increasing glory, which comes from the *Lord,* who is the *Spirit.*

Once more we are presented with an enigma: is the Spirit the same as the Father, or the same as Christ, or is he a distinct personality in his own right?

A similar issue arises in 1 Corinthians 12.4–6 (RSV): 'Now there are varieties of gifts, but the *same Spirit*; and there are varieties of service, but the *same Lord*; and there are varieties of working, but it is the *same God* who inspires them all in every one.' Here again, the boundaries are not entirely clear: is Paul, in fact, saying three different things here about three different persons, or is he, in the manner of Hebrew poetry, saying the same thing about the same person in three different ways?

We have to conclude, therefore, that not only does Jesus' identity appear to overlap with the Spirit just as much as it does with God the Father, but that all three exist in a relationship with each other which is, at least in some aspects, mutually interchangeable.[29] Trying to understand any one of them as fundamentally different *in kind* from the others simply does not do justice to the evidence in the New Testament. It seems clear, in other words, that our questions about Jesus go to the heart of the very identity of Yahweh himself.

Conclusion: Fitting the Pieces Together

In the last few chapters we have considered how the Messiah, the angel of the LORD, the Son of Man and the Wisdom and Word of God seem at one level to be indistinguishable from Yahweh, and yet at another to possess an entirely separate existence from him.[30] Moreover, when we add the Spirit of God into the equation, we end up with a remarkable *three-way* paradox.

The picture of God that this throws up is one that would probably make our Witness friends very uncomfortable. But, however much they would like to pin the blame for the problem on the councils of the early church in the fourth century AD, the issue is one that, as we have seen, is completely rooted in the Old Testament. Commenting on this apparent contradiction with respect to the angel of the LORD and God himself in Exodus 23.20–21 and 33.18–23, the Jewish scholar Alan Segal remarks that: 'Yahweh himself, the angel of God, and his Glory are peculiarly melded together, suggesting a deep secret about the ways God manifested himself to humanity.'[31]

What is this 'deep secret?' It becomes clear that, from whichever angle we look at it, the very essence of God's being consists of a *relationship* which has always existed, defined by love (1 John 8–12,16) and one in which Jesus lies at the very centre.

But what does this mean for us? Can we participate in this relationship? How would an infinite, transcendent God connect with ordinary mortals like ourselves? And why is it important for us that he should walk the earth as a real, tangible historical figure? These are issues that we will begin to explore in the next chapter.

Ten key statements about Yahweh	Ten key statements about Christ
• He is infinite (Jer. 23.24)	• He is infinite (Eph. 4.10)
• He is incomparable (Isa. 40.25)	• He is incomparable (John 7.46)
• He is all-powerful (1 Chr. 29.11)	• He is all-powerful (Matt. 28.18)
• He is all-pervasive (Acts 17.28)	• He is all-pervasive (Col. 1.17)
• He is all-sustaining (Neh. 9.6 RSV)	• He is all-sustaining (Heb. 1.3)
• He is all-encompassing (1 Cor. 15.28)	• He is all-encompassing (Col. 3.11)
• He is all-seeing (Zech. 4.10)	• He is all-seeing (Rev. 5.6)
• He is all-knowing (Ps. 139.1–4)	• He is all-knowing (John 21.17)
• He is everlasting (Ps. 90.2)	• He is everlasting (John 8.58)
• He is never-changing (Mal. 3.6)	• He is never-changing (Heb. 13.8)

Questions to consider:

(i) In a surprising twist to the predominantly male imagery of Scripture, the 'Wisdom of God' is presented in the feminine both in Proverbs and the Apocrypha. Does this affect your understanding of God in any way? Is there significance in the fact that the opening chapters of Proverbs describe Wisdom as a feminine co-creator, while the last chapter presents the capable wife as the ideal co-worker?

(ii) Both Jesus and the Bible are described in different places as the 'Word of God'. What is the relationship between these two statements? Does the Bible express the inner nature of God in the same way that Jesus does? If so, what implications might this have for our understanding of Scripture? If not, why not?

(iii) Many Christians pay lip-service to the idea of God as 'Trinity'. But to what extent is this worked out in our everyday walk with God? How might relating to God distinctly as Father, Son and Holy Spirit differ from experiencing him as a single individual? To what degree are we open to the presence and power of the Holy Spirit in our lives?

6.

Jesus as Immanuel

And I heard a loud voice from the throne saying, 'Look! God's dwelling-place is now among the people, and he will dwell with them. They will be his people, and God himself will be with them and be their God' (Rev. 21.3).

God in Miniature?

One day every year a huge segment of the industrialized world grinds to a standstill. Shops and offices close; long-lost family members gather together; children wait in excitement; gifts are exchanged; and food and drink are consumed in large quantities.

However far we may have drifted from their actual purpose, the origin of these celebrations is the birth of arguably the most influential figure in history, Jesus of Nazareth. And however marked his absence from so many of the festivities called in his honour, they serve as a small reminder of the immensity of his overall influence on Western culture, an influence that is still evident today in virtually every field of human endeavour. Even the most committed atheist cannot escape the fact that the entire dating system for world history, past, present and future, centres on him.

But can the significance of Jesus' birth be measured solely in terms of his historical and cultural impact? Or could there be more to it? What are we to make of the words that are sung again and again each Christmas:

Lo, within a manger lies
He who built the starry skies.

Words like these slide easily off the tongue but their potential implications are staggering. Could God, the Creator of the entire universe, really have come to earth as a helpless infant?

Even if we pass over all the evidence we have considered so far, there remains a series of clear pointers throughout the New Testament to this idea of 'incarnation' (a word that comes from the Latin translation of John 1.14), as the following verses suggest:

> In the beginning was the Word, and the Word was with God, and *the Word was God . . . The Word became flesh and made his dwelling among us* (John 1.1,14).

> *God was in Christ* reconciling the world to himself, no longer holding people's misdeeds against them (2 Cor. 5.19 REB).

> For in Christ *all the fulness of the Deity lives in bodily form* (Col. 2.9).

These passages raise two very important questions. The first is: *could* God come to earth as a man? For second-century Greek and Roman culture, which was rich in stories of gods becoming human (see Acts 14.11–12), the idea seems to have caused few real problems. Ignatius, for example, writing early in the second century (maybe less than twenty years after John's gospel) comments that at the birth of Jesus 'God was appearing in human form'.[1] In the same way Tatian, writing around AD 170, declares that 'God was born in the form of a man',[2] while Tertullian, shortly after the end of the century, talks of the 'nativity and incarnation of God',[3] keenly defending the idea that God 'has been born . . . of a virgin, and of a fleshly nature too'.[4]

Similar descriptions of Jesus can be found in other second-century Christian writings: to Melito of Sardis, around AD 175, for example, he was 'at once both God and perfect man',[5] while Irenaeus, around AD 185, declares that: 'He received testimony from all that He was very man, and that He was very God.'[6]

For many Jews, on the other hand, as we noted at the beginning of chapter two, the idea of the incarnation is almost nonsensical. Philo, for example, never contemplates such an idea.[7] Most Jewish writers would see it as a gross violation of God's nature to equate him with any human being, however exalted. Leslie Edgar expressed a typical view when he wrote that 'the belief that Jesus was God is an impossibility for Jewish thought'.[8]

This, however, is not necessarily the final word on the matter. We have already discussed accounts of the 'mysterious stranger' who in Genesis 18 shares in the normal human activities of eating, washing, resting and talking, and the similar stories which appear concerning the 'angel of the LORD' in the Old Testament and the 'Word of the Lord' in the Targums. The distinguished Jewish scholar Jacob Neusner mentions examples in later Jewish literature of God nodding his head to a rabbi, organizing his day with different activities, engaging in debate and even praying![9]

Elsewhere we find descriptions of the 'name' and the 'glory' of the LORD also occasionally showing personal qualities.[10] In 1 Kings 9.3, for instance, Yahweh says: 'I have consecrated this temple, which you have built, by putting my Name there for ever. My eyes and my heart will always be there.' Here the reference to God's 'Name', together with his 'eyes' and his 'heart', suggests something both identified with Yahweh and yet able to exist separately from him.

In later Jewish literature these ideas were summed up in the *shekinah*,[11] the active, personal presence of God in the midst of his people.[12] In some of the passages where the word is used it is indeed apparent that God could reduce himself to a human level. For instance, in *Exodus Rabbah*, Yahweh says to Moses, 'I will descend and even confine My *Shekinah* within one square cubit.'[13] Explaining a similar idea to a Samaritan, the famous second-century sage Rabbi Meir asks the questioner to look at himself through large mirrors and then through small mirrors. Commenting on the changing size of the reflected image, the rabbi observes, 'If you, who are but flesh and blood . . . can change yourself at will, how much more so He at whose word the world came into existence!'[14]

Lying behind these thoughts was the ark of the covenant, which occupied the central position in the Most Holy Place in the temple. While at one level this was simply a small box-shaped container constructed from acacia wood, at another level it was considered not just to represent, but actually to embody, the presence of Yahweh himself. Not only is the ark called by 'the name of the LORD' (2 Sam. 6.2), but it seems almost to possess a personality of its own. The physical symbol, in other words, *actually becomes* the reality it seeks to convey: it was, in some real sense, God on earth.

There are several verses where this becomes particularly apparent. For instance, the Israelites bring the ark from Shiloh into the battlefield 'that it may come among us and save us from the power of our enemies' (1 Sam. 4.3 ESV); its capture means that 'the Glory has departed from Israel' (1 Sam. 4.21); and when the ark arrives at Ekron the Philistines plead, 'Send away the ark of the God of Israel, and let it return to its own place, that *it may not slay us and our people*' (1 Sam. 5.11 RSV).

More remarkable still is the connection between the ark and God himself in the account which appears in Numbers 10.33–36: 'The ark of the covenant of the LORD went before them during those three days to find them a place to rest . . . Whenever the ark set out, Moses said, "Rise up, LORD! May your enemies be scattered; may your foes flee before you." Whenever it came to rest, he said, "Return, LORD, to the countless thousands of Israel."'

In the same way, when David laments in 2 Samuel 7.2 that 'the ark of God remains in a tent', Yahweh seems to link his own existence with that of the ark when he replies, 'I have not dwelt in a house from the day I brought the Israelites up out of Egypt to this day. I have been moving from place to place *with a tent as my dwelling*' (v. 6).

However, it is the verses which follow which are particularly intriguing from a New Testament viewpoint. After David offers to build a house for the LORD, God then replies that, actually, *he* will build the house (v. 11). There is a significant double meaning implied here as the word 'house' in Hebrew, *ba·yit*, can also mean 'family line'. Yahweh goes on to promise that he will do so by providing David with a 'seed' (v. 12 NKJV) who would also be God's 'son' (v. 14).

On the surface the meaning of this statement is obvious: it refers to David's son Solomon building the temple. Yet in the New Testament the word 'seed' also points to the promised Messiah (Rom. 1.3 NKJV; Gal. 3.16), himself described as the 'son of David' (Matt. 1.1), whose physical body would replace the ark, the dwelling-place of God, and the sanctuary or 'house' which contains it (John 2.21). Jeremiah 3.16–17 seems to confirm this: the ark is just a temporary sign pointing ahead to the real presence of God with his people.[15] Indeed, it may be significant that one of the titles which apparently refers to the Messiah in the Old Testament, 'Shiloh' (Gen. 49.10 NASB), was the very name of the place the ark was kept in Israel during the time of the judges (Judg. 18.31).

It is interesting in this respect that God underlines his promise to David in 2 Samuel 7.11 by one of the double uses of the divine name that, as we suggested previously, may sometimes carry particular significance: 'The LORD declares to you that *the LORD* himself will establish a house for you.'

Could this second 'LORD' in the sentence be a veiled hint here of the Messiah as *Yah·weh ṣiḏ·qê·nū*, ('the LORD our Righteousness' [Jer. 23.6 NASB]) with the 'house' as his physical body? It is striking that Zechariah 12.8 talks of a time when 'the *house of David* will be *like God*, like the angel of the LORD going before them', and almost immediately afterwards appears to describe the suffering Messiah as Yahweh in person (v. 10).

A similar link appears to be suggested in Psalm 132.11–14, where, as we saw in chapter one, the promise of Yahweh that 'one of your own descendants I will place on your throne . . . for ever and ever' is followed almost immediately by God's declaration that 'this is *my* resting place for ever and ever; here *I* will sit enthroned.'

In other words, Yahweh is showing that his promise to dwell among his people will be fulfilled not through the house of the LORD, the temple itself, but rather through the chosen descendant of the house of *David*, the promised Messiah. The ark, therefore, acts as a picture or 'sign' pointing us to the reality of Christ, in whom '*all the fulness* of the Deity lives *in bodily form*' (Col. 2.9).

From this perspective, the New Testament presents what later Jewish writings were to call the *shekinah* of God as being *physically present in Jesus himself*. We have already seen how John 1.14, translated literally, talks of the Word becoming flesh to 'tabernacle' among us, reminding us of the way that God dwelt among his people before the temple was built. This idea is pursued in Matthew 18.20 (RSV) where Jesus says, 'where two or three are gathered in my name, there am I *in the midst of them*.' Again there is a clear parallel in the Jewish Mishnah, which records that where two or three gather to study God's word, the Shekinah comes to rest upon them.[16]

Finally, it is striking to see that in a much later Jewish document entitled *Lamentations Rabbah*, the Shekinah is shown dwelling on the Mount of Olives (a place, as we have shown, intimately connected with Jewish hopes for the Messiah) for three and a half years – precisely the length of Jesus' ministry – before crying out in despair, 'I will return to my place', borrowing an image from Hosea 5.15.[17] It would be difficult to find a closer echo of Jesus' impassioned cry:

> Jerusalem, Jerusalem, you who kill the prophets and stone those sent to you, how often I have longed to gather your children together, as a hen gathers her chicks under her wings, and you were not willing. Look, your house is left to you desolate. For I tell you, you will not see me again until you say, 'Blessed is he who comes in the name of the Lord' (Matt. 23.37–39).

The Immanuel Enigma

One of the most intriguing titles for Jesus in the New Testament is 'Immanuel' (Hebrew for 'God with us'). It seems potentially packed with meaning, yet it makes only one solitary appearance before vanishing as quickly as the star which led the wise men to Bethlehem!

The name, which appears in Matthew 1.23, is taken from an obscure verse in chapter 7 of Isaiah ('Therefore the Lord himself will give you a sign: the virgin will conceive and give birth to a son, and will call him Immanuel' [v. 14]). At first sight, there seems to be no obvious reason why Matthew should have used this scripture. The chapter in which the prophecy appears concerns an alliance against Judah between the king of Israel and the king of Syria. There is nothing in the original passage that necessarily suggests a miraculous or unusual birth – the reference to a 'virgin' is debatable and the Hebrew word used, it is often argued, could equally refer to any young woman,[18] while the prophecy seems to find a natural fulfilment in the birth of Isaiah's own son in 8.3.

However, it is worth considering the immediate background to this passage. In chapter 6 Isaiah has a vision of 'the Lord, high and exalted, seated on a throne' (Isa. 6.1), who is worshipped as 'holy, holy, holy' (6.3). Here, for the first time since Genesis 11, God seems to reveal himself clearly both as *one* and as *more than one* ('Whom shall I send? And who will go for *us*?' [6.8]).

There are some intriguing parallels between this vision and chapter 3 of Zechariah.[19] Of particular interest is the way that Yahweh is again presented in the plural both here (v. 2) and also almost immediately beforehand, as we see in this quite remarkable statement:

> 'Shout and be glad, Daughter Zion. *For I am coming, and I will live among you,' declares the* LORD. 'Many nations will be joined with the LORD in that day and will become my people. I will live among you *and you will know that the* LORD *Almighty has sent me to you*' (Zech. 2.10–11).

The implications of this riddle are extraordinary. For Yahweh to dwell among his people and also remain as God, he must, inevitably, 'send' himself!

However strange the idea might seem, we have already encountered something similar with the angel of the LORD. Could the appeal of Yahweh in Isaiah 6.8, therefore, also point beyond Isaiah's own immediate response ('Here am I. Send me!') to the idea that, in the same way, *Yahweh will respond in his own person*?

A series of linked images may help us here. Shortly afterwards in Isaiah we read of a 'holy seed' which becomes a 'stump' (6.13). In 11.1 the 'stump' in turn gives rise to a 'Branch' (cf. Zech. 3.8), an image which in Jeremiah 23.5–6 describes the Messiah as God himself. In Isaiah 11 verses 1 and 10 this Branch is referred to both as the 'root' and the 'shoot' of David (in other words, he is both David's 'ancestor' and 'descendant' at the same time!).[20] Through him the earth returns to the conditions it lost in the Garden of Eden (11.6–9), which elsewhere results from the sovereign act of Yahweh alone (Isa. 65.17–25).

The background to the 'holy seed' of Isaiah 6 is also highly significant. It emerges as a symbol of hope against the backdrop of human banishment and the desolation of the land resulting from the rebellion of sin (6.9–13). This inevitably takes us back to the third chapter of Genesis, where, in very similar circumstances, we read of another 'seed' who will be born to a 'woman' (v. 15 NASB) who will crush the head of the serpent (an action which, according to Psalm 74.14, Yahweh performs unaided).

This connection with Genesis 3 means that the mention so soon afterwards in Isaiah of a 'young woman' bearing a 'child' (7.14 REB) whose name means 'God [is] with us', and who will also grow up in an empty and desolate land (vv. 18–25) has potentially huge significance. On closer inspection, it appears to point beyond a normal birth to something far more remarkable. The fact that the Septuagint translates the Hebrew word for 'young woman', '*al·māh*, as 'virgin', underlines the point that the word is *never* used elsewhere in the Old Testament to describe a married woman. And the reference in Isaiah 7.11 to 'a sign, whether in the deepest depths or in the highest heights', would appear to suggest a unique and miraculous intervention of God in human affairs (particularly if we compare it with the 'sign' described in Isaiah 38.7–8, where the sun travels backwards!).

A parallel reference in Micah, written just thirty years later, appears to underline the extraordinary nature of the event, talking of the time when 'she who is in labour' gives birth to a son 'whose origins are from of old, from ancient times' (Micah 5.2–3). And in the Septuagint translation of Psalm 110.3, God says to the man who is 'at my right hand' in verse 1 that 'from the womb, *before the morning star*, I have begotten you'.

Moreover, the child is no ordinary child. In Isaiah 7.15 he is said to eat 'curds and honey', considered in other ancient cultures to be the food of the gods. And in 8.8 the entire land is said to belong to him, despite the fact that, according to Leviticus 25.23, the land is the property of Yahweh himself.

But it is the child's name, 'Immanuel', meaning 'God is with us' which appears to give Isaiah 7.14 its full significance, particularly if we compare it with the much more direct prophecy which appears shortly afterwards:

For to us *a child is born*,
        to us a son is given,
        and the government will be on his shoulders.
And he will be called
        Wonderful Counsellor, *Mighty God*,
        Everlasting Father, Prince of Peace (Isa. 9.6).

In other words, just two chapters after we are told of the birth of a son named *God with us*, we are told that *to us* a child is born, to us a son is given, who will be called 'Mighty God', with both children, as Alec Motyer points out, possessing a fourfold name (*ma·hêr-šā·lāl-ḥāš-baz* in Isaiah 8.3 and 'Wonderful Counsellor, Mighty God, Everlasting Father, Prince of Peace' in 9.6).[21]

Jehovah's Witnesses sometimes counter this rather uncomfortable fact by reminding us that the child is 'Mighty God' but not 'Almighty God', conveniently forgetting that the same title is applied to Yahweh himself in the following chapter of Isaiah (10.21)! In fact, they are missing a powerful irony here. In Isaiah 9.6 the child born is named 'mighty God'. In Isaiah 42.13, Yahweh is said to go out as a 'mighty man' (RSV). Perhaps, as we go on to argue later, these passages are showing two angles on the same extraordinary idea.

So why might the virgin birth be so important for our understanding of the person of Christ? It is, after all, barely developed as a theme within the gospels, and, barring possible hints in Galatians 4.4, Jude 1.1 and Revelation 12.1–5, never mentioned outside them.

There are several answers we could give to this question. Firstly, it establishes in a very clear manner that Jesus is both *completely* human and *completely* divine. It is clear in both Matthew and Luke's accounts that God is the father while Mary is the mother. In his own body, therefore, Jesus provides an open doorway between our nature and God's nature (an idea touched on in Hebrews 10.19–22).

A second point has to do with the holiness of God. In the Old Testament, a thing set apart for sacred use is *never* used beforehand for any other purpose. For example, the sacrificial altar in Exodus 20.25 had to be made of 'natural, uncut stones' (NLT) that had never been shaped by a chisel. The ashes used in the 'water of cleansing' had to be taken from a red heifer 'without defect or blemish and that has never been under a yoke' (Num. 19.2). The colt on which Jesus made his entry to Jerusalem on Palm Sunday had never been ridden before (Mark 11.2). The virgin birth points to the fact that God has a special way of doing things which highlights the 'otherness' of his being. '*Make a sanctuary for me*, and I will dwell among them,' says Yahweh in Exodus 25.8.

Finally, the virgin birth reminds us that God has come to his people – *in person*! In other words, if the ultimate answer to the

question 'Who will go for us?' of Isaiah 6.8 is not the 'Here am I.
Send me!' of Isaiah himself, it points us to Christ's own 'Here am
I' of Hebrews 10.7 (NEB).

It is surely significant that this divine 'us' appears clearly on
only two more occasions in Scripture,[22] this time on the lips of
Jesus himself, as one 'sent' by God and yet also *completely identified*
with him:

> Jesus replied, 'Anyone who loves me will obey my teaching. My
> Father will love them, and *we* will come to them and make our home
> with them . . . These words you hear are not my own; they belong to
> *the Father who sent me*' (John 14.23–24).

> I pray also for those who will believe in me through their message,
> that all of them may be one, Father, just as you are in me and I am in
> you. May they also be in *us* so that the world may believe that *you have
> sent me*' (John 17.20–21)

Not only does the first of these passages extend Yahweh's promise
to dwell with his people down to the individual believer, but the
second example turns this promise upside down: now we are
called to dwell together in the incomparable unity between Father
and Son! Here the divine 'us' appears to extend back beyond Isaiah
6 to its original appearance in Genesis 1.26 ('Let *us* make man in
our image') where the inner fellowship of God's being becomes a
blueprint for the 'togetherness' of humankind.

The result for us is that God has indeed 'sent' himself through
someone who belongs to his innermost self. The huge gulf of
separation between God and humankind that Isaiah experiences
in his vision no longer exists. As Immanuel, Jesus creates a new
reality: not just *God with us*, but *us with God*. Through him we may
'participate in the divine nature' (2 Pet. 1.4). As Jürgen Moltmann
remarks, 'God became man, so that men could partake of God.'[23]

The Love that Paid the Ultimate Price

We have already begun to answer the question as to *why* God
would choose to appear on earth in human form. To see the full

significance of the incarnation, however, we need to explore more deeply the problem of human rebellion. Sin separates us from God, and even our righteous acts are like filthy rags in his sight (Isa. 64.6–7). As we have already pointed out, in Isaiah 6, the immediate background to the 'Immanuel' passage, the prophet feels the consequences of the huge gulf between sinful humanity and a holy God.

To discover the solution to this problem as Isaiah presents it, we need to turn to another of the passages announcing the 'coming' of God to earth that appears later in the book:

> When the LORD returns to Zion,
>> they will see it with their own eyes . . .
> The LORD will lay bare *his holy arm*
>> in the sight of all the nations (Isa. 52.8,10).

At first sight, the 'arm' through which God will accomplish his 'return' to Zion seems to be, by its very nature, an extension of his own being, a fact confirmed elsewhere in the book, where the 'arm of the LORD' appears to be another way of describing the action of Yahweh alone. For instance, like the angel of the LORD, God's 'arm' is described as going forward with Moses across the Red Sea (Isa. 63.12). Moreover, in Isaiah 51.9 it is said to have slaughtered the dragon Rahab, which, according to Psalm 89.10, was the act of Yahweh himself. And in Isaiah 63.5, the words '*my own arm* worked salvation for me, and *my own wrath* sustained me', suggest that the 'arm' is none other than God in person (compare 30.30 and 40.11).

However, at other points in these chapters, the 'arm of the LORD' is identified with the 'servant of the LORD' who, by contrast, is sharply distinguished from Yahweh. This becomes apparent, for example, if we compare two more passages where the 'servant' and the 'arm' are clearly one and the same:[24]

> Here is *my servant*, whom I uphold,
>> my chosen one in whom I delight;
> I will put my Spirit on him
>> and *he will bring justice to the nations* . . .
>> *in his teaching the islands will put their hope* (Isa. 42.1,4).

. . . my arm will *bring justice to the nations*
The islands will look to me
     and *wait in hope for my arm* (Isa. 51.5).

This identification between the 'arm' and the 'servant' of the Lord becomes even clearer if we compare two more passages slightly later in the book:

See, *my servant* will act wisely;
     he will be raised and lifted up and highly exalted.
Just as there were many who were appalled at him –
     his appearance was so disfigured
     beyond that of any human being
     and his form marred beyond human likeness
so he will sprinkle many nations . . . (Isa. 52.13–15)

Who has believed our message
     and *to whom has the arm of the Lord been revealed*?
He grew up before **him** like a tender shoot,
     and like a root out of dry ground.
He had no beauty or majesty to attract us to him,
     nothing in his appearance that we should desire him.
He was despised and rejected by mankind,
     a man of suffering, and familiar with pain (Isa. 53.1–3).

Here the contrast between the two pronouns 'he' and 'him' in bold type clearly *identify* the arm of the Lord with the suffering servant of the previous chapter while at the same time *distinguishing* him from God himself.

Let us summarize briefly. We have *two* sets of descriptions of the 'arm of the Lord' from the *same* section of Isaiah, the first of which seems to identify him with God in person, and the second with the fallen condition of humanity. As God, he is going to manifest himself in some form to us (Isa. 52.8,10); as man, he is going to suffer the consequences of sin on our behalf, a fact made clear in one of the most moving verses in the Old Testament:

But he was pierced for our transgressions,
     he was crushed for our iniquities;

the punishment that brought us peace was upon him,
    and by his wounds we are healed (Isa. 53.5).

Here lies the central irony of Isaiah. As Richard Bauckham points out, there is a remarkable similarity between the descriptions of Yahweh on his throne in Isaiah 6.1 as 'high' and 'exalted' and 52.13 where *the same* picture is used of the suffering servant.[25] He later goes on to observe a very similar doubling of ideas in John's gospel, where the expressions 'lifted up' and 'glorified' are used to describe both the raising up of Jesus on the cross *and* his ultimate enthronement in heaven.[26] Bauckham goes on to conclude that 'God is seen to be God in his radical self-giving, descending to the most abject human condition and, in that human obedience, humiliation, suffering and death, being no less truly God than he is in his cosmic rule and glory on the heavenly throne.'[27]

For many, this may not be the dominant picture of God that we carry from the Old Testament. But hidden in this section of Isaiah lies an important key to a deeper understanding of his nature and purpose. Immediately after discussing the mission of the servant in Isaiah 42.1–7, Yahweh insists that 'I will not yield my glory to another'. Instead, he talks of 'new things' that are to take place (vv. 8–9), and shortly afterwards (as we saw earlier) portrays *himself* coming as a 'man' (v. 13 RSV). Could there be a connection between these different ideas?

The clue lies in chapter 48. Here we see the *same* reference to 'new things' (v. 6) coupled with the *same* insistence that Yahweh cannot share his glory with another (v. 11). We then find another extraordinary description of Yahweh 'sending' himself, very similar to the one we saw earlier in Zechariah:

Listen to Me, O Jacob, even Israel whom I called;
I am He, I am the first, I am also the last …
From the first I have not spoken in secret,
From the time it took place, I was there.
And now the LORD GOD has sent Me, and His Spirit (Isa. 48.12,16 NASB).[28]

This marks a watershed in Isaiah. Up to this point Yahweh has been speaking uninterrupted for almost eight chapters. From this

moment it is no longer Yahweh alone who speaks, but a mysterious second person in alternation with him (Isa. 49.1–6; 50.4–9;
61.1–4). Is this finally the promised 'Immanuel'?

If so, the real purpose of Yahweh 'sending' himself, partially
revealed in Zechariah 2 and Isaiah 6 – 11, now becomes fully clear.
For Yahweh himself to dwell among sinful humanity, a *separation* has to take place within his being. (As if to underline this, the
Septuagint version of Isaiah 48.16 doubles up the divine name here
by declaring that '*the Lord, the Lord* sent me and his Spirit'!) In other
words, while Yahweh remains in heaven as Judge (51.17–23), he
also comes himself as the servant (49.3,6) to face the consequences
of that judgement (53.4–6) and bear the sin of many (53.11).

Echoes of this idea can be found in Zechariah 13.7:

'Awake, O sword, against my shepherd,
     against the man who stands next to me,'
declares the Lord of hosts (esv).

The Hebrew word used here for 'the man who stands next to me'
(which so powerfully recalls the second 'Lord' at the right hand
of Yahweh in Psalm 110) is found elsewhere in the Old Testament
only in Leviticus, where it describes a kinsman or neighbour, equal
in status.[29] The tragic consequences of human rebellion are spelt
out in full: Yahweh as Judge must pass judgement, but Yahweh as
Victim must suffer the result.

A clue to the significance here lies in Genesis 15.9–21, where God
makes a binding covenant with Abraham in which, according to
the custom of the times, several sacrificial animals are killed and
split in half.[30] Normally at this period both parties would walk
between the broken carcasses to enact the dire consequences that
would fall on either party should the terms of the covenant be
broken. Yet, with great significance for the future course of events,
it is only God himself, in the form of a smoking brazier and a
blazing torch, who does this, suggesting that he alone would bear
the consequences should Abraham's descendants break the terms
of the covenant.[31]

It is striking, therefore, that when in Revelation 5.6 John is
confronted by a vision of the throne of God it is 'a Lamb looking
as if it had been slain' that he sees standing at the centre of it. In

other words, the 'arm of the LORD', so closely identified with God (Isa. 59.16) and the Holy Spirit (Isa. 63.11–12) on the one hand, and yet whose form was 'marred beyond human likeness' (Isa. 52.14) and who was 'led like a lamb to the slaughter' (Isa. 53.7) on the other, occupies the very focal point of heaven. Ultimately this poses us with a profound mystery, a mystery that leads us back once more to the puzzling shift of personal pronoun that we noted previously in Zechariah 12.10: 'And I will pour out on the house of David and the inhabitants of Jerusalem a spirit of grace and supplication. They will look on *me*, the one they have pierced, and they will mourn for *him* as one mourns for an only child, and grieve bitterly for him as one grieves for a firstborn son.'

Conclusion: The Upside-Down God?

In this chapter, we have established a number of points about the incarnation. Firstly, the idea of God coming into the world and sharing in the sufferings of his people *has a clear background in the Old Testament*. This is expressed beautifully in the remarkable statement made in 1921 by the Jewish writer Franz Rosenzweig (the italics are mine):

> The Shekinah, God's descent upon man and his sojourn among men, is pictured as a dichotomy taking place in *God himself. God himself separates himself from himself*, he gives himself away to his people, he shares in their sufferings, sets forth with them into the agony of exile, joins their wanderings . . . Nothing would be more natural for the 'God of our Fathers' than that he should *'sell' himself for Israel and share its suffering fate*. But by doing so, *God puts himself in need of redemption*. In this suffering, therefore, the relationship between God and the remnant *points beyond itself.* [32]

Secondly, the gospel accounts clearly show this idea of God's 'coming' to his people *being fulfilled in Christ himself*. In John 12 Jesus is revealed successively as the 'king of Israel' inheriting David's throne (v. 13); as the promised 'seed' of Genesis 3 who overcomes Satan (vv. 24,31); as the suffering servant of Isaiah 53 (v. 38); and as the exalted Yahweh of Isaiah 6 (v. 41). Shortly afterwards there are hints at the theme of 'Yahweh sending Yahweh' that seems to play such a crucial role in these passages: 'Then Jesus cried out, "Whoever believes in me does not believe in me only, but in *the one who sent me*. The one who looks at me is seeing *the one who sent me*"' (John 12.44–45).

Thirdly, the incarnation tells us *something remarkable about the character of God*. One aspect of this is shown through the ark of the covenant itself. However great the power contained in the ark, it had to be *carried from place to place*. It was totally reliant on those chosen to carry it, to the point that it could even potentially be dropped (1 Chr. 13.9) or lost (1 Sam. 4.11). Are there the faintest glimmers here of the Creator of the universe coming to earth as a helpless, vulnerable baby?

More striking, however, is the fact that the ark had to be raised up high on *beams of wood* to achieve its ultimate purpose. Through a bizarre twist of imagery, the throne of divine glory in the Old Testament is transformed in the gospels into an execution stake! Should we be surprised that a version of Psalm 96.10 which appeared in some copies of the Septuagint, 'God reigns *from the wood*'[33] (presumably referring to the two beams supporting the ark itself), later became the basis of an early Christian hymn about the crucifixion?[34]

This extraordinary reversal of images reminds us to an almost shocking degree of the extent of God's love for us. As a modern hymn reminds us, 'hands that flung stars into space' were 'to cruel nails surrendered'. In Isaiah 52.14 the servant is 'disfigured' to the point where he is *not even human*; the Hebrew word is closely related to one used in Malachi 1.14 to describe animals unfit for sacrifice. Nowhere is this expressed more clearly than in the remarkable statement in Philippians 2.6–8, paraphrased in the original version of the New Living Translation as follows: 'Though he was God, he did not demand and cling to his rights as God. He made himself nothing; he took the humble position of a slave and appeared in human form. And in human form he obediently humbled himself even further by dying a criminal's death on a cross.'

The reference to a 'criminal's death' here is a telling one. In the heavenly courtroom the Creator and Judge of the universe does not stop merely at being *humiliated* like a slave, but, by exchanging places with us, the accused, *he himself* stands in the dock and faces the punishment that should have been our own. In words that simply take one's breath away, 'He made the One who did not know sin to be sin for us, so that we might become the righteousness of God in Him' (2 Cor. 5.21 HCSB).

It becomes more and more clear, therefore, that the Divine Paradox is a *necessary* paradox. As we shall see in the conclusion to chapter eleven, the entire Christian doctrine of salvation depends upon it! For this reason, belief in the incarnation is not an 'optional extra', but stands at the very heart of Christian belief.

Increasingly, today, however, it is under attack. The virgin birth, which so clearly portrays Jesus as both fully man and yet also fully God (more about this in chapter ten) is repeatedly called into question. The deity of Christ is frequently dismissed as an invention of the later church. Likewise Jesus' death is often portrayed merely as a heroic example of suffering or even as a tragic mistake. Such beliefs may make the Christian faith more palatable, but they deny its very essence.

At the same time, it is all too easy to accept Christ as Immanuel ('God with us') without grasping the extraordinary implications of such a belief. We can study the life of Jesus in depth without ever really seeing the bigger picture. The incarnation shows us how God invades history and changes it for ever. As the great twentieth-century Swiss theologian Karl Barth writes:

> This Jesus of Nazareth, who passes through the cities and villages of Galilee and wanders to Jerusalem, who is there accused and condemned and crucified, this man is the Jehovah of the Old Testament, is the Creator, is God himself. A man like us in space and time, who has all the properties of God and yet does not cease to be a human being and a creature too. The Creator himself, without encroaching upon his deity, becomes, not a demi-god, not an angel, but very soberly, very really a man.[35]

There is a mystery here that our human minds can never fully comprehend. But the more we look at the human Jesus, the more his ultimate divinity seems to shine through the pages of the gospels. Moreover, as we do this, the more aware we become that a huge shift of focus has taken place between the Old and the New Testaments. In the next three chapters we will attempt to investigate this 'bigger picture' as the New Testament reveals it, to see how Jesus embodies 'all the fulness of the Deity' (Col. 2.9) and brings it into our midst.

Ten key statements about God the Father	Ten key statements about Christ
• He gathers his children (Isa. 43.5)	• He gathers his children (Matt. 24.31)
• He rescues us (Col. 1.13)	• He rescues us (1 Thess. 1.10)
• He sets us free (Ps. 146.7)	• He sets us free (John 8.36)
• He redeems us from our iniquities (Ps. 130.7–8 RSV)	• He redeems us from our iniquities (Titus 2.13–14 RSV)
• He saves us by grace (Titus 2.11)	• He saves us by grace (Acts 15.11)
• He gives us a new name (Isa. 62.2)	• He gives us a new name (Rev. 2.17)
• He teaches us to love one another (1 Thess. 4.9)	• He teaches us to love one another (John 15.12)
• He grants us eternal life (Rom. 6.23)	• He grants us eternal life (John 10.28)
• He dwells within us (1 John 4.12)	• He dwells within us (Eph. 3.17)
• He prepares a place for us (Heb. 11.16)	• He prepares a place for us (John 14.2)

Questions to consider:

(i)   What does it mean to you that the Creator of the universe should become one of us? How might this affect our understanding of the value of humanity and of the world in which we live? Why would God involve himself so deeply in our broken, hurting world?

(ii) Reflecting on the miracle of the incarnation prompted many to ponder on the role of Mary, the mother of Jesus. How important is the part she played? Why has this become a topic of so much controversy in church history, and what should our attitude be towards her today? Which, if any, of the following scriptures are relevant to this question: Mark 3.31–35; Luke 1.48; 11.27–28; John 19.26–27; Rev. 12.1–5,17?

(iii) 'The story of Israel was to be the story of how God was going to deal with evil. He would draw it into one place, allowing it to do its worst at that point. And he himself would go to that place, would become Israel-in-person, in order that evil might do its worst for him and spend its force once and for all' (Tom Wright, *How God Became King* [SPCK, 2012], p. 207). What light does this throw on the nature and character of God? If Wright is correct, why is evil still such a problem in our world?

7.

Jesus as Yahweh

You who bring good news to Jerusalem, lift up your voice with a shout . . . say to the towns of Judah, 'Here is your God!' (Isa. 40.9)

Old Wine in New Bottles?

Thirty years ago, if I wanted to clean my kitchen, I would have drawn some money from Midland Bank, bought some 'Jif', and maybe treated myself to a 'Marathon' or some 'Opal Fruits' as a reward at the end of the task. Now I would need to go to HSBC, buy 'Cif', and have to make do with a 'Snickers' or 'Starburst' as my treat!

I am, of course, a victim of the well-worn practice of rebranding, where a product with previously limited commercial appeal is launched into a wider and more lucrative market. Very often the substance remains exactly the same: it is the name, the labelling or the packaging which changes.

Did God adopt the same approach two thousand years ago, expanding from targeting a limited 'niche' market to launch a new international brand that would touch every corner of the globe? If so, one major aspect of his strategy clearly stands out. Remembering from chapter five that Jesus is God's *logos* might remind us that one of the English words to come from *logos* is 'logo'. In other words, we might describe Jesus as the new 'logo' of God!

Certainly, such a major rebranding would explain the dramatic change of emphasis between the Old and New Testaments. Indeed, the entire centre of gravity has now shifted to the extent that, as Henry Liddon states, 'in the spiritual teaching of St. Paul, Christ eclipses God if he is not God'. [1]

For instance, whereas in the Old Testament people were told to look to Yahweh for redemption (Isa. 45.22 NEB), they are now told to look to the Son (John 6.40). Whereas under the old covenant people were told to come to the LORD (Isa. 55.3) and trust in the LORD (Ps. 4.5), they are now told to come to Jesus and believe in *him* (John 6.35). Whereas God once said, 'Let my people go' (Exod. 5.1), it is Jesus who now offers freedom from bondage (John 8.36). And while later in Exodus God promises to dwell among his people (25.8), it is now Jesus who dwells in our midst (Matt. 18.20 RSV).

In the same way, Jesus now plays a central part in the *life* of the believer. For instance, the psalmist writes that 'Unless the LORD builds the house, its builders labour in vain' (Ps. 127.1), but Jesus now declares that 'apart from *me* you can do nothing' (John 15.5). In Isaiah 43.10 Israel are God's witnesses (literally, 'Jehovah's witnesses'!), but in Acts 1.8 Jesus tells his disciples that they are *his* witnesses. And whereas previously Israel had waited with trepidation for 'the day of the LORD' (Joel 2.1), we are now told to prepare for 'the day of our Lord Jesus Christ' (1 Cor. 1.8).

There are substantial shifts, too, in the ceremonial law. As we saw in the last chapter, the temple, the very dwelling-place of God in the midst of his people, has now been replaced by the body of Jesus himself (John 2.19–21). Similarly, the weekly day set aside to Yahweh, the 'sabbath to the LORD your God' (Exod. 20.10) has now become 'the Lord's [i.e. Jesus'] Day' (Rev. 1.10), while the great milestone in Israel's calendar, 'the LORD's Passover' (Exod. 12.11), has now become 'the Lord's [i.e. Jesus'] Supper' (1 Cor. 11.20).

What is more, the central focus on the *name* of the LORD in the Old Testament has also been transferred to include that of Jesus. Those who formerly used to 'call on the name of the Lord' (Gen. 4.26) now call on 'the name of our Lord Jesus Christ' (1 Cor. 1.2); those who once found salvation and forgiveness through God's name (Pss 54.1; 79.9) can now find them through the name of Jesus (Acts 4.12; 10.43); and those who originally trampled on their foes in God's name (Ps. 44.5) now trample on the enemy in the name of Christ (Luke 10.17–19). Once Old Testament prophets spoke 'in the name of the Lord' (1 Chr. 21.19); but Paul now speaks fearlessly 'in the name of *Jesus*' (Acts 9.27). Similarly it is now the name of Jesus that is trusted in (John 2.23 HCSB; cf. Ps. 33.21), proclaimed (Acts 8.12 / Deut. 32.3) and glorified (2 Thess. 1.12 / Ps. 86.12).

Given the immense reverence given to the name of God in the Old Testament, this shift of authority is utterly remarkable. Blaspheming the name, for example, was an offence punishable by death (Lev. 24.16). Yet Paul's description of himself as a 'blasphemer' (1 Tim. 1.13) hardly makes sense for a model Jew (Gal. 1.14; Phil. 3.4–6) unless the name he was 'blaspheming' was actually that of Christ himself. Indeed, a couple of New Testament passages (Acts 5.41 and 3 John 7) suggest the 'name' of Jesus acquiring the same sense of awe as that of Yahweh in the Old Testament. We will touch on this matter again later in the chapter, but it is worth noting here that the similarity between several other passages concerning the 'name' of Christ and that of God in the Old Testament suggest a pattern emerging:

Whose name? Jesus and Yahweh compared	
'Many will say to me on that day, "Lord, Lord, did we not *prophesy in your name* . . .?" Then I will tell them plainly, "I never knew you. *Away from me, you evildoers!*"' (Matt. 7.22–23).	'I have heard what the prophets say who *prophesy lies in my name*. They say, "I had a dream! I had a dream!" . . . Therefore, I will surely forget you and *cast you out of my presence* . . .' (Jer. 23.25,39).
'You will be delivered up even by parents and brothers . . . you will be *hated by all for my name's sake* . . . But when you see Jerusalem surrounded by armies, then know that its desolation has come near . . . for these are *days of vengeance*, to fulfil all that is written' (Luke 21.16–17,20,22 RSV).	Your brothers . . . *hate you*, and cast you out *for my name's sake* . . . but it is they who shall be put to shame. The sound of an uproar from the city! A sound from the temple! The sound of the LORD rendering *recompense to his enemies!* (Isa. 66.5–6 ESV)
'This man is *my chosen instrument* to *proclaim my name to the Gentiles and their kings* and to the people of Israel' (Acts 9.15).	I have *raised you up for this very purpose*, that I might show you my power and that *my name might be proclaimed in all the earth* (Exod. 9.16).

This same sense that Jesus is taking on the mantle of God from the Old Testament is also clear in his teaching. Like Yahweh, he tells stories, using familiar images to convey timeless truths. However, his message is at first targeting a restricted audience. Just as God reveals himself to prophets in dreams and visions, but speaks directly to Moses 'clearly and not in riddles' (Num. 12.6–8), so Jesus speaks in parables to the masses, but reveals their secrets only to the disciples (Matt. 13.10–17), who later comment that he has spoken 'clearly and without figures of speech' (John 16.29). And strikingly, the roles in which Jesus portrays himself – as sower, harvester, vineyard owner, shepherd, bridegroom, judge and king – are ones that in the Old Testament were descriptions of the LORD himself in his relationship to Israel.

It is not only Jesus' subject-matter, however, which proves to be so suggestive, but the very choice of words he uses. We have just seen how, in his sayings, Jesus sometimes seems to place Old Testament utterances of or about Yahweh onto his own lips. If this were just an occasional practice, we might be tempted to explain it away as coincidence. But the frequency with which Jesus does this suggests a conscious (or subconscious) identification with God at the deepest level, as we can observe in another (more detailed) chart:

Ten statements of Jesus echoing Yahweh in the Old Testament	
I am sending you out like sheep among wolves . . . *do not worry* . . . At that time *you will be given what to say* (Matt. 10.16,19).	Go to the people *I send you to* . . . *Do not be afraid* . . . *I am giving you the words you must speak* (Jer. 1.7–9 GNB).
Come to me . . . and *I will give you rest*. Take my yoke upon you . . . *and you will find rest for your souls.* (Matt. 11.28–29).	*Come to me* and listen to my words (Isa. 55.3 REB). ———— My Presence will go with you, *and I will give you rest* (Exod. 33.14). ———— . . . ask where the good way is, and walk in it, *and you will find rest for your souls.* (Jer. 6.16).

Ten statements of Jesus echoing Yahweh in the Old Testament	
Jerusalem, Jerusalem . . . how often I have longed to *gather your children together,* as a hen gathers her chicks *under her wings* (Matt. 23.37).	I, the LORD All-Powerful, will protect *Jerusalem* like a *mother bird* circling over her nest (Isa. 31.5 CEV). ——— . . . *the children of mankind* take refuge in the *shadow of your wings* (Ps. 36.7 ESV).
Whoever rejects you rejects me (Luke 10.16).	. . . it is *not you that they have rejected,* but they have *rejected me* (2 Sam. 8.7).
I have given you authority to *trample on snakes* and scorpions and to overcome all the power of the enemy; *nothing will harm you* . . . rejoice that *your names are written in heaven.* (Luke 10.19–20).	. . . *no harm will overtake you* . . . *you will trample* the great lion and *the serpent* . . . I will . . . *show him my salvation* (Ps. 91. 10,13,16).
Come to me and drink. Whoever believes in me, as Scripture has said, *rivers of living water* will flow from within them (John 7.23).	*Come,* all you *who are thirsty* (Isa. 55.1). ——— . . . they have forsaken me, *the spring of living water* (Jer. 2.13).
If you *love me,* you will *keep my commandments* (John 14.15 RSV).	I, the Lord your God, am a jealous God . . . showing love to a thousand generations of those who *love me and keep my commandments* (Exod. 20.5–6).
If you dwell in me, and my words dwell in you, *ask whatever you want, and you shall have it* (John 15.7 REB).	*If . . . you make the Most High your dwelling . . . He will call on me, and I will answer him* (Ps. 91.9,14).

Ten statements of Jesus echoing Yahweh in the Old Testament	
'I have loved you,' says the LORD (Mal. 1.2).	*'I have loved you* even as the Father has loved me. Remain in my love.' (John 15.9 NLT).
'I said nothing in secret . . . the reson I was born and came into the world is *to testify to the truth'* (John 18.20,37).	*I have not spoken in secret* . . . I, the LORD, *speak the truth;* I declare what is right (Isa. 45.19).

This freedom in 'taking over' declarations made by Yahweh in the Old Testament is even more marked in the book of Revelation, where Jesus claims to:

- be the first and the Last (Rev. 2.8; see Isa. 44.6)
- give us a new name (Rev. 2.17; see Isa. 62.2)
- search hearts and minds (Rev. 2.23; see Jer. 17.10)
- blot out from the book of life (Rev. 3.5; see Exod. 32.33)
- rebuke and discipline those he loves (Rev. 3.19; see Prov. 3.12)
- be the Lord of Lords (Rev. 17.14; see Deut. 10.17)
- carry his reward with him (Rev. 22.12; see Isa. 40.10)
- give to everyone according to what he has done (Rev. 22.12; see Ps. 62.12)

Most significantly, perhaps, the absolute title 'the Alpha and the Omega' (the first and last letters of the Greek alphabet) applied to the Father in Revelation 1.8, marking his unending existence as the source of all creation, becomes Jesus' own name by the end of the book (22.13,16)!

Finally, we should note the authority that Jesus claimed for his own words (see accompanying inset). As Millard Erickson rightly observes, 'the impression one obtains is that Jesus did not expect his words to be supplanted, or even supplemented or interpreted'.[2] His claim not merely to bring truth, but to *be* that truth (John 14.6) was a claim that only God could make (Ps. 31.5 NASB). In the same way, he does not come merely to obey Scripture, but to *fulfil* it (Matt. 5.17; Luke 24.27,44; John 5.39–40). Unlike the prophets before him who *spoke out* God's word, Jesus *is* that Word in person (John 1.1). With a thrilling sense of climax, the Old Testament train pulls in at its final, long-awaited destination, compared to which even the most amazing stops on the way fade into the shadows of history (Matt. 11.11; Luke 10.23–24; Heb. 1.1–2; 1 Pet. 1.10–12).

Ten insights into the words of Jesus

- Deuteronomy 11.1 says, 'Love the LORD your God and keep his requirements . . . and his commands always.' But Jesus says, 'If you love me, you will keep *my* commandments' (John 14.15 RSV).
- In Psalm 119.25 it is God's word that brings life. But in John 5.24 and 6.63, life comes through the word of *Jesus* himself.
- In Deuteronomy 4.2 the people are warned not to add or subtract from God's commands. But Jesus says several times in Matthew 5, 'You have heard that it was said . . . But *I* tell you . . .'
- Proverbs 30.6 further warns about placing anything alongside the words of Scripture. But Jesus prefaces many of his statements with 'Amen', giving them an authority level with that of the words of Yahweh in the Old Testament.
- Isaiah 46.5 insists that no one can be likened to God or counted his equal. Yet in 1 Timothy 5.18, the words of Christ from Luke 10.7 are placed on an equal footing with the words of Yahweh from Deuteronomy 25.4.
- In Isaiah 48.11 God declares that 'I will not yield my glory to another.' Yet in 2 Peter 3.2, the words of Christ to the apostles are ranked equally with the words of Yahweh to the Old Testament prophets.
- In Deuteronomy 28.1–14, obedience to God's commandments is critical to success or failure in life. But in Matthew 7.24–25 it is obedience to the teaching of *Jesus* which is the decisive factor.
- Psalm 119.89 declares that God's word 'stands firm in the heavens'. But Jesus claims in Mark 13.31 that his word will *outlast* the heavens.

- Despite the declaration in Psalm 119.89–91 that it is *God's word* that sustains the universe, Hebrews 1.3 declares that it is the word of *Christ* which upholds the laws of the cosmos.
- In Isaiah 30.12–13 Yahweh uses the image of a collapsing wall to warn Israel of the consequences of ignoring his message. But in Matthew 7.26–27 the entire *house* collapses when Jesus' message is ignored!

A New Face at the Top?

If Jesus is the new 'logo' of Yahweh, then the statement 'Jesus is Lord' was the trailblazing slogan of the early church. It provided, according to Paul, a litmus test of true faith (Rom. 10.9; 1 Cor. 12.3). Yet the significance of calling Jesus 'Lord' (*kyrios*) can hardly have been lost on the Greek-speaking Jews who were the focus of some of Paul's early evangelistic efforts. In the Greek Septuagint, which provides the source for many of the scriptural quotations in the New Testament, the word *kyrios* was used overwhelmingly to translate the Hebrew 'Yahweh' ('the LORD' or 'Jehovah'). Charles Cranfield concludes from this that 'the confession "Jesus is Lord" was a confession that the exalted Jesus was in the fullest sense divine'.[3]

Jehovah's Witnesses have often attempted to question the truth of this by suggesting from a few variant early manuscripts that it was *the church* which originally substituted *kyrios* for the divine name 'Yahweh' in the Septuagint. Indeed, they have even attempted to 'restore' this situation in the New World Translation by a selective replacement of 'Lord' (*kyrios*) with 'Jehovah' in the New Testament, where they feel the term clearly refers to God the Father. However, the evidence they offer for this rests on nothing better than *translations from Greek into Hebrew made well over a thousand years later*! This conveniently ignores the overwhelming fact that it was Jews rather than Christians who felt reluctant to use the divine name, and therefore used *'ă·ḏō·nāy* (the Hebrew equivalent of *kyrios*) or other substitutes instead.[4] In fact, Josephus tells us that Jews of the first century AD refused to address the emperor as 'kyrios' *precisely because* they reserved it as a name for God alone.[5]

Given that this is the case, it is all the more striking that, in the New Testament, the word *kyrios*, with all its associations with Yahweh in the Greek Septuagint, is applied far more often as a title for Jesus than for God the Father. We can see the possible overlap of meaning that can arise from this in Luke 1.45, where Elizabeth says of Mary, 'Blessed is she who has believed that *the Lord* [i.e. Yahweh] would fulfil his promises to her!' But two verses previously, she applies exactly the same title to Jesus, when she says, 'Why am I so favoured, that the mother of *my Lord* should come to me?'

On many occasions in the New Testament this extraordinary merging of titles means that it is impossible to tell who is being described. As an example of the potential confusion that can arise, the word 'Lord' appears seven times in James chapter 5 with no obvious indication as to whether James is referring to Yahweh or Jesus in alternation, or is simply presenting them as one and the same:

> The cries of the harvesters have reached the ears of the Lord Almighty (v. 4).

> Be patient, then, brothers and sisters, until the Lord's coming (v. 7).

> The Lord's coming is near (v. 8).

> Take the prophets who spoke in the name of the Lord (v. 10).

> The Lord is full of compassion and mercy (v. 11).

> Anoint them with oil in the name of the Lord (v. 14).

> The Lord will raise him up (v. 15).

This apparent overlap between Yahweh and Jesus is particularly striking here, not only because James is, by common consent, one of the most theologically 'conservative' books in the New Testament, but because, according to church tradition (as we noted previously with the letter of Jude), the writer was none other than Jesus' own brother!

It can of course be pointed out that the Greek term *kyrios* has a whole range of connotations, including simply polite respect (equivalent to 'sir' in English), and there are certainly occasions in the gospels where Jesus is addressed in these terms. However, on many other occasions, the title seems to carry the full weight of divinity, as the following examples suggest:

- In Matthew 9.38 Jesus refers to the Father as 'Lord of the harvest', yet he also calls himself 'Lord of the Sabbath' (Matt. 12.8).
- In Matthew 22.32 Jesus describes the Father as 'God not of the dead, but of the living' (NRSV), yet in Romans 14.9 Paul calls Jesus 'Lord of both the dead and the living'.
- In Acts 4.24 the church prays to God as 'Sovereign Lord', yet in Jude 4 Jesus is described as 'our only Sovereign and Lord'.
- In Acts 17.24 God the Father is described as 'Lord of heaven and earth', yet in Acts 10.36 Jesus is described as 'Lord of all'.
- Most significantly, in 1 Timothy 6.15, God receives the ultimate title of 'King of kings and Lord of lords', yet, as we have already seen, the *identical* title is given to Jesus in Revelation 19.16. (In Hebrew thought, such a description is expressing an absolute superlative – you can't get any higher than this!)

It is of particular interest in the latter case that in Philippians 2.9 Jesus is given 'the name that is above every name'. Commenting on this, Alan Segal observes in his book *Paul the Convert* that 'for a Jew this phrase can only mean that Jesus received the divine name Yahweh, the tetragrammaton YHWH, translated as the Greek name <u>kyrios</u>, or Lord.'[6] Richard Bauckham stresses similarly that 'it is inconceivable that any Jewish writer could use this phrase for a name other than God's own unique name'.[7]

It is perhaps significant in this regard that Jesus prays in John 17.11, 'Holy Father, protect them by the power of your name, *the name you gave me*, so that they may be one as we are one.' Again, we are left with little alternative: it is difficult to see how this name could be anything other than the title Yahweh itself.

It is not surprising, therefore, to see passages originally describing Yahweh in the Old Testament being *altered* to apply to Jesus in the New. For instance, both Peter and Paul quote from Joel 2.32 ('everyone who calls on the name of the LORD will be saved'). But in context the 'Lord' they are describing seems to be Jesus himself (cf. Acts 2.21 with 2.36, and Rom. 10.13 with 10.9).

Similar examples appear elsewhere in their writings. For instance, in Ephesians 4.8, Paul applies a version of Psalm 68.18 about God's triumphant enthronement as King directly to Christ, while his description of Jesus as 'the Lord of glory' in 1 Corinthians 2.8 directly echoes that of Yahweh as 'the King of glory' in Psalm 24.7–10. In the same way, Peter describes Jesus as 'a stone that causes people to stumble and a rock that makes them fall' (1 Pet. 2.8) which in Isaiah 8.13–14 refers to God himself (compare Luke 20.18). And when he says '*Have no fear of them* . . . but in your hearts *honour Christ the Lord as holy*' (1 Pet. 3.14–15) he is echoing the same passage, which says, '*Do not fear* . . . but the LORD *of hosts*, him you shall *honour as holy*' (Isa. 8.12–13, both taken from the ESV).

Even more startling is the way that the writer to the Hebrews applies to Jesus a passage about Yahweh from Psalm 102.25–27, verses which are about as emphatic a declaration of divinity as one could possibly imagine:

> But about the Son he says . . .
> 'In the beginning, Lord, you laid
>   the foundations of the earth,
>   and the heavens are the work of your hands.
> They will perish, but you remain;
>   they will all wear out like a garment.
> You will roll them up like a robe;
>   like a garment they will be changed.
> But you remain the same,
>   and your years will never end' (Heb. 1.8,10–12).

The important thing to note here is that there is *nothing* in the original context of these verses to suggest that they apply to the Messiah or to anyone other than God. The writers are clearly discarding a few theological wineskins at this point! Robert Bowman and Ed Komoszewski conclude from passages such as these that 'the basic confession of early Christianity . . . turns out to entail the most astonishing and radical claim that any first-century Jew might have made: that the crucified man, Jesus of Nazareth, was Jehovah.'[8]

The Divine Signature

One statement which sums up the prevailing thought of our modern age was actually made as long ago as 1637. 'I think, therefore I am.' On its own, the idea demonstrates perfectly how increasingly we define the universe around us in relation to our own self-awareness. Carrying an intriguing echo of Babylon's stubborn declaration, *'I am, and there is none besides me'* (Isa. 47.8), it hints at how far we have moved from a truly biblical outlook where God alone is the ground of all being, the true 'I am' around which everything else revolves.

Rather neatly, in the French language with which René Descartes originally penned his statement, 'I am' (*je suis*) is just one letter different from the name 'Jesus' (the familiar Latin version *cogito ergo sum* actually came later). Although this is just a happy accident, it does serve to remind us how emphatically Jesus ties the words 'I am' to his own identity. Particularly within the Gospel of John, they receive a prominence which should make us sit up and take notice.

In Greek, the English words 'I am' (*egō eimi*) can be expressed easily by one word – *eimi* – or even by the pronoun *egō* on its own. Sometimes, for heightened emphasis, both the pronoun *egō* and verb *eimi* are used, but are separated within the sentence, as in *egō Israēlitēs eimi* ('I am an Israelite', Rom. 11.1). When *egō* and *eimi* are used next to each other, however, the effect is very strong. Yet we find this happening over twenty times in John's gospel, more than in the rest of the New Testament books put together.

The background to this usage is the Septuagint, where, particularly in the first three books of the Bible, the words *egō eimi* act as a 'calling card' through which Yahweh displays his identity, as the following three examples show:

I AM your God . . . (Gen. 17.1)

I AM the God of your father Abraham and the God of Isaac . . . (Gen. 28.13)

I AM the God that appeared to you . . . (Gen. 31.13)[9]

We also find *egō eimi* used on a number of occasions in the latter part of Isaiah to translate the Hebrew expression *'ă·nî hū* (normally translated 'I am he') which expresses the absolute uniqueness and transcendence of God.[10] Indeed, on three occasions in Isaiah the effect is increased by repetition: for example, in the Greek, Isaiah 51.12 ('I, even I, am he who comforts you') is expressed by the doubly emphatic *egō eimi egō eimi*.[11]

The most frequent usage of *egō eimi*, however, particularly in the book of Leviticus, is to translate the phrase '*I AM* the LORD'. The significance of this form of words is that, in the original Hebrew, the name 'LORD' (YHWH or Yahweh), considered by Jews too sacred to pronounce, probably had its origin in the Hebrew for *I AM* ('*eh·yeh*). This link is clearly explained in Exodus 3.13–15:

> Moses said to God, 'Suppose I go to the Israelites and say to them, "The God of your fathers has sent me to you," and they ask me, "What is his name?" Then what shall I tell them?'
> God said to Moses, 'I AM WHO I AM.[12] This is what you are to say to the Israelites. "I AM *has sent me to you.*"'
>
> God also said to Moses, 'Say to the Israelites, "The LORD [*Yahweh*], the God of your fathers – the God of Abraham, the God of Isaac and the God of Jacob – *has sent me to you.*"
>
> 'This is my name for ever,
>   the name you shall call me
>   from generation to generation.'

Jesus' consistent and emphatic use of the 'I AM' formula throughout John's gospel, therefore, appears to give us further strong evidence that he was identifying himself with Yahweh of the Old Testament. Ethelbert Stauffer describes the expression as 'the most authentic, the most audacious, and the most profound affirmation of Jesus of who he was'.[13] Clear evidence for this can be seen in the way that the seven best known of these I AM sayings act as markers announcing Jesus' true identity, in much the same way that God uses key statements to reveal his own nature in Genesis ('I am El Shaddai', 'I am the God of Bethel', etc.):

I AM the bread of life (6.35)

I AM the light of the world (8.12)

I AM the gate for the sheep (10.7)

I AM the good shepherd (10.11)

I AM the resurrection and the life (11.25)

I AM the way and the truth and the life (14.6)

I AM the true vine (15.1)

Significantly, two of these are well-known Old Testament descriptions of God: as 'light' (Ps. 27.1; Isa. 60.19–20)[14] and as the 'good shepherd' (Ps. 23.1–2; Ezek. 34.11–16), and this link is reinforced by the uncompromising way that Jesus presents them, without qualifying them in any way. Commenting on his use of the second of these two images, Peter Lewis observes that:

> Jesus does not say, 'I am a good shepherd' (in contrast to a bad one), nor does he say, 'I am *like* the good shepherd of Israel's history'. But he says, without qualification, 'I am the good shepherd' (v 11), and the definite article combined with the divine signature leads us to the recognition that Jesus is consciously and deliberately taking the name and the claim of Yahweh, the Shepherd of Israel (Ps. 23.1; 78.52), and applying it to himself. What Yahweh was to the old Israel, Jesus is to the new.[15]

The same is true of the way that some of Christ's other 'I AM' statements appear to echo closely Old Testament passages where Yahweh is the major focus, as we can see in the inset on the next page. Given that two of these refer to the aftermath of Jesus' betrayal and crucifixion, while another two are made by the risen Christ, it is striking that Luke also records Christ as saying after his resurrection, 'Why are you so frightened? Why do you doubt? Look at my hands and my feet and see who **I am** [*egō eimi*]' (Luke 24.38–39 CEV).

The significance here is that it is Christ's nail-scarred hands which are the actual means by which Thomas comes to recognize him as 'God' a week later (John 20.27–28).

The divine signature: Yahweh and Jesus compared	
Therefore My people shall know . . . That **I am He** *who speaks* (Isa. 52.6 NKJV).	Jesus said to her, '**I am he**, the one *who is speaking* to you' (John 4.26 NRSV).
. . . so that *you may know* and believe me and understand that **I am he** (Isa. 43.10).	When you have lifted up the Son of man, then *you will know* that **I am he** (John 8.28 RSV).
When this happens, you will know that **I am** the Sovereign LORD (Ezek. 24.24).	I am telling you now before it *happens*, so that *when it does happen* you will believe that **I am who I am** (John 13.19).
Don't be afraid. **I am** with you . . . Everyone who hates you will be terribly disgraced; *those who attack will vanish* into thin air (Isa. 41.10–11 CEV).	*Do not be afraid . . .* For **I am** with you, and *no one is going to attack* and harm you . . . (Acts 18.10).
'For **I am** the LORD your God . . . *Lead out those who have eyes* but are blind . . . You are *my witnesses*,' declares the LORD, 'and *my servant* whom *I have chosen*' (Isa. 43.3,8,10).	The Lord said, '**I am** Jesus . . . *I have chosen* you to be my *servant* and my *witness* – you will tell people the things that you have seen . . . I am sending you to them to *open their eyes*' (Acts 26.15–18 NCV).

Although most of the examples of *egō eimi* on Jesus' lips appear in John's gospel, the words are also prominent at significant points in the Gospel of Mark. For instance, when Jesus walks on the Sea of Galilee, the words translated 'It is I! Don't be afraid' by the NIV at Mark 6.50 appear in the original Greek as the infinitely more awe-inspiring 'I AM! Don't be afraid' (see also Matt. 14.27 and John 6.20). This underlines the fact that, according to Job 9.8 and Psalm 77.19, walking on water is the preserve of Yahweh alone.

A more indirect but equally telling clue to the way Jesus saw himself appears at Mark 13.6, where he says, 'Many will come in my name, claiming "*I am he* [*egō eimi*]," and will deceive many.'[16]

The meaning here becomes clearer when we read in 2 Thessalonians 2.3–4 of the 'man of lawlessness' who 'sets himself up in God's temple, *proclaiming himself to be God*'. It is not hard to see that if Jesus believed others would come in his name, claiming to be God, he must also have understood himself in the same terms.[17]

But the climactic use of 'I AM' in Mark's gospel appears in Jesus' testimony before the high priest in chapter 14, where he is tried and condemned to death for blasphemy. The background to such a trial is set out in the Mishnah, a Jewish handbook of rabbinic teaching compiled around AD 200, but containing a great deal of earlier material. According to the Mishnah, the *only* ground for a blasphemy sentence was to unlawfully pronounce the divine name, 'Yahweh', which only the high priest himself could utter and only once a year on the Day of Atonement.[18]

The rules for such a blasphemy trial, as set out in Sanhedrin 7.5, are as follows. Firstly, two or three witnesses are called to give evidence. Secondly, while the accused is being questioned, a substitute name for God must be used instead (it was customary at this time to use various alternatives such as 'Heaven', 'the Name' or 'the Holy One').[19] Thirdly, if the accused is found guilty of pronouncing the divine name, the high priest is required to tear his robes and pass the sentence of death. Finally, according to Josephus, the body of a man executed for blasphemy would be left without burial until sunset.[20]

It is interesting to see how closely this comes to the actual sequence of events described in Mark 14. Firstly, the witnesses are called to give evidence against Jesus, but, as Mark reports, 'their statements did not agree' (Mark 14.56). Then the high priest asks Jesus, using a customary substitution for God's name, 'Are you the Messiah, the Son of *the Blessed One?*' (Mark 14.61). And, interestingly enough, in his reply, Jesus responds with another alternative name: 'you will see the Son of Man sitting at the right hand of *the Mighty One* and coming on the clouds of heaven.'

Now affirming that he was the Christ (i.e. the Messiah) was not in itself blasphemy, as other figures around this time were to make such claims. Nor was his description of himself as the 'Son of Man', since, as we noted in chapter four, this was a term that could be understood in a number of ways. And Jesus was careful to use the words 'Mighty One' as a substitute for 'Yahweh' in his answer.

What, however, could potentially have provoked such an outburst of rage were the two words that Mark records him using before this in his reply: *egō eimi* – '*I AM*'. Was Jesus once more, at this defining moment, applying the very name of God (on which 'Yahweh' is directly based) to himself?[21] If so, the reaction of the High Priest is understandable: immediately he tears his robes and Jesus is condemned to death.

This sense of the absolute sanctity of the divine name helps to throw light on a couple of further incidents in John's gospel. In the first, Jesus seems to be understood, in his use of the words 'I AM', to be committing the ultimate heresy:

'Your father Abraham rejoiced at the thought of seeing my day; he saw it and was glad.'

'You are not yet fifty years old,' they said to him, 'and you have seen Abraham!'

'Very truly I tell you,' Jesus answered, 'before Abraham was born, I am!' **At this, they picked up stones to stone him**, but Jesus hid himself, slipping away from the temple grounds (John 8.56–58).

There can be little doubt here that Jesus was being accused of blasphemy *because he was declaring his own divinity*. This can be judged by the similar reaction we find in John 10.33, where his accusers declare, 'you, a mere man, *claim to be God*'.

It is, indeed, not hard to see why those present would have been so shocked. Jesus' remarkable change of tense mid-sentence ('before Abraham *was* born, I *am*') seems deliberately to mimic the contrast of tense in Psalm 90.2 ('Before the mountains *were* born . . . from everlasting to everlasting you *are* God'). In fact, there is an even closer link with the Septuagint, where the psalmist simply addresses Yahweh with the words, 'Before the mountains were born . . . *you are*'.

The full force of these words is brought out by Liddon who comments that in this passage '[Christ] does not merely claim pre-existence; He unveils a consciousness of Eternal Being. He speaks as One on Whom time has no effect, and for whom it has no meaning. He is the I AM of ancient Israel; He knows no past, as he knows no future; He is unbeginning, unending Being . . . the eternal "Now".'[22]

Equally striking is another incident reported in John 18.2–6:

> Now Judas, who betrayed him, knew the place, because Jesus had often met there with his disciples. So Judas came to the garden, guiding a detachment of soldiers and some officials from the chief priests and the Pharisees. They were carrying torches, lanterns and weapons.
>
> Jesus, knowing all that was going to happen to him, went out and asked them, 'Who is it you want?'
>
> 'Jesus of Nazareth,' they replied.
>
> 'I am he,' Jesus said. (And Judas the traitor was standing there with them.) When Jesus said, 'I am he,' they drew back and fell to the ground.

Here the description of a coterie of soldiers and officials suddenly collapsing to the ground like a pack of cards seems comically improbable until we realize that Jesus had again pronounced the divine name – the two words translated 'I am he' are simply *egō eimi* ('*I AM*'). The significance of this becomes clearer when we consider a Jewish tradition recorded by Eusebius which states that Pharaoh fell to the ground unconscious when Moses whispered the name 'Yahweh' in his ear,[23] and another in a Jewish commentary on Exodus, where Moses kills the Egyptian by pronouncing the name of God over him.[24] A further insight appears in the Mishnah, where it tells us that worshippers would fall flat on their faces in the temple court when the high priest pronounced the divine name on the Day of Atonement.[25]

It is, of course, possible to explain away all these statements, and Greg Stafford makes a brave attempt to do so in his book *Jehovah's Witnesses Defended*.[26] But looking back on this apparently random series of references we see an extraordinary pattern. The Hebrew phrase *'ă·nî hū* appears *seven* times in the Old Testament.[27] There are *seven* descriptions attached to *egō eimi* in John's gospel (for instance, 'I am the bread of life', 6.35)[28] along with *seven* absolute uses applied to Jesus (such as 'before Abraham was, *I am*', 8.58).[29] There are also *seven* absolute uses linked to Jesus in the three other gospels (Matthew, Mark and Luke).[30] We are faced with a choice, therefore: either we have a remarkable coincidence, a suspicious level of collusion between the biblical authors – or a divine signature!

It is hardly surprising, then, to see *egō eimi* appearing on *seven* more occasions in the book of Revelation, especially given the central role that this number plays in the organization of the book. Here, however, underlining the essential unity between Father and Son that underpins the book, they are divided up: while three of these occurrences refer to God the Father (1.8,11; 21.6), the other four clearly refer to Jesus:

> *I AM* the First and the Last (1.17).

> *I AM* he who searches hearts and minds (2.23).

> *I AM* the Alpha and the Omega, the First and the Last, the Beginning and the End (22.13).

> *I AM* the Root and the Offspring of David, and the bright Morning Star (22.16).

Since two of these are titles elsewhere in Scripture applied to Yahweh himself (cf. 1.17 with Isa. 44.6, and 2.23 with Jer. 17.10), such statements can only serve further to identify Jesus with the Old Testament God of Israel.

Does it matter if we believe this? There is one verse in John's gospel that should make us painfully aware that it does: 'That is why I told you that you will die in your sins. And you will die in your sins if you do not believe that "I Am Who I Am"' (John 8.24 GNB).

Jesus' sober warning here reminds each one of us that there may be a great deal more at stake in this issue than at first meets the eye. As Ethelbert Stauffer comments on this verse, 'this is the critical point on which the waves of world history break'.[31]

Conclusion: A Man Like No Other

In this chapter we have considered a huge, almost unthinkable shift of emphasis between the Old and New Testaments. It would be difficult to see how such claims would have been given any legitimacy at all if Jesus were believed to be anything less than

God in human form. Despite the clear warning in Jeremiah 17.5 ('Cursed is the one who trusts in man'), Jesus has now become the central object of faith, as everything in the Old Testament seems to find its fulfilment in him: he *is* the law (Rom. 10.4); he is the Sabbath (Matt. 11.28); he *is* the temple (John 2.21); he *is* the priesthood (Heb. 4.14); he *is* the kingdom (Luke 13.18–19); he *is* the resurrection (John 11.25); he *is* life itself (John 14.6).

Moreover, the gospels are very definite in according to Christ the full attributes of deity: he is omnipotent (Matt. 28.18), omniscient (John 21.17) and omnipresent (Matt. 28.20). Elsewhere in the New Testament this picture is expanded to present a cosmic Christ, self-existent (John 5.26), pre-existent (Heb. 7.3), indestructible (Heb. 7.16), standing outside time itself (Heb. 13.8), the author of life (Acts 3.15), filling every corner of the universe (Eph. 4.10), sustaining every particle of matter (Heb. 1.3) and encompassing the entire created order within himself (Col. 1.17). In the colourful paraphrase of Eugene Peterson, expressed using the imagery of our own time, 'You don't need a telescope, a microscope, or a horoscope to realize the fullness of Christ, and the emptiness of the universe without him' (Col. 2.8–9, *The Message*).

While the ancient pagan world was full of stories of gods and demigods, it is difficult to conceive of *any* historical figure portrayed with the boldness that the New Testament presents Jesus, and that within decades of his death. Moreover, the writers that were making such statements about Jesus were brought up, not within pagan society, but within a culture of strict Jewish monotheism. What was it about Jesus that caused them to respond in such a way? In the next chapter we will shift the spotlight from what Jesus *said* to what he *did*, and will consider how such actions might affect our picture of his ultimate identity.

Ten key statements about Yahweh	Ten key statements about Christ
• He is the King of Israel (Zeph. 3.15)	• He is the King of Israel (John 12.12)
• He is the King of all the earth (Ps. 47.7)	• He is the King of all the earth (Ps. 72.8)
• He is the King of glory (Ps. 24.10)	• He is the Lord of glory (1 Cor. 2.8)
• He is the Lord of the Sabbath (Exod. 20.10)	• He is the Lord of the Sabbath (Mark 2.28)
• He is the Lord of the living and the dead (Ruth 2.20)	• He is the Lord of the living and the dead (Rom. 14.9)
• He is the Lord of all (Ps. 97.5)	• He is the Lord of all (Acts 10.36)
• He is the King of kings and Lord of lords (1 Tim. 6.15)	• He is the King of kings and Lord of lords (Rev. 19.16)
• All things were made by him (Ps. 102.25)	• All things were made by him (Heb. 1.8,10)
• All things were made through him (Rom. 11.36)	• All things were made through him (John 1.3)
• All things were made for him (Heb. 2.10)	• All things were made for him (Col. 1.16)

Questions to consider:

(i) Jesus said, 'Why do you call me, "Lord, Lord," and do not do what I say?' (Luke 6.46). What areas of your life are not fully under his lordship at present? What steps can you take to address this issue? Could there be consequences if we deliberately refuse to tackle such matters? (Read Matt. 7.21–23; Acts 5.1–11; 1 John 2.4.)

(ii) Jesus' literal words to his disciples on the Sea of Galilee were 'I AM! Don't be afraid.' What situations at present are causing concern or anxiety for you? How can this statement be a comfort to us in the uncertainty of our daily lives? Is Jesus calling you, like Peter, to step out of the security of the boat?

(iii) In his letter to the Colossians, Paul writes that 'in him [Christ] all things hold together' (1.17). At what levels is this apparent? How might it relate to those things in rebellion against God (such as the powers of darkness)?

8.

Jesus the Miracle Worker

What shall we do? Look at all the miracles this man is performing! If we let him go on in this way, everyone will believe in him (John 11.47–48 GNB).

Signposts to the Infinite

In Luke 5.17–26 a remarkable incident takes place. Jesus is at home, his house packed with visitors, when suddenly a hole starts appearing in his roof, through which a paralysed man slowly appears! No doubt impressed by this novel means of entry, Jesus tells the man, 'Friend, your sins are forgiven.'

The religious authorities present are, quite rightly, scandalized. 'Who can forgive sins but God alone?' they mutter to themselves. The crowd, of course, also knows that only God can take away sin. The paralytic knows it. Jesus knows it, too. And yet, to prove that he does have the authority to forgive sins, he heals the paralytic anyway.

The crowd are stunned. 'We have seen remarkable things today,' they say (v. 26). The word Luke uses for 'remarkable things' is *paradoxos*, the root of our English word 'paradox', with which, by now, we should be quite familiar! Since it is the only time this Greek word appears in the whole of the New Testament, it must have some special significance. In context, it simply means that they have never seen anything like this before (cf. Mark 2.12). In the English sense of the word, the paradox here is, of course, that Jesus is a man who seems to be doing what only God can do.

One of my earliest memories at infant school is of a rather graphic demonstration by my teacher of how Jesus might have performed some of his signs and wonders by what can only be described as a cheap conjuring trick. Attempting to reproduce the first of Jesus' miracles from the wedding at Cana in Galilee, she mixed some water with what appeared to be dried paint at the bottom of a jar, gave it a few shakes and – in a flash – it turned into a convincingly wine-coloured liquid! I remember being quite impressed, at the time, by the demonstration.

In retrospect, however, I am somewhat less impressed. Had Jesus served such a concoction to the unfortunate guests at the wedding feast, I rather doubt that they would have exclaimed, 'You have saved the best till now'. In fact, I suspect that he would have had to make a fairly rapid exit! As an 'explanation', it ranks in implausibility with one I was given at school a few years later of how the Israelites crossed the Red Sea through what was actually just an area of marshy ground (how, in that case, did the entire Egyptian army drown in just a few inches of water?)

By contrast, there can be little doubt that the miracles Jesus performed were indeed genuine. Quite apart from the New Testament, there is a considerable body of Jewish evidence which testifies to this fact.[1] The questions raised were always about their legitimacy, not whether they had taken place at all. Moreover, compared to the clearly legendary stories about Jesus that appear in some of the later apocryphal writings, one is immediately struck by the sober matter-of-factness of the New Testament accounts.

But the miracles also tell us something about Jesus. They are not simply there for their own sake. We have already noted how Christ's healing of the paralytic in Luke 5.17–26 represented an implied claim to divinity. Similarly, we saw in chapter one how, after Jesus raises the widow's son from the dead, the crowd exclaim, 'A great prophet has appeared among us . . . *God has come* to help his people' (Luke 7.16).

We also noticed how, in response to a question from John the Baptist, Jesus gave a spectacular demonstration of healing and deliverance, which he then went on to explain by referring back to Isaiah 35.4–6, a passage which describes the miraculous deeds that would accompany the *coming of God* to earth.

If, then, Jesus' miracles are outward declarations that God has 'come' through his ministry, or, as he later said himself, 'it is the Father, living in me, who is doing his work' (John 14.10; cf. 10.38), they are not merely acts of mercy, but demonstrations of who he is. In other words, they are 'mighty works' intended to lead people to repentance (Matt. 11.20–24; Luke 10.13–14), or, to use the language of John's gospel, 'signs' which reveal his ultimate divinity.

In the Old Testament such 'signs', whether miraculous or prophetic, are almost always demonstrations of the uniqueness and sovereignty of Almighty God himself: they reveal his glory (Num. 14.22) and act as a basis for belief in him (Exod. 4.8–9,30; 14.31). But in John's gospel the signs now reveal *Jesus'* glory (2.11), a term that for John, as we noted in chapter three, seems to mean nothing less than deity itself. Furthermore, they bear witness to *him* (5.36; 10.25) and, repeatedly, act as a basis for belief in *him* (2.11; 3.2; 10.38; 14.11; 20.30–31). The last of these 'signs', moreover, is linked to a conclusive proof of Christ's own divinity (compare 20.30 with 20.24–29).

There can be little doubt, therefore, that by using the word 'signs', John intends to connect us to the acts of Yahweh in the Old Testament. The strongest evidence for this appears in John 12.37, where he writes that 'even after Jesus had *performed so many signs* in their presence, they *still would not believe in him*.' This clearly recalls the words of Yahweh in Numbers 14.11: 'How long will they *refuse to believe in me*, in spite of *all the signs I have performed* among them?'

Moreover, in selecting miracles to include in his gospel, John seems to deliberately choose examples that elude all natural explanation, and sometimes go far beyond what is required in the situation, defying every conceivable law of space, time and matter. For example, Jesus produces at the wedding feast in Cana not a few choice bottles but somewhere between 120 and 180 *gallons* of the best wine; he heals an official's son *instantly* and *at a distance*; he feeds *five thousand* people from a few loaves and fish, and still has twelve baskets left over (one for each of the disciples!); he walks *three and a half miles* across the Sea of Galilee to reach his disciples, and then immediately transports the boat to the other side; he gives sight to a man blind since birth; and finally raises a man who has been dead *for four days* and whose body, in the normal run of things, would already have started decomposing.

Some equally spectacular accounts appear in Mark's gospel. For instance, in chapter 5, Jesus commands a 'legion' of demons to leave a man (in the Roman army, this consisted of up to six thousand troops) and two thousand pigs are drowned as a result. It is small wonder that the region's Gentile population, gripped by fear and perhaps concerned about the impact on the local economy, implore Jesus to leave the area!

Luke, in his version of the same miracle, hints at Christ's true identity here by observing that 'the man from whom the demons had gone out begged to go with him, but Jesus sent him away, saying, "*Return home and tell how much* **God** *has done for you."* So the man went away and told all over the town *how much* **Jesus** *had done for him'* (Luke 8.38–39).

The fact that this act of deliverance was performed in a Gentile area shows how Jesus crossed boundaries in a manner flagrantly unacceptable to many of his Jewish contemporaries. This is equally apparent in the fact that a number of his miracles were performed on the Sabbath. As we saw in the last chapter, the justification that Jesus gave for breaking the Sabbath regulations was that he himself was 'Lord of the Sabbath' (Matt. 12.8), a claim that in the Old Testament only Yahweh could make (Exod. 20.10–11).

Bearing this in mind, there may be a deeper significance to Jesus' repeated act of healing on the Sabbath beyond a simple impatience with well-worn tradition. In Jewish thinking, Yahweh himself continued to work on the Sabbath day and alone had the right to do so.[2] Philo, for example, remarks that 'God never ceases from making something or other'.[3] In a similar manner, when Jesus is challenged about the healing of a paralysed man in John chapter 5, he responds by saying, 'My Father is always at his work to this very day, and I too am working' (John 5.17). As we shall see in chapter ten, John goes on to argue from this statement that Jesus was actually claiming equality with the Father.

The same willingness to challenge age-old traditions can be seen in his apparent disregard of Old Testament cleanliness laws. According to purity regulations (based on chapters 11 – 15 of Leviticus) he should in theory have become defiled through physical contact with those such as lepers who were ritually unclean. The gospels, however, betray no trace of concern that this had taken place. The North African writer Tertullian, writing around AD 200,

regarded this as further evidence of Christ's deity, commenting
that 'The Lord . . . touched the leper, by whom (even although as
man He might have been defiled) He could not be defiled as God,
being of course incorruptible.'[4]

Similarly he writes of the woman with the flow of blood who
touches the edge of Jesus' cloak in Mark 5.25–29 that 'she touched
him, not as a holy man, or as a prophet, who she would know was
because of his human substance capable of defilement, but as God
himself, whom she had assumed to be incapable of pollution by
any manner of uncleanness.'[5]

Such incidents serve to remind us that, as with the miraculous
cure of the paralytic in Mark's gospel, healing, forgiveness and
restoration belong together in Jesus' ministry, qualities that, in
Psalm 103, bear the fingerprints of Yahweh himself:

Praise the LORD, my soul,
    and forget not all his benefits –
who *forgives all your sins*
    and *heals all your diseases*,
who *redeems your life* from the pit
    and crowns you with love and compassion,
who satisfies your desires with good things
    so that your youth is renewed like the eagle's (Ps. 103.2–5).

The Footprints of God

Even if Jesus' physical healings do not provide categorical evidence
for his claims to divinity (we find similar acts attributed to other
Jewish figures of this period),[6] the same could not be said about his
nature miracles, where he seems to exert a creative power over the
laws of physics, chemistry and biology together! The fact that he
turned water into wine (John 2.1–11) and could, if he had chosen,
have turned stones into bread (Matt. 4.3) recalls the instantaneous
creation of matter by God in the opening chapter of Genesis.

This apparent total authority over the forces of nature is
particularly evident in Mark 4.37–41, where the vivid description
of Christ's unbroken calm contrasts sharply with the disciples'
state of panic:

> A furious squall came up, and the waves broke over the boat, so that
> it was nearly swamped. Jesus was in the stern, sleeping on a cushion.
> The disciples woke him and said to him, 'Teacher, don't you care if
> we drown?'
>
> He got up, rebuked the wind and said to the waves, 'Quiet! Be still!'
> Then the wind died down and it was completely calm.
>
> He said to his disciples, 'Why are you so afraid? Do you still have
> no faith?'
>
> They were terrified and asked each other, 'Who is this? Even the
> wind and the waves obey him!'

The emphasis in this story clearly lies in the final question, '*Who
is this?*' (perhaps recalling the comment of the Pharisees and the
teachers of the law that we noted in Luke 5.21: '*Who* can forgive
sins but God alone?') – or, as Matthew pointedly words it here,
'*What kind of man* is this' (Matt. 8.27) But the strongest clue to
the 'message' underlying the story comes from Psalm 89, wich
declares:

> *Who is like you,* LORD God Almighty?
>   You, LORD, are mighty, and your faithfulness surrounds you.
> You rule over the surging sea;
>   when its waves mount up, you still them (Ps. 89.8–9).

The same echo of Yahweh in the Old Testament can also be felt
in the initial urgency to wake Jesus, which carries echoes of God
being 'roused' from sleep at a time of great crisis:

> Awake, Lord! Why do you sleep?
>   Rouse yourself! Do not reject us for ever (Ps. 44.23).

This sense of Jesus acting as Yahweh in person is also apparent
in the story of him walking on the Sea of Galilee (Mark 6.45–52),
where, as we have already noted, he utters the divine name 'I AM'
(Mark 6.50; cf. John 6.20). If the disciples had been alert to this
action they would have recognized that it bore the very footprints
of the Creator himself, who alone, according to Job 9.8, 'stretches
out the heavens and treads on the waves of the sea'. Even the
detail, added by Matthew, of Jesus reaching out and catching hold

of Peter when he steps out of the boat and starts sinking (Matt. 14.28–31) recalls the words of Psalm 94.18:

When I said, 'My foot is slipping,'
   your unfailing love, LORD, supported me.

It is small wonder that, according to Matthew, the disciples fell down and worshipped Jesus there and then!

The authority that Jesus possesses here over the created order is also apparent in the miraculous catch of fish described in Luke 5.4–11. With striking echoes of the way that Yahweh caused innumerable species of mammals, reptiles, birds and insects to converge on Noah's Ark, Jesus seems to go one stage further here by actually causing the boat to start sinking! The breathtaking extravagance of this miracle illustrates in a spectacular fashion the explosive nature of the kingdom that Jesus is inaugurating, and it acts as a curtain raiser to Christ's ministry in Luke's gospel in a manner similar to that played by the miracle at Cana in the Gospel of John.

Perhaps the most spectacular demonstration of Christ's power over the physical laws of the universe, however, can be seen in the feeding of the five thousand. Moreover, this happens to be the best reported of his miracles, the only one (apart from his own resurrection) to appear in all four gospels, with three of the writers (Matthew, Mark and John) supplying their own unique details.[7]

Several factors contribute to the particular significance of this miracle. At one level it shows Jesus being able to cause inanimate objects to multiply as if they were actually alive, overcoming the normal rules of arithmetic just as surely as he seems to alter the known laws of science! At another level it shows him able to satisfy the needs of countless individuals at the same time, giving a foretaste of the way, on the day of Pentecost, the life-giving gift of the Spirit would be multiplied to fill thousands of people at once. Jesus, moreover, links the miracle directly with the breaking and sharing of his own body enacted in the Lord's Supper (John 6.50–51).

Again, we find in this miracle various parallels with the activities of Yahweh in the Old Testament. We read in the Psalms that it is God who fills the hungry with good things (Pss 104.27–28; 136.25) while in Isaiah God feeds his people on a mountainside (25.6; cf. John 6.3–6). In addition Mark's reference to Jesus' 'compassion' on the crowd recalls a later passage from Isaiah:

> They will feed beside the roads
>> and find pasture on every barren hill.
> They will neither hunger nor thirst,
>> nor will the desert heat or the sun beat down on them.
> He who has compassion on them will guide them . . .
> *For the* LORD *comforts his people*
>> *and will have compassion on his afflicted ones* (Isa. 49.9–10,13).

We should also notice two little details in Mark's version of the story that also bring to mind familiar passages of the Old Testament. Jesus' observation that 'they were like sheep without a shepherd' (Mark 6.34; compare the words of Yahweh in 1 Kgs 22.17) and the apparently unnecessary detail that the grass was 'green' (6.39)[8] both provide an interesting link with the opening of Psalm 23, which describes Yahweh's never-failing provision for his people:

> The LORD is my shepherd, I lack nothing.
>> He makes me lie down in green pastures . . .
>> he refreshes my soul (Ps. 23.1–3).

This in turn links back through a whole network of associations elsewhere in the gospels to the familiar Old Testament picture of Yahweh as the Shepherd of Israel (see insets on the next page).

Another chain of associations with Yahweh's acts in history can be seen in the events immediately following the miracle in the gospels of Matthew and Mark. Here we see Jesus calming the storm on the Sea of Galilee, healing the sick, preaching against the bondage of religious tradition, delivering a girl afflicted by an unclean spirit, before performing yet another feeding miracle (Matt. 15.32–39/Mark 8.1–10). These episodes seem to echo in reverse order the sequence of images in Psalm 107 in which God intervenes successively to feed the hungry in the desert, to set captives free, to heal those near to death, and to rescue those in danger on the sea. In each case the refrain, 'then they cried to the

L ORD in their trouble, and he delivered them from their distress' (vv. 6,13,19,28 RSV) appears to have clear parallels in Matthew (see in particular 14.36 and 15.22). The message could not be clearer: Jesus has come as Yahweh in person to deliver those who call out to him.

Ten pictures of Yahweh as Shepherd	Ten pictures of Jesus as Shepherd
• He is the true Shepherd, not a worthless one (Ezek. 34.1–12)	• He is the true Shepherd, not a worthless one (John 10.11–14)
• The sheep are his and he calls them by name (Ezek. 34.11; Isa. 43.1)	• The sheep are his and he calls them by name (John 10.3–4)
• He looks after them (Ezek. 34.12)	• He lays down his life for them (John 10.11)
• He separates out the goats (Ezek. 34.17)	• He separates out the goats (Matt. 25.32)
• He searches for the strays (Ezek. 34.16)	• He searches for the strays (Luke 15.4)
• He carries the vulnerable (Isa. 40.11)	• He carries the vulnerable (Luke 15.5)
• He brings them to safety (Ezek. 34.28)	• He brings them to safety (John 10.9)
• He gathers them as one flock (Mic. 2.12)	• He gathers them as one flock (John 10.16)
• He satisfies the hungry (Ezek. 34.14)	• He satisfies the hungry (John 21.15)
• He leads them to green pastures and quiet waters (Ps. 23.2)	• He leads them to pasture and living waters (John 10.9; Rev. 7.17)

The strongest echoes of the Old Testament in the miracle of the loaves and fishes, however, come from the feeding of the Israelites in the wilderness, particularly as Jesus himself links the miracle to the gift of manna, God's sovereign act of provision for his people (John 6.48–51). But there are also some interesting links in John's account of the miracle with Yahweh's dramatic provision of quail for the Israelites after they left the Sinai desert. This is particularly evident if we compare the reactions of Moses and Philip in the two stories:

[Moses] asked the LORD . . . *'Where can I get meat for all these people?* They keep wailing to me, "Give us meat to eat! . . ."'

The LORD said to Moses '. . . the LORD will give you meat, and you will eat it . . .'

But Moses said, 'Here I am among six hundred thousand men on foot, and you say, "I will give them meat to eat for a whole month!" Would they have enough if flocks and herds were slaughtered for them? *Would they have enough if all the fish in the sea were caught for them?'*

The LORD answered Moses, 'Is the LORD's arm too short? Now you will see whether or not what I say will come true for you.'

So Moses went out and told the people what the LORD had said . . .

All that day and night and all the next day the people went out and gathered quail. No one gathered less than ten homers (Num. 11.11–32).

When Jesus looked up and saw a great crowd coming towards him, he said to Philip, *'Where shall we buy bread for these people to eat?'* He asked this only to test him, for he already had in mind what he was going to do.

Philip answered him, *'It would take more than half a year's wages to buy enough bread for each one to have a bite!'*

Another of his disciples, Andrew, Simon Peter's brother, spoke up, 'Here is a boy with five small barley loaves and two small fish, but how far will they go among so many?'

Jesus said, 'Make the people sit down.' There was plenty of grass in that place, and they sat down (about five thousand men were there). Jesus then took the loaves, gave thanks, and d*istributed to those who were seated as much as they wanted.* He did the same with the fish (John 6.5–11).

Under these circumstances, we can hardly be surprised that the crowds intended to take Jesus and make him king by force (John 6.15)!

Death in Reverse

Let us shift our attention for a moment to two scenes from very different parts of the Bible. In the first, we are in a garden. It is the cool of the evening. Through the trees we see God walking in a garden he has planted and designed himself. There is a woman present, partly concealed from him. It is a defining moment. She has only ever known life, but now, for the first time, she must encounter death.

Now we find ourselves in another garden. It is the cool of the morning. A man is there who seems to be the gardener. There is also a woman present, but he is partly concealed from her. Again we are at a defining moment. The woman has only ever known death as an ending. Now she is to discover unending life once more.

There is a beautiful symmetry between these two accounts, which only makes complete sense if the gardener in both cases is one and the same. For the first time ever, death itself has actually been turned backwards!

Certainly, it is the authority that Jesus exercises over life and death that shows him most completely taking on a role that in the Old Testament was considered to belong to Yahweh alone. This authority is evident not only in the ending of life, as we see in the drowning of the herd of pigs (Mark 5.13) or the cursing of the fig tree (Mark 11.20–21) but also in the restoration of it, as (for example) in the raising of the widow's son in Luke 7.14–15 (which, as we have pointed out, leads to his ministry being seen as the coming of God to earth [v. 16]).

More spectacular still was the raising of Lazarus (John 11.38–44) which is presented not merely as an act of mercy (John 11.38) but as a demonstration of power (John 11.40): indeed, it was considered so threatening by the religious authorities that they convened a special meeting of the Sanhedrin to debate the matter (11.47), and even considered having Lazarus put to death to prevent a further draining of their support (12.10–11).

Such acts, however, also have a further dimension, in that they provide a foretaste of Jesus' supreme assurance of *eternal* life to all who believe in him (John 11.25), a gift which in the Old Testament had been Yahweh's alone to grant (Ps. 133.3). For example, Christ's promise to raise up the faithful on the last day (John 6.40) was an offer that previously only God himself could have made (cf. 1 Sam. 2.6). Not only is Jesus now the *source* of life (John 5.26) but he *is* that life in person (John 14.6).

In the same way, where Yahweh alone was the source of *power* in the Old Testament (Ps. 68.35; Isa. 40.29; Mic. 3.8), Jesus now takes on this role (Mark 5.30; Luke 9.1). There is a clear similarity, for example, between Jesus' words to the seventy-two that he sends out in Luke 10 ('I have given you authority *to trample* on snakes and scorpions and to overcome all the power of the enemy', v. 19) and David's words in Psalm 18.40–42, as translated in the Revised English Bible: 'You set my foot on my enemies' necks . . . like mud in the streets *I shall trample them.*'

Likewise, Jesus' role in directing and sending the Spirit closely parallels that of Yahweh in the Old Testament. He bears the Spirit in full measure (John 3.34); his words are Spirit (John 6.63 NIV margin); and he baptizes with the Spirit and with fire (Matt. 3.11; Luke 3.16). At the same time the Spirit brings to mind his words (John 14.26), bears witness to him (John 15.26) and glorifies him (John 16.14). His act of breathing the Spirit onto his disciples (John 20.22) recalls the way in which God imparts his own life-giving breath into Adam in Genesis 2.7, while the way he pours out the Spirit at Pentecost (Acts 2.17–21,33) echoes the promise of Yahweh in Joel 2.28–32.

Stressing the way Peter transfers this promised outpouring of the Spirit from Yahweh to the risen Christ, Robert Reymond observes here that 'the connection between what Peter expressly emphasized in 2.17 by his deliberate insertion of the words "God says" into the Joel prophecy ('"In the last days', *God says, 'I will pour out my spirit'"*) and his later statement in 2.33 ("he [the ascended Jesus] *has poured out* this which you now see and hear") can not have been unintentional or lost on Peter.'[9]

The greatest 'sign', however, demonstrating Jesus' authority over life and death, and eclipsing others in sheer magnitude, is the resurrection itself. Not only does this act as the final guarantee for all of Jesus' promises, but for Paul and the early church it remained the foundation stone of Christian belief, upon which the claims of Christianity stand or fall. Just as the incarnation establishes Christ's full humanity, the resurrection confirms his essential divinity. In this regard Paul says of Jesus in Romans 1.3–4 that 'as to his humanity, he was born a descendant of David; as to his divine holiness, he was shown with great power to be the Son of God *by being raised from death*' (GNB).

The full significance here becomes more apparent when we consider the Old Testament background. An indirect clue to this can be found hidden in 1 Corinthians 15.4, where Paul teaches that Jesus was raised to life on the third day *according to the Scriptures*. The key question is: to which scripture was Paul referring here? Unless one could conceivably argue that Paul was talking about *New Testament* scriptures (i.e. the gospels), which almost all scholars would argue were largely unwritten at this stage,[10] the most obvious candidate would be Jonah 1.17, given that Jesus himself referred to it in his own prophecy of his resurrection (Matt. 12.40).

When we take a look at Old Testament prophecies that specifically use the phrase 'on the third day', however, two other significant passages stand out, and both describe *a visible manifestation of God himself*. In one of these, Hosea 6.1–3, this visible 'appearing' is implied rather than clearly described, but the link with the rising sun provides an intriguing background for Mark 16.2, where the women arrive at the tomb 'just after sunrise':

Come, let us return to the LORD.
He has torn us to pieces
    but he will heal us;
he has injured us
    but he will bind up our wounds.
After two days he will revive us;
    on the third day he will restore us,
    that we may live in his presence.
Let us acknowledge the LORD;
    let us press on to acknowledge him.
As surely as the sun rises,
    he will appear;
he will come to us like the winter rains,
    like the spring rains that water the earth.

In the other, which we have already referred to in chapter three, we are left in no uncertain terms that we are witnessing a visitation from Yahweh in person: 'Make them wash their clothes and be ready *by the third day*, because on that day *the LORD will come down on Mount Sinai* in the sight of all the people' (Exod. 19.10–11).

It is interesting in this regard to compare the later part of this account in Exodus 24 with Peter's reference to the resurrection in his speech to Cornelius in Acts 10:

> Moses and Aaron, Nadab and Abihu, and the seventy elders of Israel went up and *saw the God of Israel* . . . But God did not raise a hand against these leaders of the Israelites; *they saw God, and they ate and drank* (Exod. 24.9–11).

> They killed him by hanging him on a cross, but God raised him from the dead on the third day *and caused him to be seen*. He was not seen by all the people, but by witnesses whom God had already chosen – *by us who ate and drank with him after he rose from the dead* (Acts 10.39–41).

Had Peter understood a connection here? The fact that Jesus appeared to his disciples over forty days, the *same* length of time Yahweh spent with Moses on Mount Sinai (Exod. 24.18), only serves to strengthen the link. If it has any bearing on what Paul meant when he talked of rising on the third day 'according to the Scriptures' then it helps further to remind us how loudly the resurrection proclaims the deity of Christ. It is small wonder that Thomas, confronted with the proof, should exclaim, 'My Lord and my God!' (John 20.28).

Ten key statements about Yahweh	Ten key statements about Jesus
• He alone performs great wonders (Ps. 136.4)	• He performs great wonders (John 2.11)
• His miracles cannot be counted (Job 9.10)	• His miracles cannot be counted (John 21.25)
• He heals every disease (Ps. 103.3)	• He heals every disease (Matt. 8.16)
• He gives sight to the blind (Isa. 35.4–5)	• He gives sight to the blind (Mark 8.25)
• He straightens bent backs (Ps. 146.8 NEB)	• He straightens bent backs (Luke 13.10–13)
• He feeds the multitude (Num. 11.13,21–23,31–32)	• He feeds the multitude (John 6.5–11)
• He walks on water (Job 9.8)	• He walks on water (John 6.19)
• He calms the storm (Ps. 89.8–9)	• He calms the storm (Mark 4.39–41)
• He destroys death (Isa. 25.7–8)	• He destroys death (2 Tim. 1.10)
• He restores to life (1 Sam. 2.6)	• He restores to life (John 6.40)

Questions to consider:

(i) Jesus said, '*Whoever* believes in me will do the works I have been doing, and they will do *even greater things than these*' (John 14.12). Is this promise still valid today? Is it reserved for a select few? What obstacles are there to God doing 'greater things' through us? (For some ideas, read Mark 11.22–26; John 15.7; James 1.6–8; 4.3).

(ii) No two miracles that Jesus performs are exactly the same. Do we limit God by expecting him to act in a particular way? How do our initial preconceptions affect the way that we pray? Do we pin our expectations on past experience, or on what the Bible itself says?

(iii) Set aside some time to read the evangelistic sermons in Acts (2.14–40; 3.12–26; 10.34–43; 13.16–41; 17.22–31; 26.2–23). Why is so much more emphasis placed on the resurrection of Jesus than on his saving work on the cross? Has today's church lost sight of the full significance of the resurrection?

9.

Jesus Through the Eyes of Others

Then I looked and heard the voice of many angels, numbering thousands upon thousands, and ten thousand times ten thousand . . . In a loud voice they were saying: 'Worthy is the Lamb, who was slain, to receive power and wealth and wisdom and strength and honour and glory and praise!' (Rev. 5.11–12).

No One Ever Spoke Like This!

There is a well-known story of some overseas visitors who, visiting the Houses of Parliament in London in the 1980s, walked past the Lord Chancellor of the time, Lord Hailsham, looking rather imposing in his robes of office. It happened that, at that very moment, he was trying to catch the attention of the then Leader of the Opposition, Neil Kinnock, who was coming past in the opposite direction, but as he called out, 'Neil!', the awestruck visitors, mistaking it as an instruction to them, fell straight down on their knees!

Though almost certainly a fictional tale (as it exists in several versions), the story serves to remind us of the sense of awe we can feel in the presence of something much greater than ourselves. So it is hardly surprising, given the nature of the accounts that we have considered in chapter eight, that Jesus' activities produced some powerful responses. Indeed, the gospel writers seem to run out of superlatives in describing the reactions of those present at the scene. Thus we find people being 'amazed' (Matt. 7.28), 'even more amazed' (Mark 10.26), 'completely amazed' (Mark 6.51), 'overwhelmed with amazement' (Mark 7.37), 'astonished'

(John 7.21 NRSV), 'filled with awe' (Luke 5.26), 'frightened and bewildered' (Luke 8.25 PHILLIPS) and 'overwhelmed with wonder' (Mark 9.15). 'We have never seen anything like this!' exclaim the onlookers at Capernaum, after Jesus raises the paralytic man in full view of all (Mark 2.12).

Such reactions were, however, by no means restricted to those in sympathy with Jesus' ministry. Even his opponents seem to have been struck by his sheer charisma and authority. 'No one ever spoke the way this man does,' say the temple guards, explaining their failure to obey orders and arrest Jesus in John 7.46. A later detachment of soldiers, as we have already noted, simply fell backwards to the ground on encountering him (John 18.6) and even Pilate was afraid (John 19.8).

In our exploration of Jesus' true identity, however, we should note a number of other significant reactions to Jesus which suggest parallels with Old Testament responses to Yahweh himself. The first of these is a *deep conviction of sin*. 'Go away from me, Lord; I am a sinful man!' exclaims Peter in Luke 5.8, on being confronted with the miraculous catch of fish, recalling the response of such figures as Job and Isaiah when faced with the awesome majesty of God (Job 40.4; Isa. 6.5). The second, linked closely with the first, is a remarkable *transformation of character*, such as we see in the life of Zaccheus (Luke 19.1–10) which may have parallels in the lives of such Old Testament figures as Manasseh (2 Chr. 33.12–17). A third response is an *extravagant outpouring of devotion*, like that in John 12.3, where Mary of Bethany pours out a whole flask of extremely rare perfume onto the feet of Jesus (equivalent to perhaps a year's wages for a working man) and wipes them with her hair. Here we may perhaps recall David's sacrificial pouring out of precious water before the LORD that others had risked their lives to obtain (2 Sam. 23.13–17).

But perhaps the most significant reaction to Jesus is a *great emboldening of faith*. This is apparent in the centurion who places an unswerving trust in Jesus' words without needing to see the evidence for himself (Matt. 8.8–9); in the woman who touches the hem of Jesus' robe with the childlike certainty that she will be healed (Mark 5.25–29); in the dogged determination of the four friends of the paralytic man to lower him through the roof of Jesus' house (Mark 2.3–4); in the outspoken persistence of the

Canaanite woman and of blind Bartimaeus in pleading with Jesus for a miracle (Matt. 15.21–28; Mark 10.46–52) and in the sheer courage of Peter in stepping out of the boat and walking on the water (Matt. 14.28–31). To such incidents one could of course name any number of parallels in the Old Testament, in the lives of Moses, Joshua, Gideon, David, Daniel, Esther and many others, each one responding to the call of Yahweh directly.

On at least one occasion in the gospels – the appearance of the unnamed sinner in Luke 7.37–50 – all these four reactions (deep conviction, transformed personality, extravagant devotion and remarkable boldness) seem to come together. Here the woman's unrestrained devotion towards Jesus and her apparent loss of dignity contrasts sharply with the cynicism and scorn shown by others, in a manner that might remind us of David's dancing before the Ark of the LORD in 2 Sam. 6.12–22.

There are several things we should notice in this story. To begin with, we should observe not only the woman's unwavering faith in Christ's authority to forgive her sins, but also the parable that Jesus tells in response to what has taken place, which seems to suggest that her debt of sin is owed to him alone (Luke 7.41–43). Indeed, the implications of this are not lost on the other dinner guests (v. 49)! Jesus is not only offering to *forgive* sin, but in doing so is effectively claiming to be *without* sin. In the Old Testament these qualities were both the sole preserve of God himself (cf. Ps. 103.3 with Eph. 1.7 and Ps. 92.15 with 1 Pet. 1.19).

More interesting still is the way in which the woman's whole-hearted expression of commitment seems to verge on an attitude of true worship, a response which Jesus accepts without question. This point is underlined when we compare Christ's willingness to accept such devotion with the vigorous arguments of Peter and Paul when confronted by similar situations (see Acts 10.25–26; 14.8–18). They both knew that for any being other than God to receive anything approaching worship was the ultimate sacrilege – a fact that Jesus himself makes clear when he rebuffs Satan in the wilderness by quoting the words of Deuteronomy 6.13: 'Away from me, Satan! For it is written: "Worship the Lord your God, and serve him only"' (Matt. 4.10).

It is striking, therefore, that several times in his gospel, Matthew records that Jesus accepted the worship of others without rebuke or query.[1] While it is true that the Greek verb *proskyneō* that he uses carries wider notions of reverence or homage than the modern English word 'worship', we should note that, as Richard Bauckham points out, 'Matthew's consistent use of the word . . . and his emphasis on the point show that he intends a kind of reverence which, paid to any other human being, he would have regarded as idolatrous.'[2]

A similar situation arises in Luke 17.15–16, where the restored Samaritan leper returns to throw himself at Jesus' feet (an action, note, which is understood in v. 18 as *praising God*). Here Luke employs the same Greek word that is used for worship before the heavenly throne in Revelation 5.14. Yet far from repudiating such an action, Christ rebukes the other nine for not doing the same!

If the instances we have described so far come across less as premeditated actions, and more as responses performed on the spur of the moment, the same can be said about the way those around Jesus sometimes spoke to him as if they were addressing God himself. Frequently on these occasions the person speaking seems moved, in a moment of heightened awareness, to honour Jesus with titles that in the Old Testament would have belonged to Yahweh alone, even before they had worked out the real implications of what they were saying. As a result, their exclamations appear not as carefully thought-out statements of doctrine, but as spontaneous expressions of wonder and praise.

We can see numerous examples of this throughout Jesus' lifetime. For example, as we have already seen, Elizabeth, suddenly filled with the Spirit (Luke 1.41) is moved to speak of the unborn Christ using the same word *kyrios* (Lord) in verse 43 that she gives to God the Father just two verses later. Likewise in John 1.49 Nathanael is prompted to call Jesus the 'king of Israel' (applied to Yahweh in Zeph. 3.15); Peter in John 6.69 names him as the 'Holy One' (another divine title frequently used by Isaiah) and both felt moved to hail him as 'Son of God' (John 1.49; Matt. 16.16) as Martha does later (John 11.27), which, as we shall see in chapter ten, was also effectively a declaration of divinity.

It is striking that such spontaneous declarations of faith also provide a climax to each of the gospels. In Matthew 27.54 and Mark 15.39 we hear 'Truly this man was God's Son!' [NRSV] from the lips of the centurion, a title which in a Roman context might well imply a divine or semi-divine being. Similarly, the words 'remember me when you come into your kingdom' from the crucified thief in Luke 23.42 carry equal significance, given that, as Stauffer points out, the words 'remember me' are prominent in the Jewish liturgy as a form of address to God.[3] And most remarkable of all, of course, is Thomas's awestuck exclamation 'My Lord and my God' in John 20.28, recalling the psalmist's impassioned cry to Yahweh, 'my King and my God', in Psalm 84.3.

The new theological ground that statements such as these open up provides further evidence that Jesus was actively worshipped as God by his followers long before any clear framework of doctrine had been worked out to justify such a practice. Arthur Wainwright, for example, has suggested that 'their faith outstripped their reason, and they were able to give joyful utterance to a belief which they felt incapable of expounding'.[4] Ralph P. Martin concludes that 'the first Christians made *in worship* the decisive step of setting the exalted Christ on a par with God as the recipient of their praise'.[5]

Can We Pray to Him?

Remarkable though reactions to Jesus were during his lifetime, the weeks and months after his resurrection signal an important shift in the way he was viewed by those around him. Larry Hurtado comments that 'devotion to Jesus as divine erupted suddenly and quickly'.[6] Already during the resurrection appearances the worship of Jesus is being mentioned prominently (Matt. 28.9,17; Luke 24.52). This fuller understanding seems to deepen in the fascinating transitional period that we see in the first chapter of Acts. Although the outpouring of the Spirit at Pentecost has yet to take place, the disciples are convinced that, in some sense, Jesus is with them, even after he has finally disappeared from their midst at the ascension (Acts 1.9–12).

The problem at hand was how to replace Judas, who had met an untimely end. 'Lord,' they call out, 'you know everyone's heart. Show us which of these two you have chosen to take over this apostolic ministry, which Judas left to go where he belongs' (Acts 1.24–25). At first sight this looks like a straightforward prayer to

God the Father. The form of address here is almost identical to that used by Solomon in his prayer to Yahweh when he dedicated the temple ('for *you alone know the human heart*', 2 Chron. 6.30).

Yet closer inspection reveals something more startling. In context, the 'Lord' they are calling on here appears to be none other than Jesus himself. Not only has Peter just talked of him as 'Lord' three verses earlier, but the question about 'which of these two you have chosen to take over this apostolic ministry' clearly ties in with the description in verse 2 of 'the apostles he [Jesus] had *chosen*'.

The significance of this first example we have of a prayer made to Jesus is huge. For a devout Jew, the idea of directing prayer to anyone other than God was a shocking one. Larry Hurtado says that 'Jewish opponents would likely have seen it as an unwarranted and dangerous innovation'.[7] Acts does not make clear how quickly the practice took root in the early church, but it clearly came out into the open when Stephen, the first Christian martyr, calls out in his final moments, 'Lord Jesus, receive my spirit' (Acts 7.59), borrowing a form of address almost identical to the one used by Jesus in praying to the Father before his own death. Bowman and Komoszewski underline the implications here: 'Clearly, Luke understands Jesus to be performing a function of deity by receiving Stephen's spirit – and in this context Stephen's calling on Jesus is as significant an act of prayer as one could imagine.'[8]

For a young man named Saul of Tarsus, who was present at Stephen's death, this apparent act of sheer idolatry may have been the final straw. He embarks on a frenzied campaign of persecution, culminating in a trip to Damascus to destroy the emerging church there. The irony is, of course, that the vision that overtakes him on the way there causes him to do the very thing that has most shocked him, forcing him, the arch-enemy of the church, to address Jesus as 'Lord' (Acts 9.5). As a result, when he is told by a Christian in Damascus named Ananias to 'call on the name' of Jesus (Acts 22.16), the phrase is loaded with heightened significance for him. As Paul would have known only too well from his rigorous Old Testament study, the expression 'calling on the name of the Lord' was a standard description of prayer to Yahweh himself (see, for example, Gen. 4.26).

It is striking, therefore, that he later describes the church as 'all those everywhere who *call on the name of our Lord Jesus Christ*' (1 Cor. 1.2). As Bowman and Komoszewski point out, 'this statement, written about AD 54 (just over twenty years after Jesus' death), in effect defines believers in Christ . . . as those who pray to him as Lord'.[9]

But why did the early church adapt so easily to what, from a Jewish viewpoint, would have been a completely heretical practice? One possible source is the promise that Jesus makes in John 14.14 (according to the earliest and most reliable manuscripts) that he would both *hear* and *answer* prayer made to him. 'You may ask me for anything in my name, *and I will do it*.'

The same suggestion seems also to be present in 1 John 5.13–15, according to the most natural reading of the Greek. In the RSV this is translated as follows:

> I write this to you who believe in the name of the Son of God, that you may know that you have eternal life. And this is the confidence which we have in him, that if we ask anything according to his will he hears us. *And if we know that he hears us in whatever we ask, we know that we have obtained the requests made of him.*

Elsewhere Paul underlines the fact that Christ both hears and answers prayer. When, in Romans 10.12, he writes that 'the same Lord is Lord of all and richly blesses all *who call on him*', the 'Lord' to whom he is referring is Christ, as verse 9 makes clear. To Timothy he writes, 'I *thank* Christ Jesus our Lord, who has given me strength, that he considered me trustworthy, appointing me to his service' (1 Tim. 1.12). And where he, Barnabas and other prophets and teachers from Antioch are said to be 'worshipping the Lord and fasting' in Acts 13.2, it is very likely that their praises were directed towards Jesus, since from Acts 5 onwards the title 'Lord' is almost always describing Christ himself.

We also have one example of an *unanswered* prayer to Jesus. In 2 Corinthians 12.8, Paul says of his 'thorn in the flesh' that 'three times I pleaded with the Lord to take it away from me.' Given that the title 'Lord' is Paul's normal description for Christ, it is almost certainly Jesus whom Paul is addressing here; this becomes more obvious in verse 9, where after recording the response to his request ('My grace is sufficient for you, for *my power is made perfect in weakness*'), Paul adds the comment, 'Therefore I will boast all the more gladly about my weaknesses, so that *Christ's power* may rest [literally, *tabernacle*] on me.'

It is perhaps significant that almost the very last words of the New Testament are a prayer to Christ: 'Come, Lord Jesus' (Rev. 22.20). A similar expression appears in Aramaic (*Marana tha*) at the end of 1 Corinthians, and its preservation in this form is yet another reminder of how quickly the practice of praying to Jesus became established in the months and years immediately following Pentecost, when Aramaic was still the dominant language within the church.

Other indications of the growing focus on Christ in the prayer life of the early church can be seen in the changing use of 'benedictions'. In the Old Testament these were short prayers of blessing offered in the name of Yahweh as, for example, we find at the beginning of Psalm 67:

> May God be gracious to us and bless us
>   and make his face shine on us.

In Paul's letters, however, we often find these prayers of blessing given in the name of Christ himself, either in addition to God the Father (as at the beginning of most of his letters) or, as we see at the end of 1 Corinthians, in Jesus' name alone: 'The grace of the Lord Jesus be with you' (1 Cor. 16.23).[10]

The same can be said of 'doxologies', which in the Old Testament were brief expressions of praise and worship to God, such as we find in 1 Chronicles 29.10–11:

> Praise be to you, LORD,
>   the God of our father Israel,
>   from everlasting to everlasting.
> Yours, LORD, is the greatness and the power
>   and the glory and the majesty and the splendour,
>   for everything in heaven and earth is yours.

In the New Testament, however, some of these outbursts of praise are now directed to Christ. For instance, Peter writes at the end of his second letter: 'But grow in the grace and knowledge of our Lord and Saviour Jesus Christ. To him be glory both now and forever! Amen' (2 Pet. 3.18). The placing of this seems to be deliberate, balancing Peter's statement in the opening verse of the letter that Jesus is 'our *God* and Saviour'.

Similar in style, if not a prayer as such, is Romans 9.5, which as we saw in chapter two appears to be another rare instance of the New Testament describing Christ directly as 'God', and where once more he is described as deserving the highest praise and worship: 'Abraham, Isaac and Jacob are their ancestors, and Christ himself was an Israelite as far as his human nature is concerned. And he is God, the one who rules over everything and is worthy of eternal praise! Amen' (Rom. 9.5 NLT).

There is good evidence from second-century writers to suggest that Christians continued praying to the risen Christ on a regular basis, even if prayer to God the Father remained the norm. Liddon observes that such prayer addressed to Christ, 'far from being a devotional eccentricity, was the universal practice of Christians; it was the act of devotion *which specially characterized a Christian*' (my italics).[11] As the late second-century writer Tertullian comments, 'This bodily patience adds a grace to our prayers for good, a strength to our prayers against evil; *this opens the ears of Christ our God.*'[12]

In conclusion, reverence and praise for Jesus seems to have arisen quite naturally from the impact he made, both during and after his life on earth. From that viewpoint, little has changed in the centuries that have followed. In the context of our own day, Murray Harris sums up the situation quite neatly when he writes that: 'He is unique, in a category of his own, both as a historical figure and as an ever-present person. If Caesar or Kennedy entered the room, we would all immediately stand up. If Jesus came in, *we would all instinctively bow down.*'[13]

Should We Worship Him?

On a wall of a house in the Palatine district of Rome, a striking example of second-century graffiti was discovered in 1857. A cartoon of a crucified man with an ass's head appears, with the caption 'Alexamenos worships his God.'

Unflattering though it is, this spontaneous piece of artwork is one of a number of fascinating clues that the worship of Jesus was becoming a central aspect of Christian life across much of the Roman Empire in the centuries after his death. Further evidence emerged in the 1990s when an ancient church was discovered at Megiddo in Israel containing the earliest definite reference to Christ yet discovered in the Holy Land, with the inscription 'The God-loving Akeptous has offered this table to *God Jesus Christ* as a memorial.'

Even earlier evidence comes in what is one of the first references to Jesus in a secular source. Writing to the emperor Trajan in about AD 113, Pliny, the governor of Pontus in Asia Minor, points out that Christianity in his province has taken over to such a degree that the pagan temples have almost been deserted. He comments that, instead, Christians in the region were accustomed to meet on one day of the week 'to sing hymns to Christ as if to a god'.[14]

It is clear from the New Testament that such 'hymns to Christ' were not new. In Ephesians 5.19, Paul mentions such 'hymns' in the same breath as 'psalms', the familiar Old Testament songs of praise to Yahweh (some of them, as we see in Hebrews 1, now being understood as addressed to Jesus). Furthermore, Paul continues by exhorting his readers to 'sing and make music from your heart to the Lord', the 'Lord' in this context being none other than Christ himself (as v. 20 makes clear).

We can make an educated guess as to the ingredients of these 'hymns' and 'spiritual songs' from what appear to be fragments of such material preserved for us in the New Testament. Given that, by definition, such extracts must date from before the passages in which they appear, it is entirely possible that some of them go back to the earliest years after Jesus' death; yet together they provide some of the strongest declarations of Jesus' deity in the Bible. Possible examples include John 1.1–18, which twice describes Jesus as 'God'; Philippians 2.6–11, which sees him being 'in the form of God' (RSV); Colossians 1.15–20, where he is called 'the image of God'; and Hebrews 1.3, which calls him 'the exact representation of his being'.

Some of the pointers in these apparent song fragments are less obvious without reference to the Old Testament. For instance, in Ephesians 2.14–16 Christ is described as 'our peace', a title applied to Yahweh himself in Judges 6.24. Similarly in 5.14 the verse:

Wake up, O sleeper,
    rise from the dead,
    and Christ will shine on you

seems to be modelled on Isaiah 60.1, which in the New English Bible is translated:

    Arise, Jerusalem,
rise clothed in light; your light has come
    and the glory of the LORD *shines over you.*

More remarkable is a passage in the letter to the Philippians, where two verses from Isaiah:

before me *every knee will bow;*
    by me every tongue will swear.
They will say of me, 'In the LORD alone
    are deliverance and strength' (Isa. 45.23–24)

have now become:

. . .that *at the name of Jesus every knee should bow,*
    in heaven and on earth and under the earth,
and every tongue acknowledge that Jesus Christ is Lord
    to the glory of God the Father (Phil. 2.10–11).

As Hurtado points out, 'the utterly remarkable allusion to Isaiah 45.23 . . . involves finding a reference to Christ as *kyrios* as well as God in what is perhaps the most stridently monotheistic passage in the Old Testament!'[15] Bowman and Komoszewski comment here that 'God wants all creation to recognize Jesus as no one less than the Lord YHWH himself'.[16] Reymond concludes that the Philippians passage is 'as bold and unqualified an assertion of both the pre-existence and the full unabridged deity of Jesus Christ as one could ever hope to find in the pages of the New Testament'.[17]

Two more examples of hymn-like material can be seen in Revelation 5.9–10 and 5.12, heavenly songs of praise to the exalted Christ. Here, as in Philippians 2, we are presented with a stark contrast between glory and sacrifice, with an abrupt shift from descriptions of Christ as 'the Lion of the tribe of Judah' and 'the Root of David' (5.5) to the image of 'a Lamb, looking as if it had been slain' (5.6).

However, it is clear that this Lamb is also divine: it stands at the centre of God's throne, and possesses the threefold attributes of omnipotence ('seven horns'), omniscience ('seven eyes') and omnipresence ('seven spirits of God sent out into all the earth'). Moreover, it seems to receive both the prayers of the saints and the worship of the elders in heaven (v. 8; see also Rev. 5.13–14) despite the clear instruction at three points in the book of Revelation (14.7; 19.10; 22.8–9) that worship should be directed to God alone. And we should note how closely the song of praise to the Lamb in verse 12 resembles the one to the Father in 4.11: *both* are counted worthy of receiving honour, glory and power. As Hurtado points out, 'it would be difficult to imagine a more direct and forceful way to express Jesus' divine status'.[18]

Carey Newman concludes that 'Revelation legitimates and promotes . . . the worship of Jesus as God – and it does so at the very places where God is worshipped and with the very language that is used to venerate God. Revelation shows how . . . psalms originally addressed to God, under the inspiration of the Spirit, were redirected to Jesus.'[19]

If such hymns focusing on Christ played a significant role in the worship of the New Testament church, there is good evidence to suggest that the use of such material continued with little interruption during the centuries which followed. The *Gloria in Excelsis* and the Vesper Hymn of the Orthodox Church *Phos Hilaron* probably also date back to the second century AD, as does the vision section of the *Ascension of Isaiah*, where Christ is described as being worshipped alongside the Father and the Holy Spirit,[20] and the *Paedagogus* of Clement of Alexandria, which ends with a hymn of praise to Christ. Along with a number of statements by the early church fathers, these testify to a continuing focus on the worship of Christ (see inset).

The Church Fathers on the Worship of Jesus

- Justin Martyr (c.150): 'Some Scriptures which we mention ...expressly prove that Christ was to suffer, to be worshipped, and [to be called] God.'[21]
- Melito of Sardis (c.175): 'We are worshippers . . . of His Christ, who is veritably God the Word – existing before all time.'[22]
- Irenaeus (c.185): 'The Church . . . has received from the apostles and their disciples this faith . . . that to Christ Jesus, our Lord, and God, and Saviour, and King, according to the will of the invisible Father, "every knee should bow".'[23]
- Clement of Alexandria (c.195): 'Let us sing together simple praises, true hymns to Christ [our] King.'[24]
- Tertullian (c.210): 'Christ's Name is extending everywhere, believed everywhere, worshipped by all . . . reigning everywhere, adored everywhere, conferred equally everywhere upon all.'[25]
- Origen (c.240): 'We worship with all our power the one God, and His only Son, the Word and Image of God, by prayers and supplications.'[26]
- *Martyrdom of Polycarp* (anonymous, 2nd century AD): 'It is neither possible for us ever to forsake Christ . . . nor to worship any other.'[27]
- *Phos Hilaron* (anonymous, 2nd century AD): 'You are worthy at all times to be praised by happy voices, O Son of God, O Giver of Life, and to be glorified through all the worlds.'[28]
- *Odes of Solomon* (anonymous, 2nd century AD): 'Glory to thee, our Head, the Lord Messiah. Hallelujah.'[29]

It is not surprising that the church historian Eusebius later remarked, 'How many psalms and hymns, written by the faithful brethren *from the beginning*, celebrate Christ the Word of God, speaking of him as Divine?'[30]

To these we can add some significant evidence from pagan sources. We have already commented on Pliny's remark to the emperor Trajan that the early Christians were accustomed to sing hymns to Christ 'as if to a god'. Similarly we find Lucian of Samosata, in *The Passing of Peregrinus*, written around AD 170, referring to 'that one whom they still worship today, the man in Palestine who was crucified'.[31] In the same vein the pagan philosopher Celsus, writing at approximately the same time, comments that, 'If these people worshipped one God alone, and no other, they would perhaps have some valid argument against the worship of others. But they pay excessive reverence to one who has but lately appeared among men, and they think it no offence against God if they worship also his servant.'[32]

Similarly in the early third century the pagan Caecilius is reported as mocking 'the worship of a criminal and his cross',[33] while Porphyry (late third century) comments that 'Here it was said that he was a very religious man, and that his soul, like that of other persons, became immortal after his death: and this the Christians in their folly worship.'[34]

Arnobius quotes another pagan view from around this time which attacks Christians 'because you both allege that one born as men are, and put to death on a cross . . . was God, and because you believe that he still lives, and because you worship him in daily supplications'.[35] In the same way, Lactantius records the widespread reproach of pagans that 'we worship a man, and one who was visited and tormented with remarkable punishment'.[36]

Clearly no pagan writer of the period was prepared for the extraordinary transformation in the standing of the church which took place in the fourth century AD. Yet this very leap forward from a small handful of believers to a world-changing movement that within three centuries had effectively taken over the Roman Empire is difficult to explain in purely natural terms. Rather, it testifies to the everyday reality of those who experienced Christ not just as a great teacher, but as the awesome power of God active daily in their midst. The simple sequence opposite, charting this exponential growth, provides a striking background to everything we have discussed so far.

The church: A divine Masterplan		
John 6.66–7	AD 32	From this time many of his disciples turned back and no longer followed him. 'You do not want to leave too, do you?' Jesus asked the Twelve.
Acts 1.15	AD 33	In those days Peter stood up among the believers (a group numbering about a hundred and twenty)
Acts 2.41,47	AD 33	Those who accepted his message were baptised, and about three thousand were added to their number that day . . . And the Lord added to their number daily those who were being saved.
Acts 4.4	AD 33	But many who heard the message believed; so the number of men who believed grew to about five thousand.
Acts 6.7	AD 34	So the word of God spread. The number of disciples in Jerusalem increased rapidly, and a large number of priests became obediant to the faith.
Acts 17.6	AD 49	'These men who have turned the world upside down have come here also' (RSV)
Acts 21.20	AD 58	'many thousands of Jews have believed, and all of them are zealous for the law'
Rom. 1.8	AD 58	'your faith is being reported all over the world'
Col. 1.6	AD 62	'the gospel is bearing fruit and growing thoughout the whole world'
Tacitus	AD 64	Talks of 'an immense multitude' of Christians in Rome[37]
Pliny	AD 113	'many of all age and every rank . . . from . . . not the cities only, but also villages and the country'[38]
Tertullian	AD 200	'We are but of yesterday, and we have filled every place among you – cities, islands, fortresses, towns, market-places . . . tribes, companies, palace, senate, forum . . . we have left nothing to you but the temples of your gods.'[39]

Conclusion: The Witness of the Early Church

The observations of both pagan and early Christian writers provide compelling evidence for the almost universal belief in the deity of Christ in the early church. Indeed, in the centuries before the Nicene Creed was formulated, we find a wealth of references to Jesus as 'God'. Even as early as the *Didache*, possibly dating from the late first century AD, 'Hosanna to the Son of David' (Matt. 21.9) has become 'Hosanna to the *God* of David',[40] while in the writings of Ignatius, at the beginning of the second century, Jesus is described as 'God' on at least twelve separate occasions.[41] In addition, Polycarp talks of 'our Lord and God, Jesus Christ';[42] *2 Clement* appears to refer to Jesus as 'God' at least twice;[43] the *Epistle to Diognetus* also describes Jesus as 'God'[44] and the references to Jesus as 'God' in the surviving works of Justin Martyr, Irenaeus, Clement of Alexandria, Tertullian and Hippolytus, all of whom were active in the second century AD, run into double figures in each case.

There is also a large body of material recording the dying words of Christian martyrs from this and later centuries, which, as Bauckham states, 'whether or not their records . . . are accurate, are evidence of Christian views on this issue'.[45] As one example, the African bishop Felix, who was beheaded at Venusium in AD 303, is recorded to have addressed his dying prayer to the 'Lord God of heaven and earth, Jesus Christ, to whom belong glory and majesty, world without end. Amen'.[46]

Liddon, citing numerous such prayers made by early Christian martyrs, comments that 'they prayed to Christ as God, they confessed that Christ is God, they died for Christ as God'.[47] There is only one conclusion we can sensibly draw from this. The fact that Jesus 'not only taught that he was God but demonstrated that fact by what he did' provides, according to Gerald Bray, the only explanation for his 'unique place . . . in early Christian worship, and the willingness of his followers to stand up for it in the face of persecution and death'.[48]

To add to this evidence are several Jewish texts which, while clearly hostile to Christianity, seem to show a widespread knowledge of the church's belief in the deity of Christ. The most extraordinary of these comes from the famous second-century sage Rabbi Meir (who, remarkably enough, is said to have been descended from the emperor Nero).[49] He once described God as having a twin brother who is crucified for robbery. Their appearance is so similar, however, that it leads the onlookers to mistake the man on the cross for Yahweh himself![50]

Other Jewish texts also pick up on Jesus' claim to be God. In the early third century Rabbi Eleazar ha-Kappar states that:

> [God] beheld that there was a man, son of a woman, who should rise up and seek to make himself God, and to cause the whole world to go astray. Therefore . . . he spoke: Give heed that you go not astray after that man, for it is written, 'God is not man that he should lie' (Numbers 23.19), and if he says that he is God he is a liar; and he will deceive and say that he departs and comes again in the end, he says and he shall not perform.'[51]

A similar text from the end of the third century declares that 'If a man says to you, "I am God," he is a liar; if [he says, "I am] the son of man," in the end people will laugh at him; if [he says], "I will go up to heaven," he says, but he shall not perform it.'[52]

From around the same period we find the following passage: 'If the son of the harlot shall say to you, "These are two Gods," say to him [Deut. 5.4], "Face to face the Lord [singular] spoke with you."'[53]

This wealth of evidence from a variety of sources sharply contradicts the frequent claim of the Jehovah's Witnesses that the church of the apostolic and post-apostolic periods knew nothing of the belief in Jesus as God incarnate: indeed, it is a fabrication of the most remarkable proportions! The sheer fact that there is no obvious attempt to argue or debate the topic in the New Testament (with the possible exception of Hebrews 1) suggests that, by and large, it was *not* a subject of controversy in the early church. Quite apart from the ten or more possible descriptions of Jesus as 'God' in the New Testament, and the volume of supporting evidence presented in the last few chapters, there is a striking unanimity of evidence from Christian, pagan and Jewish sources that the church really did believe Jesus to be 'God with us'. Moreover, even in the vast majority of the sects, both heretical and orthodox, that broke off from the church, be they Docetists, Marcionites, Montanists, Modalists or Novatianists, this belief was never seriously challenged until the fourth century AD.[54] The question to ask, therefore, is not 'Was Jesus God?' but rather 'How can he share such a title with the Father?' This is an issue that we will begin to tackle in the next chapter.

Ten key statements about God the father	Ten key statements about Jesus the Son
• He receives prayer (Matt. 6.9)	• He receives prayer (John 14.14)
• He receives thanksgiving (Col. 1.3)	• He receives thanksgiving (1 Tim. 1.12)
• He receives glory (1 Tim. 1.17)	• He receives glory (2 Pet. 3.18)
• He receives honour (Rev. 4.11)	• He receives honour (John 5.23)
• He receives power (1 Pet. 5.11)	• He receives power (Rev. 1.6)
• He is worshipped by Jews (Acts 26.7 RSV)	• He is worshipped by Jews (Matt. 28.17)
• He is worshipped by Gentiles (Acts 10.2)	• He is worshipped by Gentiles (Matt. 2.11)
• He is worshipped by children (Ps. 8.2)	• He is worshipped by children (Matt. 21.15–16)
• He is worshipped by angels (Rev. 7.11)	• He is worshipped by angels (Heb. 1.6)
• All creation will bow before him (Rev. 5.13)	• All creation will bow before him (Phil. 2.9–11)

Questions to consider:

(i) Read the story of Mary and Martha (Luke 10.38–42). Do we spend enough time listening to Jesus? Are we too busy to timetable him in? What is he trying to say to us at present? Are we trying to operate in our own strength, or in his?

(ii) Jesus taught that our attitude in prayer should be like that of an expectant child (Matthew 7.9–11). A loving parent sometimes says 'no' to their children's requests (see 2 Cor. 12.8–9). How can we reconcile this with Jesus' statement that 'you may ask me for anything in my name, and I will do it' (John 14.14)?

(iii) To what extent is worship a lifestyle? Is it possible to live every moment of each day for Jesus, and how would that work out in practical terms? What obstacles are there to us yielding every aspect of our lives to him?

10.

Jesus and the Father

In a lawsuit the first to speak seems right, until someone comes
forward and cross-examines (Prov. 18.17).

Less Than God?

The Witnesses are back at the front door! This time, however, we
feel more relaxed, more certain of the Scriptures, and more confi-
dent in our theology. But not for long. Soon our visitors have us
squirming on the spot!

The difficulty, as they are only too happy to remind us, is that
both the Old and New Testaments repeatedly insist that there is
only one true God.[1] Our problem, then, is that we seem to have too
many beings called 'God' to fit the bill! Only the most contrived
arguments, for example, could be used to suggest that God was
talking to himself on the Mount of Transfiguration, or that Jesus
was praying to himself in the Garden of Gethsemane. More prob-
lematic still is the fact that Jesus refers to the Father repeatedly
not just as 'God' but as 'my God' (see, for example, Mark 15.34;
John 20.17; Rev. 3.2,12). Something has to be wrong with our case
somewhere!

Certainly, our friends do seem to have a point. Moreover, if
Jesus was consciously attempting to *identify* himself as God, he
was going a very strange way about it! In fact, on some occasions
he seems rather to go out of his way to *deny* such a notion. 'Why do
you call me good?' he asks, when addressed as 'Good teacher' in
Mark 10.17–18. 'No one is good – except God alone.' This conclusion seems to be backed up by several other incidents in Mark's

gospel which suggest a distinct limit to the power that Jesus was able to exercise: he is, for instance, *unaware* of who touched him in Mark 5.30; *unable* to heal many people in Nazareth in Mark 6.5; and only *half-successful* in his initial attempt to restore the sight of the blind man in Mark 8.22–24.

While we might allow that Jesus claimed to be the *Son* of God (see John 10.36), his use of the expression often seems to imply a position much lower than that of the Father. In Mark 13.32, for instance, he tells us that the Father possesses knowledge apparently unknown to himself (cf. Rev. 1.1). And similar statements appear in John's gospel, as the following verses show:

> *The Son can do nothing by himself;* he can do only what he sees his Father doing (John 5.19).

> *I seek not to please myself* but him who sent me (John 5.30).

> *For I have not spoken on my own authority;* the Father who sent me has himself given me commandment what to say and what to speak (John 12.49 RSV).

> *The words I say to you I do not speak on my own authority.* Rather, it is the Father, living in me, who is doing his work (John 14.10).

> If you loved me, you would be glad that I am going to the Father, for *the Father is greater than I* (John 14.28).

> Now this is eternal life: that they know you, *the only true God,* and Jesus Christ, whom you have sent (John 17.3).

Examples like these can also be seen in the writings of Paul, as we can see from the following list:

> All things are yours . . . and you are of Christ, and *Christ is of God* (1 Cor. 3.21,23).

> But I want you to realise that the head of every man is Christ, and the head of the woman is man, and *the head of Christ is God* (1 Cor. 11.3).

When he has done this, then *the Son himself will be made subject to him* who put everything under him, so that God may be all in all (1 Cor. 15.28).

For there is *one* God and *one* mediator between God and mankind, the *man* Christ Jesus (1 Tim. 2.5).

There are other problems, as well. We have already pointed out the complete lack of agreement between different Bible translations as to which verses in the New Testament actually describe Jesus as 'God'. What is more, the Greek word for 'God', *theos*, can itself sometimes refer to a created being (as in John 10.34–35; Acts 17.23; 2 Cor. 4.4), a point which our Witness friends are only too keen to mention if we start discussing the first verse of John's gospel. The same can be said about the word for 'Lord', *kyrios*, which carries an even wider range of meaning.

Some of the other arguments that we have used in previous chapters can also be challenged. For example, one of Jesus' key 'I AM' statements is tied to a declaration of total submission to the Father (John 8.28); the miracles he performs are 'from the Father' (John 10.32); and where Jesus is 'worshipped', the same Greek word is used for those who 'fall down' at the feet of the church in Revelation 3.9.

So have we come to a dead end in our investigation of the nature of Christ? Should we, in fact, admit that the Watchtower organization was right all the time? Or is there another answer?

A Partnership of Equals?

On the face of it, the statements above might seem to provide a fairly compelling reason for setting aside much of the evidence for the deity of Christ that we have been considering so far. But the issue is just not that simple. The problem is that, alongside those scriptures which suggest a clear distinction in position between Father and Son, we find a number of other verses which seem to mark out a completely level playing field between them! Indeed, it is particularly notable that, with the exception of Acts, Colossians and 3 John, *every* New Testament book from John's gosʳ

onwards begins with a clear suggestion that they are equal part-
ners together. In Paul's letters, for example, they are presented as
joint sources of blessing to the churches, as we see in Romans 1.7,
which reads: 'Grace and peace to you from God our Father *and*
from the Lord Jesus Christ.'

This is repeated elsewhere in a variety of ways. James describes
himself as 'a servant of God *and* of the Lord Jesus Christ' (Jas
1.1); Peter talks of being 'chosen according to the foreknowledge
of God the Father . . . *to be obedient to* Jesus Christ' (1 Pet. 1.2);
Jude addresses those 'loved in God the Father *and* kept for Jesus
Christ' (Jude 1); John describes 'fellowship . . . with the Father
and with his Son, Jesus Christ' (1 John 1.3) and Revelation refers
to 'the word of God *and* the testimony of Jesus Christ' (Rev. 1.2).
This equality is expressed more forcefully in the opening chapters
of John's gospel and Hebrews, in verses such as John 1.1,18 and
Hebrews 1.8–12.

Moreover, in Paul's letters to the Thessalonians, probably the
earliest literature in the New Testament, written only two decades
after the death of Christ, we find Father and Son acting together in
the lives of believers with such unity of purpose that *only singular
verbs are used*:

Now may our God and Father himself and our Lord Jesus clear [*singular*] the way for us to come to you (1 Thess. 3.11).

May our Lord Jesus Christ himself and God our Father . . . encour-
age [*singular*] your hearts and strengthen [*singular*] you in every good
deed and word (2 Thess. 2.16–17).

A similar thing happens on three occasions in the book of Revelation (6.17; 11.15; 22.3–4) where *joint* references to Father and Son
are followed by *singular* pronouns. In addition, where 14.1 says of
the Lamb that 'his name and his Father's name [were] written on
their foreheads', the Greek word for 'written' is singular where
it would normally be plural, suggesting that they both share the
same name.

We find a number of other interesting pairings of Father and
Son in the New Testament. Faith is to be placed in them equally
(John 14.1); eternal life depends on a personal relationship with

both of them (John 17.3; Rev. 7.10); and both are actively present together in the lives of believers (John 14.23), as with Paul when he gives instructions to Timothy 'in the presence of God *and of* Christ Jesus' (2 Tim. 4.1). Likewise the church is said to be '*in* God the Father *and* the Lord Jesus Christ' (1 Thess. 1.1) with believers remaining 'in the Son and in the Father' (1 John 2.24). Jointly Father and Son are said to possess the divine name (Matt. 28.19), the divine glory (John 17.5), the temple (Rev. 21.22) and the throne (Rev. 22.1,3).

Furthermore, many of these terms prove to be completely inter-changeable. For example, the word of God (1 John 2.14) is also the word of Christ (Col. 3.16 RSV); the Spirit of God (1 Cor. 3.16) is also the Spirit of Christ (1 Pet. 1.10–11); and the life of God (Eph. 4.18) is also the life of Christ (2 Cor. 4.10). The same could be said about the angels (Rev. 3.5/Matt. 13.41), the blood (Acts 20.28/Eph. 2.13), the church (1 Cor. 11.16/Rom. 16.16), the gospel (1 Thess. 2.9/ Rom. 15.19), the kingdom (1 Thess. 2.12/Col. 1.13) and the final judgement seat (Rom. 14.10/2 Cor. 5.10); it also embraces such absolute qualities as love (Rom. 5.5/Eph. 3.18), truth (Rom. 1.25 NASB/2 Cor. 11.10), grace (1 Cor. 15.10/16.23), peace (Phil. 4.7/ John 14.27) and righteousness (Rom. 10.3/2 Pet. 1.1).

It is interesting in this regard to see how many statements in the New Testament seem to identify our attitude to Christ with our attitude to the Father. Apart from the verse, 'he who receives me receives him who sent me', which unusually appears almost unchanged in all four gospels (Matt. 10.40; Mark 9.37; Luke 9.48; John 13.20), we find a whole network of similar statements following the same basic pattern, mainly in John's gospel, as we can see from the list below:

- To see Jesus is to see the Father (John 12.45; 14.9)
- To know Jesus is to know the Father (John 8.19; 14.7)
- To believe in Jesus is to believe in the Father (John 12.44)
- To acknowledge Jesus is to acknowledge the Father (1 John 2.23)
- To dishonour Jesus is to dishonour the Father (John 5.23)
- To deny Jesus is to deny the Father (1 John 2.23)
- To reject Jesus is to reject the Father (Luke 10.16)
- To hate Jesus is to hate the Father (John 15.23)

Indeed, so close is the link for many of the New Testament authors that such correspondences seem sometimes to creep almost subconsciously into their writing. In Acts 16.31, for example, Paul says to the Philippian jailer, '*Believe in the Lord Jesus*, and you will be saved', yet just three verses later we are told that he was filled with joy 'because he had come to *believe in God*'. Likewise in Acts 18.25–26 Luke slides effortlessly from 'the way of the Lord' (that is, Jesus) to 'the way of God', while a similar shift takes place from 'the day of the Lord' (again referring to Christ) to 'the day of God' in 2 Peter 3.10–12. We also find a number of similar examples of this in the letters of Paul.[2]

Most interestingly of all, Paul takes the *Shema'*, the uncompromising declaration of the uniqueness of God which provides the bedrock of Jewish faith to this day, and splits it quite shamelessly down the middle. So while Deuteronomy 6.4 (RSV) states, 'Hear O Israel: The LORD our God is one LORD,' it is now altered by Paul in 1 Corinthians 8.6 to become: 'there is but *one* God, the Father, *from* whom all things came and for whom we live; and there is but *one* Lord, Jesus Christ, through whom all things came and *through* whom we live.' For a devout Jew of the time, this would have been about as shocking as seeing the veil of the temple tear in two from top to bottom!

Our visiting Witnesses, however, will be quick to raise an objection here. The subtle change in the sentence ('from' becoming 'through') appears to suggest that the Father and the Son are not, in fact, performing equal roles. And, more significantly, it is still only the Father that is called 'God' here. Jesus is merely 'Lord', a fact that, with only a very few debatable exceptions, holds true throughout almost the entire body of Paul's letters.

However, these objections are by no means watertight. In Romans 11.36, for example, it is the Father *through* whom all things were made, while in Hebrews 1.10 it is the Son *from* whom all things originate. And while it is tempting to think that Paul is suggesting a difference in rank between the titles 'God' and 'Lord', we should remember that the Old Testament switches quite freely between them in its descriptions of Yahweh.

Paul may, in fact, have been reflecting a tradition which extends back at least as far as Philo and which appears again in later rabbinical literature, where the titles 'God' and 'Lord' reflect different aspects of Yahweh's character.[3] The distinction between them in Paul's writings, in other words, may simply have been an arrangement of convenience, to avoid confusion. It would be difficult otherwise to explain such verses as 1 Corinthians 6.14 ('*God* raised the *Lord* from the dead') and 7.17 ('each person should retain the place in life that *the Lord* assigned to him and to which *God* has called him'). As Charles Moule writes, Paul 'seems to reflect an experience of Christ which implies such dimensions as any theist would ascribe to God himself'.[4]

A Family Business?

At this point our visiting Witnesses might change tack. Jesus is only the *Son* of God, they tell us. He was *sent* by the Father (John 3.17), *imitates* the Father (5.19), is *obedient* to the Father (8.28) and acts *only* on the Father's will, not his own (Mark 14.36; John 5.30). It all seems very persuasive on the surface. At first sight, the titles 'Father' and 'Son', by their very nature, might seem to suggest a much greater contrast of status than 'God' and 'Lord'.

On closer examination, however, the argument does not stand up quite so well. In the Old Testament, for example, as we noted in chapter one, there are several passages where there seems to be a mysterious overlap between 'God' and the 'Messiah', and this is particularly apparent in two that make reference to a divine 'Son'. In one of these, Zechariah 12.10, we saw that God seems to portray *himself* both as a human martyr and as a firstborn son, while in the other, Isaiah 9.6, the 'son' is described not only as 'Mighty God', a title given to Yahweh himself in the following chapter, but even as 'Everlasting Father'.

The curious nature of this relationship between 'God' and his 'Son' is reflected in the intriguing riddle we met in chapter five, which appears in Proverbs 30:

> Who has gone up to heaven and come down?
>> Whose hands have gathered up the wind?
> Who has wrapped up the waters in a cloak?
> Who has established all the ends of the earth?
>> What is his name, *and what is the name of his son*?
> Surely you know! (Prov 30.4)[5]

Since the form of the last part of this proverb is similar to that of Numbers 23.19 ('God is not a man, that he should lie, or a son of man, that he should change his mind' ESV), and since, as we saw in chapter four, 'son of man' is in this case simply another way of saying 'man', could we, by the same token, suggest a similar kind of exchange of meaning here between God and his 'son'? Put simply, if 'son of man' (in its everyday Hebrew usage) means, in essence, 'man', then might it be possible to argue by the same logic that 'son of God' means, in essence, 'God'?

Certainly Jesus' contemporaries seem to have understood his claim to be the Son of God as effectively being a declaration that he is on a par with Yahweh himself. In John 10 Jesus is threatened with stoning because, according to his own account of events, he said, 'I am God's Son' (John 10.36); yet the crowd read far more into what he said, protesting that 'you, a mere man, *claim to be God*' (John 10.33). The same hint may be present in John 19.7, where the Jewish authorities say, 'We have a law, and according to that law he must die, because *he claimed to be the Son of God*.' Bowman and Komoszewski comment here that 'they clearly mean that Jesus claimed to be divine, God's "Son" in a sense that made him . . . uniquely like him in his prerogatives, attributes, and works'.[6]

In fact, in other places in his gospel such as 1.18 and 20.28–31, it seems quite clear that John means by the word 'Son' nothing less than total divinity. In the second of these passages, for example, he concludes that Jesus is the 'Son of God' by placing Thomas's staggering description of Christ as 'Lord' and 'God' immediately beforehand. Robert Reymond points out here that:

> If John had intended by the title 'Son of God' in his stated purpose for his Gospel something other than or less than an ascription of full deity to Jesus, one can only impute unforgivable ineptitude to him for bringing this lesser title into such close proximity to Thomas' confession of Jesus' unabridged deity . . . To be the Son of God in the sense that John intended it of Jesus is *just to be God the Son* [italics mine].[7]

Elsewhere the same thought seems to surface repeatedly. At the end of John's first letter, for instance, he appears to suggest that the Son of God 'is the true God and eternal life' (1 John 5.20). A similar idea is expressed by Tertullian, who writes that 'even the

Son of the Almighty is as much almighty as the Son of God is God'.[8]

But even when the words 'Father' and 'Son' appear together, we should not automatically assume that the Father is always occupying a greater role. Indeed, as the following verses suggest, there are a number of passages where it is the *Son* who seems to take the limelight:

> For my Father's will is that everyone who looks to *the Son* and believes *in him* shall have eternal life, and I will raise them up at the last day (John 6.40).

> Everyone who has heard the Father and learned from him *comes to me* (John 6.45).

> No one who denies the Son has the Father; *whoever acknowledges the Son has the Father also* (1 John 2.23).

> And this is his command: *to believe in the name of his Son, Jesus Christ* (1 John 3.23).

> And this is the testimony. God has given us eternal life, a*nd this life is in his Son*. Whoever has the Son has life; *whoever does not have the Son of God does not have life* (1 John 5.11–12).

More significant, perhaps, are the passages which seem to point to an exact equality between Father and Son. In John 5.23, for example, Jesus insists that all should honour the Son '*just as* they honour the Father', implying that he and the Father are worthy of equal dignity and reverence. The same point is made more powerfully just five verses earlier, where the writer tells us that Jesus was 'calling God his own Father, *making himself equal with God*'. It is difficult to escape the full force of such a statement: the Greek word *ison* used here does not imply a vague equivalence but an exact identity (an isosceles triangle, for example, has two sides *of the same length*).

As far as our visiting Witnesses go, this is our one 'knockout' verse which demolishes their entire argument in a single stroke! If they stick to their 'official' line, they will try to argue that it was Jesus' *opponents* who were saying this of him. In fact, this is a completely bizarre interpretation of the text, since even an elementary grasp of English grammar shows that it is *John himself* who is making the statement! Such an unqualified claim to exact equality with the Father must rank (along with Phil. 2.6) among the most remarkable declarations in the whole of Scripture, and its potential consequences for our understanding of Jesus' sonship are far-reaching.

When One Plus One Equals One

We have already commented briefly on the central role played by the *Shema'* ('Hear O Israel: The LORD our God, the LORD is one,' Deut. 6.4) in Judaism. It plays a central role in synagogue services: orthodox Jews pronounce each word with the utmost care (particularly the word '*one*') and cover their eyes with their hand while doing so. It is the first Bible verse that a Jewish child learns and, traditionally, the last words that are spoken before death. Rabbi Akiba famously emphasized the word 'one' as he was being martyred by the Romans around AD 135.[9]

In John 10, however, Jesus moves the same word in a completely new direction, when he makes the remarkable statement: 'I and the Father are *one*' (10.30). Like Paul in 1 Corinthians 8.6, he has apparently taken the *Shema'*, which he himself later declared to be part of the greatest of all Old Testament declarations (Mark 12.29), and divided it equally between himself and the Father.[10] This is all the more shocking because he mentions himself first and the Father *second*!

Geza Vermes comments here that:

> the blunt assertion . . . is framed as an unequivocal affirmation of equality . . . Consideration of the context strengthens the impression that John meant real parity . . . The implied assertion is that the Father and the Son possess the same power and strength, that is to say that they are of the same stature. They are co-equal, to use the jargon of later Christian dogmatic theology.[11]

Coming from a writer celebrated for his thoughtful reflection on Jesus from a *Jewish* perspective, this remark has immense value.

Although Vermes follows the line, shared by many other modern scholars, that John's gospel presents a later, idealized portrait of Jesus, far removed from reality, his understanding of the *implications* of such a statement hits the nail firmly on the head.

Furthermore, it is hard to ignore the fact that a very similar saying appears in the so-called 'Q' segments of Matthew and Luke, widely considered (even by sceptics) to date back to a period much closer to Jesus' lifetime. Here Jesus says that 'no one knows the Son except the Father, and no one knows the Father except the Son and those to whom the Son chooses to reveal him' (Matt. 11.27; see also Luke 10.22).

Peter Lewis observes here of this deep unity between Father and Son that:

> he does not say 'no-one *knows* the Father as well as I know him'; he says 'no-one knows the Father *except* the Son' . . . He is speaking of an inter-trinitarian relationship: coequal, coeternal, infinite. Because of that relationship the Son knows the Father as well as the Father knows the Son; and each knows the other as well as each knows himself! In a word, Jesus Christ is part of the *self*-knowledge of the Godhead. He is part of God's *self-consciousness*! That is the core truth of this unsurpassed revelation of Jesus' full identity.[12]

Reymond concludes that 'a higher expression of parity between the Father and the Son . . . is inconceivable'.[13]

Indeed, some writers have pursued the picture of mutual dependence between the Father and the Son in this verse even further. Stanley Grenz and Denise Muir Kjesbo have suggested that, while Jesus willingly submits to the Father, the Father actually *depends* on the Son for his own deity: 'In sending his Son into the world, the Father entrusted his own reign – indeed his own deity – to the Son . . . Likewise, the Father is dependent on the Son for his title as Father. As Irenaeus pointed out in the second century, without the Son the Father is not the Father of the Son.'[14]

The inevitable conclusion that Father and Son must *together* constitute God is amply backed up by 2 John 9, which, while not directly balancing the picture of 'God the Father' with 'God the Son', comes remarkably close to doing so: 'Anyone who runs ahead and does not continue in the teaching of Christ *does not have God*; whoever continues in the teaching has *both the Father and the Son.*' This is not saying that the Son is the *same* as the Father, but rather, as we have shown repeatedly in this chapter, that both Father and Son *are equally God.*

Within the context of the Old Testament, as viewed through the lens of Judaism, such ideas are revolutionary. In Isaiah, for example, as we noticed in chapters two and three, we find the traditional belief in the absolute uniqueness of Yahweh expressed in no uncertain terms, with such statements as 'With whom will you compare me or count me equal?' (Isa. 46.5) and 'I will not yield my glory to another' (Isa. 48.11). Yet Jesus' statements in John's gospel imply that Father and Son possess some kind of shared existence, as the following verses suggest:

> . . . even though you do not believe me, believe the works, that you may know and understand that the Father is in me, and I in the Father (John 10.38).

> Don't you believe that I am in the Father, and that the Father is in me? (John 14.10).

> And now, Father, glorify me in your presence with the glory I had with you before the world began . . . All I have is yours, and all you have is mine . . . I pray also for those who will believe in me through their message, that all of them may be one, Father, just as you are in me and I am in you (John 17.5,10,20–21).

Most intriguing of all is the absolute union implied by John 14.23: Jesus replied, 'Anyone who loves me will obey my teaching. My Father will love them, and *we will come to them and make our home with them.*'

It is but a short step to the extraordinary statement in Matthew 28.19, in which Jesus includes *himself* within the unity of the divine name: 'Therefore go and make disciples of all nations, baptising them *in the name of the Father and of the Son and of the Holy Spirit.*' Overfamiliar though we might be with this verse, it would be difficult to overestimate its importance, given the prominent place it possesses, right at the end of Matthew's gospel. In fact, it would be hard to imagine a stronger declaration of equality between Father and Son (not to mention the fact that it introduces a *third* divine person into an already crowded billing)! Whatever one's view of the Trinity (and a detailed consideration of this subject lies outside the scope of this book), the fact that, as we saw in chapter five, the Father and the Son appear to share an *equal* relationship to the Holy Spirit would appear to provide the final proof that Christ is 'God' in every sense and shares fully in the attributes of the Father.

Conclusion: The Man Who Is God

So how do we match up the passages we have just considered with those we met at the beginning of this chapter, which seem to present Jesus on a lower rung of being from the Father? At first sight, it might seem as if we are playing 'musical chairs' with Bible verses, with increasingly less scope to accommodate both view-points at the same time!

However, like many of the passages that seem to describe Jesus as 'God', it is possible to read many of these 'problem' verses in more than one way, as we can see in the chart on the next page. In any case, many of the examples we mentioned have a much more obvious explanation. Virtually all of them are spoken from the viewpoint of Christ's union with us, as our representative, model and guide. In other words, it was not *as God* that Jesus was born in Bethlehem, that he grew in wisdom and stature, that he was baptized, tempted and crucified, or, for that matter, that he addressed the Father as 'his God' or even as 'the only true God', but *as a man*, as one of us. From this viewpoint, the limitations on Jesus' knowledge, power and status are relative, rather than absolute; they are temporary and self-imposed, and yet absolutely necessary to his sharing our humanity to the fullest degree.

The clearest passage to express this idea is Philippians 2.6–8, which seems to suggest that Jesus, although he possessed the nature of God, did not *take advantage* of his equality with the Father, but made himself nothing, and took on our nature instead. In other words, although he shared the Father's divinity, he freely chose to let go of the privileges that stem from this in order to

---

Less than God? Some possible answers

- **Why do you call me good? . . . No one is good – except God alone (Mark 10.18).**
  We then have two choices about Jesus: either he isn't truly good, or he *must* be God.
- **But about that day or hour no one knows, not even the angels in heaven, nor the Son, but only the Father (Mark 13.32).**
  Perhaps this is inevitable: Yahweh himself seems to have restricted knowledge when manifesting himself on earth in Genesis 2.19; 3.9; and 18.21. It is possible that the knowledge was present in Christ, but somehow hidden away (Col. 2.3).
- **The Son can do nothing by himself; he can do only what he sees his Father doing (John 5.19).**
  John has just stated in the previous verse that Jesus is, in fact, equal to the Father.
- **The Father is greater than I (John 14.28).**
  The context is the foot-washing at the last supper; Jesus has told us in John 13.16 that 'greater' describes a person's *role*, not their identity. He has humbled himself voluntarily as a servant.
- **Now this is eternal life: that they may know you, the only true God, and Jesus Christ, whom you have sent (John 17.3).**
  The context is the same here; elsewhere in the gospel Jesus is described both as 'truth' and as 'God' (14.6; 20.28) and the words 'true God' seem themselves to be applied to Christ in 1 John 5.20.
- **I am ascending to my Father and your Father, to my God and your God (John 20.17).**
  It is true that Jesus talks of the Father as 'God' here and elsewhere. But the Father also addresses the Son as 'God' in Hebrews 1.8.
- **The Son himself will be made subject to him who put everything under him (1 Cor. 15.28).**
  Why would he have to be *made subject* to the Father if the Son was in fact inferior by nature?
- **There is one God and one mediator between God and mankind, the man Christ Jesus (1 Tim. 2.5).**
  Why are *both* Christ and the Father clearly distinguished from 'man' in passages such as 1 Cor. 7.22–23 and Gal. 1.1,12?

---

become one of us. John Milton captured the theme beautifully when he wrote:

That glorious Form, that Light unsufferable,
And that far-beaming blaze of Majesty . . .
He laid aside; and here with us to be,
Forsook the Courts of everlasting Day,
And chose with us a darksom House of mortal Clay.[15]

But if this is really the case – if Jesus in his earthly existence truly became like us in every respect – if, in fact, everything he did was in the power and strength given by the Father – then can we really view his earthly ministry (his example, his teaching, his miracles, and so on) as reflecting anything more than a perfect human life? Were the church fathers of the second and third centuries not guilty of a grave mistake when they used such phrases as the 'birth of God' or the 'suffering of God' in their descriptions of Christ?[16] Did Paul make a serious miscalculation when he talks (apparently) about God's 'own blood' in Acts 20.28?

The answer must be that, while Jesus seems to have laid aside his divine privileges during his time on earth, they were by no means totally lost. Commenting on Philippians 2.6, for example, David Wells observes that:

> Far from qualifying or reducing the Godness of Christ Jesus, Paul has here invested it with profounder significance . . . The human Jesus provided the unique exegesis of Godness, of that God who is in essence holy love, and he did so within the limitations of being human. As this divine light passes through the darkened glass of his humanity, it is obscured but not refracted. In Jesus God became *incognito*, but he did not disappear; he is hidden, but not lost.[17]

This thought is neatly summed up in the words of Charles Wesley that are sung (probably without much thought) every Christmas:

> *Veiled in flesh* the Godhead see;
> Hail the incarnate Deity.

How such an idea might work out in practice is, of course, an entirely open question. Did Jesus possess, to use the words of Edmund Strong, 'two distinct and complete consciousnesses' seamlessly merged together within a single, undivided personality (hinted at, perhaps, in Luke 2.48–50)?[18]

One possible line of evidence for this idea of two distinct natures within Christ can be found in the way in which Jesus tends so often to speak about himself in the third person almost as an *alter ego*. We saw something similar in chapter two with many statements of Yahweh in the Old Testament which appear to reflect a dialogue within his own being. Could Jesus' own figures of speech be understood in a similar way? Why, for example, does he present most of his statements about 'the Son' or 'the Son of Man' as if they are referring to someone else? (Consider, for example, Mark 8.38: 'If anyone is ashamed of *me* and *my words* in this adulterous and sinful generation, the *Son of Man* will be ashamed of them when he comes in his Father's glory with the holy angels')?[19]

In fact, the same could be said about many other passages in the gospels.[20] While there are occasional examples of others talking in this way in Scripture,[21] the fact that Jesus does it so frequently might hint at a unique kind of self-consciousness in which two natures, human and divine, could exist together and interact with each other.

Other passages in the New Testament also appear to highlight this two-sided view of Jesus. In John 1, for example, the Word is described alongside the Father as his equal, but yet became flesh to dwell among us (vv. 1,14,18). In the letter to the Hebrews, the Son, though God (1.8), became 'flesh and blood' (2.14) through a body that had been 'prepared' for him (10.5). In Philippians, Jesus is 'in very nature God' in 2.6 but takes 'the very nature of a servant' in 2.7. In Romans he is 'descended from David according to the flesh' but 'Son of God . . . according to the Spirit' (Rom. 1.3–4 RSV). And in the accounts of the virgin birth, Jesus is equally Son of Mary (Luke 1.31) and Son of God (1.32), a contrast summed up neatly in Matthew's use of Isaiah's prophecy of Jesus as '*God* with *us*' (Matt. 1.23).

As the great Christian writers and thinkers increasingly stressed from the second century onwards, we need to hold both of these truths firmly in place. On the one hand, Jesus' life provides the perfect portrait of what we ourselves were intended to be: the only genuine example we have of what it means to be truly human. Our understanding of 'humanity' tends to be defined by weakness, insecurity and vulnerability, thinly disguised under the veneer of advancement and self-fulfilment. Jesus shows us rather that an authentically 'human' life is one that is completely 'sold out' to God, in which every moment of each day is lived out fully in the Father's presence and through the Spirit's power.

But as we have seen, Jesus shows us in an equally powerful way what *God himself* is like. Far from being the remote, inscrutable deity of some other world religions, he is a God who stoops to our level, sharing in our weakness and sorrows, and lifting us up from the dust so that, as we observed in chapter six, we may 'participate in the divine nature' (2 Pet. 1.4). This is why *both* aspects of Jesus' identity are essential for our salvation: he is the bridge that spans the ocean separating us from our true destiny. When our lives have lost all direction and meaning, Jesus meets us at the crossroads of existence, connecting us back to the very purpose for which we were made.

Ten key statements about the Father	Ten key statements about the Son
• The throne is his (Rev. 22.1)	• The throne is his (Rev. 22.1)
• The kingdom is his (Eph. 5.5)	• The kingdom is his (Eph. 5.5)
• The angels are his (Ps. 103.20)	• The angels are his (Matt. 13.41)
• The blood is his (Acts 20.28)	• The blood is his (Eph. 2.13)
• The church is his (1 Cor. 11.16)	• The church is his (Rom. 16.16)
• The gospel is his (1 Thess. 2.9)	• The gospel is his (Rom. 15.19)
• The judgement day is his (Joel 2.1)	• The judgement day is his (1 Cor. 1.8)
• We have *his* Word within us (1 John 2.14)	• We have *his* Word within us (Col. 3.16 RSV)
• We have *his* Spirit within us (Rom. 8.9)	• We have *his* Spirit within us (Rom. 8.9)
• We are sent as *his* witnesses (Isa. 43.10)	• We are sent as *his* witnesses (Acts 1.8)

Questions to consider:

(i) Jesus prayed that we should be one as he and the Father are one (John 17.20–23). Why have we fallen so far short of this? How can his perfect unity with the Father act as a model for our relationships with our brothers and sisters in Christ, both within our fellowships and across denominations?

(ii) What does it mean for Jesus to be fully human and yet fully divine? Is there a contradiction here? What might it mean, for example, for him to be 'tempted in all things as we are, yet without sin' (Heb. 4.15 NASB)?

(iii) Philippians 2 tells us that Jesus did not cling on to his exalted status but made himself nothing. How can we put this example into practice in our family lives, our church lives, and in the places where we work?

11.

Jesus and Eternity

Jesus Christ is the same yesterday and today and for ever (Heb. 13.8).

Taking to the Streets

In recent times the sight of protesters on the streets of Egypt and other Middle Eastern countries has become a rather familiar one. It may come as a surprise to learn, however, that similar demonstrations took place on the streets of what was once Egypt's greatest city, Alexandria, as far back as the year AD 318. With unrest continuing sporadically over a period of time, slogans were chanted, campaign songs were sung, and graffiti appeared on walls. The cause of these demonstrations, however, was not oppressive government, or high food prices, or corruption. Instead, they originated in what may seem today to be a very peculiar bone of contention – an argument about theology!

Strange indeed, but true. On one side of the dispute was the bishop of Alexandria, appropriately enough named Alexander, who stood by the church's traditional view that Jesus Christ before his incarnation was 'God' in the fullest sense of the word, eternal and all-powerful. On the other side was Arius, his presbyter, who was insisting that the Son of God was quite different in nature from the Father, having a definite beginning in time. Arius believed that the Son was in no sense part of God himself, but rather God's first creative act through which all other things came into being.

As we have seen in recent times, street protests can spread with remarkable rapidity. 'In every city bishops were engaged in obstinate conflict with bishops, and people rising against people,' the church historian Eusebius tells us.[1] Indeed, so concerned was the newly converted emperor Constantine about the escalating crisis that he attempted to intervene personally. 'Give me back my quiet days and untroubled nights,' he pleaded in a letter to the warring protagonists.[2] But to no avail. Soon the controversy was engulfing the entire eastern half of the Empire, causing the pagan writer Ammianus Marcellinus to declare that 'the highways were covered with galloping bishops'.[3]

Before long the conflict had reached the newly established Eastern capital of Constantinople. As Gregory of Nyssa observed: 'Garment sellers, money changers, food vendors, they are all at it. If you ask for change, they philosophise about the begotten and the unbegotten. If you inquire about the price of bread, the answer is that the Father is greater and the Son inferior. If you say to the attendant, "Is my bath ready?" he tells you that the Son was made out of nothing.'[4]

His contemporary, Gregory of Nazianzus, lamented similarly that 'it has gone so far that the whole market resounds with the discourses of heretics, every banquet is corrupted by this babbling even to nausea, every merry-making is transformed into a mourning, and every funeral solemnity is almost alleviated by this brawling as a still greater evil.'[5]

It seems extraordinary today that a theological issue of this kind should have stirred up so much popular unrest, particularly since much of the later controversy centred on a single letter which had been added to the Nicene Creed! But a great deal was at stake – not just the nature of Christ, but, as we shall see, the very question of salvation itself. During this state of ferment Arian beliefs began engulfing vast swathes of Europe and briefly threatened to become the 'official' position of the entire church.

In the end, after much heated discussion, the orthodox view won the day. However, over the centuries that followed, new challenges arose, attempting to demote Christ to a level far lower than anything Arius or his followers had ever contemplated. The first of these was Islam, which swept out from Arabia with remarkable speed in the seventh century AD, engulfing many previously Christian lands, and offering a completely new picture of Jesus as one of a line of prophets preparing the way for Muhammad. The second grew up much later *within* Christian Europe in the form of Unitarianism, which also rejected both the preexistence and the deity of Christ, and came to see Jesus more and more as merely a great moral example. Indeed, in America its influence expanded to the point where Thomas Jefferson, the third US president and one of the drafters of the American Declaration of Independence, once predicted that 'the present generation will live to see Unitarianism become the general religion of the United States'.[6]

Certainly Unitarianism can claim a dazzling array of followers, from eminent scientists such as Isaac Newton,[7] Joseph Priestley[8] and Charles Darwin[9] to writers such as Samuel Taylor Coleridge and Henry Longfellow. Many more, such as Florence Nightingale, Louisa May Alcott, Frank Lloyd Wright, Beatrix Potter, Neville Chamberlain and arguably Barack Obama, were or have been profoundly impacted by their Unitarian backgrounds.[10] Beyond this, its influence shows up in surprising places. Few people know that the much-loved Christmas carol 'It Came upon a Midnight Clear' was actually written by a Unitarian minister (and even 'Jingle Bells' was composed by a Unitarian worship leader)!

Over the last hundred years, however, Unitarianism has drifted further and further away from its (quasi-) Christian origins towards a 'pick and mix' attitude towards religious belief.[11] In its place, Arian views have made an unexpected comeback through the Jehovah's Witnesses, who, striking a very different tone from the liberal, inclusive atmosphere of Unitarianism, present a very narrow yet selective approach to Scripture, packaged as authentic, Bible-believing Christianity. Moreover, they are fired by a missionary zeal that Unitarians have rarely possessed in recent times. In Italy, for example, from where the roots of Unitarianism sprung in the sixteenth century, Jehovah's Witnesses outnumber all Protestant denominations combined, while in Japan, a country traditionally resistant to orthodox Christianity, their numbers are disproportionately large compared with mainline denominations. We ignore them at our peril.

What was it about Arius's ideas (and those of his more radical Unitarian successors, such as Fausto Sozzini) that made them so attractive? Apart from their apparent logical consistency, it was what seemed to be their clear basis in Scripture that proved a strong selling point. On the one hand they seemed to explain a number of New Testament passages which, as we saw in the last chapter, suggest that the Son possesses a status lower than that of the Father. However, they also helped to tie together several key statements in Scripture which seem to show the Son existing as *part* of creation, and therefore, however exalted he might be, being fundamentally different *in nature* from the Father himself.

There are a number of verses which played a key role in defining Arian beliefs, many of which are still frequently used by Jehovah's Witnesses today. In order to investigate these issues in more depth, we will need to unpack a number of Hebrew and Greek words in this chapter, but the end result will be well worth the effort! To begin with, therefore, we will put two of these passages under the microscope, together with another particular favourite of visiting Jehovah's Witnesses, to see whether they really do furnish grounds for overturning the evidence we have considered so far.

(i) Proverbs 8.22

> The LORD *created me* the beginning of his works,
>   before all else that he made, long ago (NEB).

This statement, placed on the lips of divine 'Wisdom' by the writer of Proverbs, seems at first sight to provide quite impressive evidence that the Son was, in fact, a created being. Given that, as we saw in chapter five, the New Testament seems to link Jesus with this pre-existent figure of Wisdom, it is striking how many modern versions use the word 'created' here.

However, while it cannot be denied that Jesus was, in terms of his human nature, created by God (see Isa. 49.5), there are several fundamental objections to this translation of the verse. Firstly, although the Hebrew word *qanah* can mean 'create', it is not necessarily its principal meaning. Indeed Derek Kidner notes that 'of its 84 Old Testament occurrences, only six or seven allow the sense "create" . . . and even these do not require it'.[12]

A much more natural meaning, rather, is 'possess', a rendering that appears in other early translations such as those of Aquila, Theodotion and Symmachus,[13] and which later found its way into the Latin Vulgate and subsequently into the Authorized Version. The logic of this translation can be judged from the fact that the nearest appearance of the same word, in Proverbs 4.7, is an invitation to 'get' wisdom: 'create' would clearly not match the context here, or in the eleven other instances of *qanah* that appear in Proverbs.

We should also note, however, that the first use of *qanah* in Scripture is at Genesis 4.1, where Eve says that 'with the help of the LORD I have *brought forth* a man' (giving rise to the name Cain). This means that the translation used in the current version of the NIV, 'the LORD *brought me forth* as the first of his works', is also possible, as it ties in well with the images of 'birth' introduced in verses 24 and 25. We need to observe, though, the subtle difference between 'brought forth' and 'create' – the offspring has to have the *same nature* as the parent for the image to hold true.

By contrast, given that Proverbs 3.19–20 implies that wisdom is an essential part of God's nature, it is difficult to see how the *same* author would try to suggest that wisdom was actually something *created* by him. Admittedly, some translations of Proverbs 8.23 talk of Wisdom being 'fashioned in times long past' (NEB), but this is hardly the best understanding of the Hebrew, which would be better expressed with the words 'established from everlasting' (NKJV). Indeed, the root Hebrew word *olam* used here is the one which appears in the infinite sweep of Psalm 90.2: 'from *everlasting to everlasting* you are God'.

In fact, this link with Psalm 90, one of the strongest declarations of God's eternal nature in Scripture, may be no coincidence. The full text of verse 2 of the psalm reads: 'Before the mountains *were* born . . . from everlasting to everlasting you *are* God.' It is surely significant, therefore, that the only other appearance of the phrase 'before the mountains' in the entire Bible is in the description of Wisdom in Proverbs 8.25, just three verses after the one we are considering.[14] The link is even closer in the Septuagint translation of Proverbs, which keeps *the same* contrast of past and present tenses: 'before the mountains *were* settled, and before all hills, *he begets* me'.

The message could not be clearer. God's wisdom is as timeless as God himself, and therefore exists completely outside the created realm. The logical alternative, that God originally 'lacked' Wisdom, is, as Athanasius once pointed out, clearly nonsensical![15]

But, in any case, although Proverbs 8 provides a very useful background for understanding some of the statements in John's gospel, as we saw in chapter five, we should be cautious about picking out clear-cut doctrines from what is obviously poetry. If we have identified Wisdom with Christ, then who are 'Understanding' (8.1) and 'Prudence' (8.12)? Such personification is not uncommon in Hebrew literature; there is a striking example in the first chapter of Lamentations, and Larry Hurtado cites a similar instance in *Joseph and Aseneth* where Penitence is portrayed as a beautiful virgin.[16] In short, given the problems in translation and the pictorial nature of the imagery used, Proverbs 8, though interesting as a source, is too shaky a foundation on which to build any major doctrine, particularly one that runs counter to the overwhelming thrust of the rest of Scripture. We need stronger evidence if we are seriously to entertain the idea of a 'created' Son of God.[17]

(ii) Colossians 1.15

> The Son is the image of the invisible God, the *firstborn* over all creation.

At first sight, this verse seems to provide much clearer grounds for believing that the Son was the first being that God created. However, we need to consider more carefully what the word 'firstborn' means. Although, in ancient Jewish custom, the rights of the 'firstborn' were normally given to the oldest male child in a family, this is by no means exclusively the case, as is clear at several points in the Old Testament.[18] In Exodus 4.22 the nation of Israel is described as God's 'firstborn', but nowhere in the Old Testament is it suggested that Israel is the first nation to appear on earth. The Authorized Version includes phrases such as 'the firstborn of death' (Job 18.13) and 'the firstborn of the poor' (Isa. 14.30) using the same Hebrew word, *bə·ḵō·wr*, but the expressions mean, in these two cases, 'the deadliest disease' and 'the poorest of the poor'. The principal meaning is, in other words, that of *greatness* or *pre-eminence*, as Psalm 89.27 makes clear:

> And I will appoint him to be my *firstborn*,
>   *the most exalted* of the kings of the earth.

(Although this is, from a prophetic viewpoint, a messianic psalm, its immediate context concerns King David, who was not even the first king of *Israel*, let alone of the entire world.)

It is worth remembering here that Colossians 1.15–20 is bringing together aspects of Christ's eternal existence ('for in him all things were created', v. 16) with aspects of his earthly existence ('making peace through his blood, shed on the cross', v. 20). It might therefore be possible to see the reference to Christ as 'firstborn over all creation', along with the description of him as 'firstborn from among the dead' (v. 18), as belonging to his earthly ministry and its aftermath. But, on the other hand, phrases such as 'all things have been created through him and for him' (v. 16) carefully *distinguish* the Son's past existence from the created order. As Bowman and Komoszewski point out, 'if verse 15 were to mean that the Son was the first thing created, Paul would be flatly contradicting himself from one sentence to the next.'[19]

This distinction is even more apparent in the following verse, 'he *is* before all things', where Paul, in switching to the present tense (rather than saying 'he *was* before all things') seems to imply that Christ stands *outside* of time and therefore outside the entire realm of creation. Despite the fact that these verses are cunningly obscured in the New World Translation by the repeated addition of the word 'other' before 'things' (an intrusion quite unwarranted by any Greek manuscript), it is the very absence of this word 'other' in the Greek which makes Paul's insistence on the uncreated nature of Christ so definite here. This is underlined by the way that the passage repeatedly applies statements to Christ which are elsewhere made about God the Father, as the pairings on the next page clearly show.

Most importantly, we should remember the main reason behind Paul's letter to the Colossians. He is writing specifically to attack a belief system which appears to see Christ simply as one of a chain of intermediate beings between God and humankind. Instead, he states quite emphatically that 'in Christ all the *fulness* of the Deity lives in bodily form' (2.9), and while in 1 Corinthians 15.28 it is the Father who will be 'all in all', Paul here applies the same description to Christ (Col. 3.11; cf. Eph. 1.23).

Finally, we should note that Paul elsewhere warns (in Rom. 1.25) of the dire consequences that faced those who 'worshipped

---

Colossians 1.15–18: Some parallels in creation

- **For by him [Christ] all things were created, in heaven and on earth (Col. 1.16 ESV)**
  In the beginning God created the heavens and the earth (Gen. 1.1)
- **. . . all things have been created through him and for him (Col. 1.16)**
  For from him [the Father] and through him an for him are all things (Rom. 11.36)
- **He *is* before all things . . . (Col. 1.17)**
  Before the mountains were born . . . you *are* (Ps. 90.2 Septuagint)
- **. . . and in him all things hold together (Col. 1.17)**
  For in him [the Father] we live an move and have our being (Acts 17.28)
- **He is the beginning . . . (Col. 1.18)**
  I am . . . the Beginning and the End . . . and I will be their God (Rev. 21.6–7)
- **. . . so that in everything he might have the supremacy (Col. 1.18)**
  The LORD has established his throne in heaven, and his kingdom rules over all (Ps. 103.1)

---

and served created things'. But given that, at the beginning of the same chapter, he has no hesitation in describing *himself* as 'a servant of Christ Jesus', how could he have included Christ in the category of 'created things'? Would Paul really have described a created being as 'God over all, for ever praised' (Rom. 9.5)? Would he really have transferred Old Testament declarations about Yahweh to such a being (e.g. Phil. 2.10–11)? Would he really have addressed such a being in prayer (2 Cor. 12.8–9)?

Considered both in its immediate setting and in the context of Paul's writings as a whole, therefore, Colossians 1.15 provides rather strong evidence that the Son stands *outside* the created realm. On the contrary, as Robert Reymond concludes, 'it is difficult to find any other biblical passage that more forthrightly affirms the full and unabridged deity of Jesus Christ'.[20]

(iii) Revelation 3.14

The words of the Amen, the faithful and true witness, *the beginning of God's creation* (RSV).

This verse, though not apparently used by Arius or his followers,[21] is often raised by Jehovah's Witnesses today. On the surface, it seems to provide better evidence for the idea that the Son was brought into being as a first step in God's process of making the universe. But again, we need to examine the wording more closely. What does it mean to call Christ 'the beginning of God's creation', and is this really the best translation of the original Greek?

It is helpful first to take a look at the key word in question here, *archē* ('beginning'). We can gain some insight into its overall meaning from its use as the root of a number of modern English words. While it can certainly imply the first of a series (as in 'archaeopteryx' – 'first bird'), it can also suggest pre-eminence (as in 'archbishop'), or, in particular, refer to the origin or originator of something (as in 'architect' – one who designs – not part of the design itself!).

When we consider the compounds of *archē* used elsewhere in the New Testament, we find, in fact, that it is the latter two senses of the word that are used almost exclusively. On the one hand, we see a number of words relating to rulership and authority, as follows:

archōn	leader (Matt. 9.18)
archiereus	high priest (Heb. 3.1)
archipoimēn	chief shepherd (1 Pet. 5.4)
archisunagōgos	synagogue leader (Acts 18.8)
architelōnēs	chief tax collector (Luke 19.2)
architriklinos	master of the banquet (John 2.8)

At the same time there are two words which also carry the suggestion of someone who creates or originates:

archēgos	author (Acts 3.15)
architektōn	master builder (1 Cor. 3.10 rsv)

By calling himself *archē* here, therefore, Jesus is probably not saying that he was the first created being, but rather, according to whichever of these interpretations we choose, that he is 'the ruler of God's creation' (NIV), or 'the prime source of all God's creation' (NEB), both of which clearly distinguish Christ from the created order itself. (The nearest comparable passage, Rev. 1.5, which describes Christ as 'the faithful witness, the firstborn from the dead, and the **ruler** (*archōn*) of the kings of the earth', would tend to support the first of these alternatives.)

The background here may help us to unlock the real meaning of the verse. For a start, just five verses later, Jesus makes the statement that 'those whom I love I rebuke and discipline' which closely resembles the words of Yahweh in Proverbs 3.12. Furthermore, in announcing himself as 'the Amen . . . the beginning of God's creation', Jesus seems to echo the words of Yahweh in Isaiah 65, where God presents himself as the 'Amen' who is the beginning of his *new* creation:

> Those who pronounce a blessing in the land
>> will do so by the *God called Amen*;
>>> those who make a solemn pledge in the land will do so by the
>>> *God called Amen* . . .
> Look! *I'm creating a new heaven and a new earth.*
>> past events won't be remembered;
>> they won't come to mind (Isa. 65.16–17 CEB).

Most significantly, *archē* is applied elsewhere in Revelation, along with the equally absolute title 'the Alpha and the Omega', both to God the Father (Rev. 21.6) and to Christ (22.13). Indeed, this sense of them sharing divinity together seems to be one of the dominant themes of the whole book, since, as we have seen, they both utter the divine name *egō eimi* (1.8,17); both occupy the divine throne (22.1,3); both share equal titles of dignity (such as 'holy and true', 3.7; 6.10); and both act together as the temple and the source of light for the New Jerusalem (21.22–23).

While none of these factors is necessarily decisive, when considered together they do seem to weigh strongly against the idea of Christ as a created being. The fact that, only two chapters after the one we are considering, John sees 'every creature in heaven and on earth' worshipping both God *and* the Lamb (Rev. 5.13–14) clearly links Christ to the Father in a single divine unity while setting him apart from those heavenly creatures whose praise he receives. As Martin Hengel points out, 'he with whom God shares his throne must be equal with God'.[22]

In fact, everything in Revelation works together to support Jesus' bold statement in John 10.30 that 'I and the Father are one.' In context, therefore, Revelation 3.14 provides no clear grounds here for suggesting a fundamental difference of nature between them.

A Timeless Existence?

One of the most familiar sights of the night sky is the constellation of Orion ('the Hunter'). It has inspired awe and wonder for thousands of years (see Job 9.9; Amos 5.8). Yet a glimpse at its distinctive pattern of stars does not reveal an instant of time but something far bigger. Because of the different lengths of time it takes for light to cross the immense distances of space, we only see the stars as they *were*, not as they *are*. For instance, the light from Bellatrix, situated on Orion's right shoulder (from our vantage point) began its journey around the time James Cook discovered Australia; Rigel, on Orion's right foot, appears as it did when the Plantagenet Henry III was king of England, while the sight of Alnilam in the middle of Orion's belt (a massive star 10,000 times brighter than our sun) takes us back to the time when the Anglo-Saxons first converted to Christianity.

In just one small segment of the night's sky, therefore, history seems to open up before our very eyes! It is a startling reminder of how God can see past, present and future together in a single instant (Ps. 139.4,16; Isa. 46.10; Luke 20.38). So is the same true of Christ? Is he confined within history, as we are, or does he, too, 'look in' at different points of time from outside? Is he eternal, like God, or a creature of time, like ourselves?

As we have already begun to demonstrate, the New Testament is not short on possible answers to this question. John 17.24 shows the relationship between Father and Son extending not only within time, but also throughout eternity, suggesting that it makes no more sense to talk of the Son having a 'beginning' than it does to make such a statement about the Father. This is particularly apparent in the way that John 1.1 changes the opening of Genesis ('In the beginning God . . .') to become 'in the beginning was *the Word*', or, as the NEB translates it (in a manner which captures some of the nuances of the Greek), 'When all things began, *the Word already was*.' A similar idea appears in 2 Timothy 1.9, where Paul talks of the grace that was 'given us in Christ Jesus *before the beginning of time*'.

Several verses in the letter to the Hebrews also emphasize this point. Hebrews 1.10–12 contrasts the timeless existence of the Son with the temporary nature of the creation itself; 7.3 hints that Christ is 'without beginning of days or end of life' while 13.8 underlines this infinite, unchanging truth when it declares that 'Jesus Christ is the same yesterday and today and for ever,' a statement that resembles that of the Jewish historian Josephus about Yahweh as 'the beginning, the middle, and the end of all things'.[23] This is backed up by the remarkable change of tense mid-sentence in John 8.58 ('before Abraham *was* born, I *am*') which seems deliberately to mimic the contrast of tense in Psalm 90.2 that we referred to earlier in this chapter ('Before the mountains *were* born . . . from everlasting to everlasting you *are* God').

If this evidence were not enough, it is worth pointing out that the description of the Son in Isaiah 9.6 as 'Everlasting Father' can literally be translated as 'Father of Eternity'. The extraordinary implication of this seems to go beyond that of the statements made so far, in suggesting that the Son, in addition to filling the whole of space/time, stands beyond such existence in terms that exceed our ability to conceive, being outside eternity, beyond infinity, and eluding all attempts to pin him down within fixed categories of knowledge.

But it is not simply the eternal nature of Christ that identifies him so closely with God himself. We also need to take account of the passages we read in the last chapter which present him with a relationship of such intimacy with the Father that would be quite impossible if they were wholly unlike one another. In particular, Jesus' prayer that 'they may be one *as we are one*' (John 17.22) presents a clear parallel between the shared *humanity* of the church and the shared *divinity* that he possesses with the Father.

The extent of this bond is demonstrated further in John 1.18. Here the description of the Son resting in the bosom of the Father suggests a picture of a baby nursing at its mother's breast, like the one we find in Ruth 4.16. Far from suggesting two very different individuals, the image is rather of Father and Son intimately bound together by a shared identity, with both being described as 'God' (according to the best manuscript evidence for this verse).

It is perhaps significant in this context that John chooses to describe the Son's relationship to the Father here with the Greek word *monogenēs* (sometimes translated 'only-begotten'). On several occasions in the Septuagint the same word is used to translate the Hebrew *ya·ḥêḏ*, from the verb *yachad* that refers to absolute singleness and unity of nature (as, for instance, in the phrase 'Give me an undivided heart' [Ps. 86.11]). In other words, *ya·ḥêḏ* could refer to one's own life as the most fundamental aspect of one's being, or, more frequently, to an only child who alone could carry forward one's name and identity. By using the word *monogenēs* in 1.14,18; 3.16–18; and again in 1 John 4.9, John is therefore specifying the closest possible bonding between Father and Son.

The same can be said about the related Greek word *agapētos* ('beloved') which was also used to translate *ya·ḥêḏ* in the Septuagint.[24] It appears in Mark 12.6 (the parable of the labourers in the vineyard) to specify the unique relationship *in kind* between the Son and the Father, as opposed to the simple sense of ownership over the servants who precede him, who are 'contrasted . . . not as predecessors or rivals, but as slaves', as Liddon comments.[25] The word also appears at Jesus' baptism, with a voice from heaven calling out, 'This is my *beloved* Son, with whom I am well pleased' (Matt. 3.17; 17.5 RSV). As a natural counterpart, we see the same intimacy expressed in Jesus' heartfelt cry of '*Abba*' ('Daddy') in the garden of Gethsemane (Mark 14.36).

This closeness is further expressed in Hebrews 1.3 which, as we have seen, describes Jesus as 'the exact representation' of the Father's being. Bowman and Komoszewski point out here that:

The Greek word literally referred to the mark or imprint reproducing the likeness of something (such as letters or a person's face), typically by a metal stamp or seal . . . Using a metaphor derived from what is now somewhat obsolete technology, we might say that the son is a '*carbon copy*' of his father . . . the book of Hebrews states emphatically the *essential likeness* of the Son to God [italics mine].[26]

It is hard to escape the conclusion, therefore, that Father and Son are bound in the deepest possible union with each other. As John 16.15 suggests, all the qualities that make the Father 'God' are attributes that the Son also possesses. On this issue Liddon observes that:

> there is no room in St. Paul's thought for an imaginary being like the Arian Christ, hovering indistinctly between created and uncreated life; since, where God is believed to be so utterly remote from the highest creatures beneath his throne, Christ must either be conceived of as purely and simply a creature . . . Or He must be adored as One Who is for ever and necessarily internal to the uncreated life of the Most High.[27]

We are left, therefore, with a very stark choice. If we are not to risk preaching 'another Jesus' (2 Cor. 11.4 RSV), we need to take the language of the New Testament very seriously. The evidence given above shows clearly that, if the terms 'Father' and 'Son' are to mean anything at all in an absolute sense, both must share the same inner nature. If the Father is eternal, the Son must also be eternal. If the Father is true God, the Son must also be true God. As Irenaeus once summed it up, 'that which is begotten of God is God'.[28]

Does It Matter?

This leaves us with a further vital question: is it important? Does it really matter what we believe about this issue? Are there not many similar questions about which Christians disagree upon?

It is true, of course, that there are a great many areas of doctrine in which Christians hold a range of different views. But some are simply non-negotiable. Paul describes anyone who 'preaches a Jesus other than the Jesus we preached' as 'false apostles, deceitful workers, masquerading as apostles of Christ' (2 Cor. 11.4,13). Is this an overreaction? Athanasius described the denial of Christ's deity as 'blasphemy against the Godhead'.[29] Was he being over-sensitive? Let us consider some of the reasons for taking this issue seriously.

To begin with, we should note that two apparently conflicting requirements for gaining salvation are laid down in Scripture. On the one hand, Psalm 49 seems to imply that no human being can achieve our salvation:

No one can redeem the life of another
> or give to God a ransom for them –
the ransom for a life is costly,
> no payment is ever enough –
so that they should live on for ever
> and not see decay . . .
But *God* will redeem me from the realm of the dead;
> he will surely take me to himself (Ps. 49.7–9,15).

On the other hand Hebrews 2 suggests that *only* a human being can achieve our salvation:

> Since the children have flesh and blood, he too shared in their human- ity so that by his death he might break the power of him who holds the power of death – that is, the devil – and free those who all their lives were held in slavery by their fear of death . . . For this reason *he had to be made like them, fully human in every way*, in order that he might become a merciful and faithful high priest in service to God, and that he might make atonement for the sins of the people (Heb. 2.14–17).

This question takes us back once more to the Divine Paradox. In the introduction we noted how the dozen or so apparently open declarations of Jesus' deity in the New Testament tilt precariously between identifying him with God, while appearing to imply the opposite as well! Then, in the chapters which followed, we saw how the Messiah, the 'angel of the LORD', the 'Son of Man', the 'Wisdom' and 'Word' of God, and the 'arm of the LORD' seem at one level to be aspects of Yahweh's own being, while also appearing to have a life of their own. Finally, in the last chapter, we consid- ered briefly how our views of Christ as 'God' and as 'man', as the Father's equal and yet his subordinate, might exist in a creative tension with each other.

The consistent pattern throughout Scripture, therefore, is that the Son is both 'God' and yet someone 'other than God'. But now it becomes even more obvious that the Divine Paradox is a *neces- sary* one. For both the requirements of salvation stated above to be met, a one-sided view of Jesus is insufficient: it is not enough for him to be simply God alone or man alone, but to embrace both natures together within a single physical body. The question of the sheer humanity of Jesus is not, admittedly, an issue for us today (though, as 1 John 4.2 seems to imply, it was a problem for a time in the late first century and beyond). The difficulty that faces us is, rather, whether Jesus can also truly be understood as 'God', and if so, what the implications of that might be for us.

We have already glimpsed the importance of answering this question. In chapter two we saw Job, in imagining a mediator who could 'arbitrate and impose his authority' in his disagreement with God, conceiving of a being who would at very least be God's equal (!) but, more importantly, Job's 'Redeemer'. In chapter four we discovered how Jesus, in likening himself to a ladder between heaven and earth, saw himself as fulfilling this role as a divine/human mediator between God and humankind. In chapter six we noted that when Yahweh made a binding covenant with Abraham he promised that *he alone* would bear the consequences on Abraham's behalf if the covenant was broken. And in chapter seven, we noticed how vital for us belief in Jesus' divine status really is: 'If you do not believe that I am what I am, you will die in your sins' (John 8.24 NEB).

A similar warning lies scarcely concealed below the surface of John 3.18, which says, 'whoever does not believe stands *condemned already* because they have not believed in *the name* of God's one and only [Greek *monogenous*] Son'. This verse is not describing Jesus as God's son in some general sense, since the word 'son' is used elsewhere for members of the church (Gal. 4.6), for Israel (Hos. 11.1) and for the angels (Job 1.6 RSV). Rather, we stand already condemned if we do not believe in the name (meaning here the true identity) of God's *monogenes* Son (that is, a Son who is unique, one of a kind, and who shares the Father's nature exclusively).

The Scripture is painfully clear. If Jesus is not both completely God and completely man, then he cannot truly be Immanuel – *God with us*. The ladder is still incomplete and we are left trying to seek other methods of bridging the gaping chasm between God and human beings. Writing about the early Arian movement, Robert Gregg and Dennis Groh comment that:

> Salvation, for orthodoxy, is effected by the Son's essential identity with the Father – that which links God and Christ to creation is the

divine nature's assumption of flesh. Salvation for Arianism is effected by the Son's identity with the creatures – that which links Christ and creatures to God is *conformity of will* [italics mine].[30]

In other words, since we can no longer trust in Christ as a secure guarantee of our salvation, we are forced to rely on our own works.[31] This is precisely the result that Paul warns about in his letter to the Colossians, who were in danger of being influenced by the 'hollow and deceptive philosophy' (2.8) advocated by those who, as we noted, saw Christ as simply one of a chain of intermediary beings between God and humanity. The end result was simply a degeneration into regulations characterized by 'their self-imposed worship, their false humility and their harsh treatment of the body' (2.23).

It is perhaps not surprising that, throughout his letters, Paul is scathing about those who, through an incomplete faith, seek to gain redemption through their own efforts. As the standard set in this regard is absolute perfection (Matt. 5.48), and as our righteous deeds are 'filthy rags' in God's sight (Isa. 64.6), what hope does anyone have of being saved? Once we embark upon this road, Christ's role is not merely downgraded, but 'will be of no value to you at all' (Gal. 5.2). To borrow Paul's words from a slightly different context, our faith has become futile and 'we are of all people most to be pitied' (1 Cor. 15.17,19).

Finally, we noted earlier Paul's stern warning of the dreadful consequences that faced those who 'exchanged the truth of God for a lie, and worshipped and served *created things* rather than the Creator' (Rom. 1.25). The results of such false devotion as he describes them make for bleak reading. In the final analysis, serving a created Son of God falls little short of idolatry.

The nineteenth-century writer Joseph Gurney sums these things up admirably when he comments that:

the scheme of religion unfolded in the New Testament, although composed of many parts, is a perfect whole, and is directed, *as a whole*, to the great end of our salvation. If then we accept it only in part, there is surely much reason to fear that, as far as we are concerned, we shall undermine its strength, and defeat its operation . . . in rejecting the divinity, incarnation, and atonement of Christ, we reject *precisely that part of the system . . . upon which all the other parts may be said to depend* [italics mine].[32]

A similar remark is made by Alan Gomes: 'It is critical to realize that the core teachings of Christianity stand or fall together. It is not possible to deny one central doctrine but then be correct about everything else; it simply does not work like that. It is like a one-piece knit sweater: if you unravel one part of the sweater you eventually wind up with a tangle of yarn at your feet.'[33]

A survey of the Unitarian Universalist denomination in the USA in 1967 seems to bear this out. Of those polled, only 3 per cent believed in a supernatural God who intervenes in human affairs, only 10 per cent believed in the immortality of the soul, while 64 per cent 'seldom' or 'never' prayed.[34] In a more recent survey, only 13 per cent described themselves as 'Christian' while 18 per cent considered themselves to be 'atheist'.[35]

The stakes, then, are very high. Gomes' conclusion is stark: 'one who rejects Christ's true deity, and accordingly his saving work, is lost for eternity'.[36] The issue of whether or not the Son is merely a created being is therefore one of the greatest importance. If Jesus stands only as a created being within time, he cannot truly exercise lordship over history, or be Ruler of our destiny; he certainly cannot connect finite human beings with an infinite God. Rather, it is only as Christ transcends the created order that he can bridge the vast gulf that would otherwise separate us from the Father.

Ten key statements about Yahweh	Ten key statements about Jesus
• He is the I AM (Exod. 3.14)	• He is the I AM (John 8.58)
• He is the Alpha and the Omega (Rev. 1.8)	• He is the Alpha and the Omega (Rev. 22.13,16)
• He is the First and the Last (Isa. 44.6)	• He is the First and the Last (Rev. 2.8)
• He is an Everlasting Father (Isa. 63.16)	• He is an Everlasting Father (Isa. 9.6)
• He is a Wonderful Counsellor (Isa. 28.2)	• He is a Wonderful Counsellor (Isa. 9.6)
• He is the Bridegroom (Isa. 62.5)	• He is the Bridegroom (Mark 2.19–20)
• He is the Saviour (Isa. 43.11)	• He is the Saviour (Luke 2.11)
• He is our Light (Isa. 60.19)	• He is our Light (John 8.12)
• He is our Hope (Ps. 71.5)	• He is our Hope (1 Tim. 1.1)
• He is our Peace (Judg. 6.24)	• He is our Peace (Eph. 2.14)

Questions to consider:

(i) So often in church history, differences of belief have sparked off great personal antagonism. Is this inevitable? Are there ways in which we can remain firm in doctrine and yet maintain the highest level of love and respect for those with whom we differ?

(ii) Jesus experienced intimacy with the Father at a level that would be difficult for us to imagine. In what areas of our lives do we need to experience more of the Father heart of God? How can that work through into the lives of those around us?

(iii) 'Any modern form of Christianity that has surrendered a whole-hearted belief in Jesus' deity has drifted from its moorings and is at sea in a vessel that has forfeited its rating as "Christian"' (Murray Harris, *Three Crucial Questions about Jesus* [Carlisle: OM, 1994], p. 103). Do you agree? What is the key thing you would want to communicate if a Jehovah's Witness knocked at your door tomorrow?

12.

Who Do You Say I Am?

Whoever wants to be my disciple must deny themselves and take up their cross daily and follow me. For whoever wants to save their life will lose it, but whoever loses their life for me will save it (Luke 9.23–24).

The most important question that has ever been asked, which forms the title of this final chapter, was put by Jesus to his disciples one day near the town of Caesarea Philippi (Mark 8.29). According to the New Testament, the way we react to it determines our future, not just in this life, but for the rest of eternity. It takes the spotlight off what theologians say, what church tradition says, even what the Bible says, to how we ourselves respond. It is not a question we can delay answering.

It was, of course, Peter who first attempted to answer the question, describing Jesus (in the gospel version which probably corresponds most closely to his original recollection) as 'the Messiah' (Mark 8.29).[1] But was this a complete answer? It is perhaps significant that Mark places his declaration immediately after the healing of blind man at Bethsaida (Peter's home town in John 1.44), whose first view of people is 'like trees walking around' (Mark 8.24). It is only after Jesus lays his hands on the man a *second* time that 'he saw everything clearly' (v. 25). Could Peter's understanding of Christ, expressed straight afterwards, have gone later through a similar sequence of stages?

If this is the case, we may need to turn elsewhere in the gospels for a definitive answer to the question, 'Who do you say I am?' Clearly all those present at Caesarea Phillipi had already wrestled with it (see John 1.41,49; Matt. 8.27, 14.33) and doubtless continued to do so. For many of us today the experience may well be the same: we may start off with a blurred impression of Jesus like 'walking trees' but, as we live out our lives for him, our understanding of him sharpens in focus and depth over time. However, our picture inevitably remains far from complete.

The irony, however, is that the person who at first seemed to get things most wrong is the one who, in the end, gets them most right. Of all the figures in the New Testament, it is Thomas who seems closest in spirit and outlook to the world in which we live today. His questioning mind, his desire for hard evidence, and his rather dark humour (John 11.16; 14.5; 20.25) all strike a chord with us in our sceptical, rationalistic age.

Yet of all the figures around Jesus, it is Thomas who is the first to offer the ultimate answer to the question, 'Who do you say I am?', describing Jesus as 'My Lord and my God' (John 20.28). It was not a conclusion he came to easily. He was not willing to live on the borrowed faith of others. He had to see for himself.

Through revealing himself to Thomas in a special way, Jesus seems to speak directly into our pessimistic, uncertain age. He shows us that God does not reject those who need to be more certain. On the contrary, it may be *precisely* because of Thomas's sceptical, rationalistic mindset that he is the first to recognize the full implications of Jesus' resurrection – that he could only be God himself – long before any of the other disciples grasp its full significance. (By contrast, we have no direct evidence of Peter calling Jesus 'God' for another thirty-five years![2])

There are probably many mysteries about Jesus that Thomas could never fully understand. Nor can we. But in this one critical question of Jesus' true identity, Christ did not want him to stay in a place of doubt. For Thomas, the newly resurrected, nail-scarred body of Jesus was proof enough that he straddled the boundaries of 'now' and eternity, of life and death, of man and God.

Like Thomas, we do not have to remain in a state of uncertainty. One important reason for God appearing in the world as a man is that *we can* be definite about his existence. While there are many aspects of God that are beyond description or definition or understanding, the sheer fact of God appearing as a man is so simple, so tangible and so immediate that even a child can grasp it ('We *saw* him with our own eyes and *touched* him with our own hands', 1 John 1.1 NLT).

But to establish this beyond doubt, God only needed to do it *once* in history (Heb. 1.1–2; 9.26). This principle of 'once, only once, and once for all' (as William Bright's hymn goes) is an important one here. Although no two versions of the Bible seem to be in agreement about *which* verses describe Jesus as 'God', on the 'Thomas' verse they are all absolutely unanimous. Even the New World Translation cannot escape the force of its testimony. Although this might seem at first sight to be a very fragile foundation on which to build a huge theological edifice, we have already seen that the volume of indirect evidence for the deity of Christ is simply enormous. And Thomas only needed to be told once. If that was enough for him, surely it is enough for us.

The fact that, two thousand years ago, God entered the world as a helpless baby and lived an ordinary human life has enormous implications for us. For him to have experienced a normal human existence, with all its highs and lows, profundity and banality, excitement and tedium, reminds us that no aspect of human life is trivial or insignificant in his sight. It shows us that everything we do, say and think *matters* to him far more than we can ever imagine.

Knowing that the Creator of the galaxies has shared in the depths of our sufferings (Heb. 5.8) and has been tempted in every way as we are (Heb. 4.15) can be an enormous source of comfort to us. But it also carries an immense challenge. Thomas recognizes Jesus not just as 'Lord' and 'God' but as '*my* Lord and *my* God'. He goes on to live out the reality of this statement by travelling to India (according to well-established tradition) and laying down his life for the gospel. All over the world today, Christians are continuing to pay the highest price for their belief: in North Korea, in the Middle East, in parts of Africa, martyrdom is an all-too-regular occurrence.

Many of us in the West could not even begin to emulate this because our picture of Jesus is, quite simply, far too small. It is one thing to recognize Jesus as 'Lord' and 'God', but quite another to make him *our* Lord and *our* God. Are we willing to submit to him in *every* area of our life? Are we willing to become *nothing* for him? Is he simply *the Lord* (an intellectual point), or *our Lord* (challenging us to the very core of our being)?

The question becomes more pointed because Jesus turns the traditional notions of 'lordship' upside down. Even before he is born, huge question marks hang over his legitimacy; his birth takes place not in a palace but in a stable; and he later grows up in an obscure town which is apparently the butt of local jokes (John 1.46) where even his fellow townsfolk misunderstand and reject him (Mark 6.4). At his 'coronation' as King his throne is a wooden torture-stake, his crown is woven together from thorns, and his royal robe is gambled away, while his 'courtiers' mock and jeer.

A telling insight into this topsy-turvy quality of God's kingdom comes at the last supper, where John paints the extraordinary picture of Jesus, the King of the Universe, adopting a stance of abject humility in washing his disciples' feet. It is a powerful and moving picture that speaks a thousand words. In later Jewish culture, the task was considered too demeaning even for a slave to perform.[3]

Yet it is against the background of this remarkable action that Jesus goes on to make the astonishing statement that 'anyone who has seen me has seen the Father' (John 14.9). He is not just demonstrating, in other words, what true humility really is. *He is using it to show us what the Father himself is like.*

Through this striking prophetic action, therefore, we see what it might *mean* for the Father to dwell amongst us and bless us. In Hebrews the concept of 'blessing' implies more than merely the transference of well-being: it actually conveys the image of 'bowing the knee'. There is an obvious logic here. In order to bless God, we have to humble ourselves. But does God, in order to bless us, have to humble *himself* as well?

It is worth noting that Jacob, when wrestling with Yahweh in Genesis 32, in a remarkable repetition of his youthful outmanoeuvring of his brother (Gen. 25.29–34), insists that he will not let go until he has received his blessing (Gen. 32.26; Hos. 12.2–5). But far from being rebuked for his arrogance, he is actually *given the very thing he asks for* and even commended for it! In other words, God has to *weaken* himself deliberately in order for Jacob to win. In an extraordinary reversal of Christ's promise to Paul (2 Cor. 12.9) Jacob's strength is made perfect *in Yahweh's weakness!* As the original NIV translation of Psalm 18.35 so beautifully declares: 'you stoop down to make me great'.

Hints of this extraordinary contrast come to the fore again and again throughout the later parts of Isaiah: we see a God who roars like a warrior, but gently leads the blind (Isa. 42.13,16); who demands universal allegiance, yet carries the weak (45.23; 46.4);

whose hands laid out the entire universe, yet are branded with the names of those he loves (Isa. 48.13; 49.16); who is awesome in holiness, yet abiding with those crushed in spirit (57.15); rising up in judgement, yet afflicted with the afflictions of his own people (63.6,9); enthroned in heaven, yet fixing his eyes on the downtrodden (66.1–2). The outstretched 'arm of the LORD' used in creation (Jer. 32.17) and in judgement (Jer. 21.5) is also the outstretched arm of redemption (Deut. 26.8; Ps. 136.11–12).

The same irony continues into the New Testament. The words of Pilate concerning Jesus, 'Here is the man' (John 19.5) and 'Here is your king' (John 19.14) together with John the Baptist's 'Here is the Lamb of God' (John 1.29 NRSV) appear as a tragic twist on the words of Isaiah 40.9: 'Here is your God!' The contrast between the two extremes is staggering. In Jesus God steps into the world as both king and servant, victor and victim, shepherd and sacrificial lamb. He is at one level a terrifying judge, and yet, exchanging places with us, the criminal in the dock.

On several occasions we have referred to the extraordinary verse at Zechariah 12.10, which sums up, with John 1.1, the mystery of the Divine Paradox, with Yahweh describing himself both as 'me' and as 'him': 'And I will pour out on the house of David and the inhabitants of Jerusalem a spirit of grace and supplication. They will look on *me*, the one they have pierced, and they will mourn for *him* as one mourns for an only child, and grieve bitterly for him as one grieves for a firstborn son.'

The strange grammatical 'twist' in this sentence (to which the repeated '*I* am *he*' statements in Isaiah offer a strange kind of answer) hints at something which, if true, is astonishing beyond words. We know from Paul that 'God made him who had no sin to be sin for us' (2 Cor. 5.21) and that Jesus cried out in agony, 'My God, my God, why have you forsaken me?' (Matt. 27.46), the only prayer where he did not address God as 'Father'. Could it be that, for a moment that may have seemed like an eternity, the Godhead itself was torn in two?

Knowing the extraordinary power that is released by the splitting of a single atom (and Matthew very graphically portrays the tearing open of the temple curtain and the *splitting open* of the tombs at the moment of Jesus' death), the thought of the very foundations of the universe breaking open for mere mortals like ourselves should take our breath away. Was this the price that was necessary to secure our salvation, and to extend the extraordinary invitation to us to share in the divine glory (John 17.22)? If so, we can only marvel, for it opens up for the first time a way for each of us into the extraordinary relationship of love that exists between Father and Son. But the invitation is urgent, and will not remain open for ever!

For this reason, the question 'Who do you say that I am?' does not invite a glib response, because it confronts us not just with the reality of Jesus' deity but also with the reality of his death, as Peter discovered in his first – only half-successful – attempt to answer it (Mark 8.27–33). Our natural instinct, like Peter's, is to gloss over the difficult consequences of our answer. Yet for Thomas, it is not a vision of glory but the *marks of the nails themselves* which convince him that his beloved friend is actually God in person.

In other words, Jesus' question to us demands, by its very nature, a personal response of faith rather than a 'correct' theological answer. It turns the questions that we have about *Christ* on their head and starts directing a lot of other questions about us instead. Are we ready to follow Jesus wherever he takes us? Are we willing to lay down our life for him? Are we willing to take up our cross and follow him every day? The challenge to us is laid down powerfully in the words of Isaac Watts:

> Forbid it, Lord, that I should boast,
> Save in the death of Christ my God!
> All the vain things that charm me most,
> I sacrifice them to his blood.

The response we give here is of the utmost importance. God's entire plan of salvation was made possible because a young, unmarried Jewish girl from a humble background dared to say 'yes', despite all the emotional turmoil, both short term and long term, that this would cause her (Matt. 1.19; Luke 2.35). Are we willing to do the same? Are we willing to surrender our all to him, come what may? God's invitation is spoken to us not merely in words, but in blood-soaked hands nailed to a bare wooden cross. As Pope Benedict XVI exhorted us, 'With Thomas let us place our hands into Jesus' pierced side and confess: "My Lord and my God."'[4] Eternity now awaits our response.

Ten invitations from Yahweh	Ten invitations from Jesus
• Come to him (Isa. 55.3)	• Come to him (Matt. 11.28)
• Hope in him (1 Tim. 6.17)	• Hope in him (1 Thess. 1.3)
• Trust in him (Ps. 25.2)	• Trust in him (Acts 14.23)
• Taste him (Ps. 34.8)	• Taste him (1 Pet. 2.3)
• Take refuge in him (Ps. 34.8)	• Take refuge in him (Ps. 2.12)
• Look to him (Isa. 45.22 NKJV)	• Look to him (John 6.40)
• Listen to him (Isa. 46.3)	• Listen to him (Mark 9.7)
• Love and obey him (Exod. 20.6)	• Love and obey him (John 14.15)
• Receive from him (1 John 3.21–22)	• Receive from him (1 John 5.13–15 RSV)
• Dwell in him (Ps. 91.9)	• Dwell in him (John 15.7 REB)

Questions to consider:

(i)   Has your overall picture of Jesus changed through reading this book? Does it affect the way you see God? How might a fuller understanding of Jesus clarify our own identity and destiny?

(ii) What does it mean to take up your cross and follow Jesus? What crosses has he called you to bear in your own life? What possessions or habits are you holding onto that he is asking you to lay down for him?

(iii) 'According to the Bible, one's eternal destiny hangs upon what he thinks about Jesus' person and work . . . I urge [the reader] to bow in faith before Christ's saving sceptre and to join Christ's witnesses in their effort to make the salvation that he accomplished at his cross known to the rest of mankind' (Robert Reymond, *Jesus, Divine Messiah*, p. 538). If you have already taken this step, what has the impact been in your own life? If not, what is your immediate personal response?

Appendix: Jesus as God

The tables, which follow on subsequent pages, show which of thirty well-known Bible translations represent Jesus (or the Messiah-King in the Old Testament) as being 'God'. In some of the verses, such as Matt. 1.23, Rom. 9.5, Phil. 2.6 and John 5.20, the assessment of whether Jesus is being described as 'God' is inevitably rather a subjective one; many translations preserve the ambiguity present in the original Greek. For a discussion of the pros and cons of different interpretations here, see our website, **www.but-is-he-God.org**, or, for a much more detailed examination of the subject, Murray Harris's authoritative work *Jesus as God: The New Testament Use of Theos in Reference to Jesus* (Grand Rapids, MI: Baker, 1992).

Key to Bible Tables

American Standard Version (asv) (originally New York: Thomas Nelson, 1901).

Amplified Bible (amp) (Grand Rapids, MI: Zondervan, NT, 1958; full Bible, 1965; rev. edn, 1987).

Common English Bible (ceb) (Nashville, TN: Common English Bible, 2011).

Complete Jewish Bible (cjb) (Clarksville, MD: Jewish New Testament Publications, NT, 1989; full Bible, 1998).

Contemporary English Version (cev) (New York: American Bible Society, NT, 1991; full Bible, 1995).

Darby Translation (dby) (originally London: G. Morrish, 1883).

English Standard Version (esv) (Wheaton, IL: Crossway, 2001).

Good News Bible (GNB) (New York: American Bible Society, NT, 1966; full Bible, 1976).

Holman Christian Standard Bible (HCSB) (Nashville, TN: Broadman and Holman, NT, 2001; full Bible, 2003).

J.B. Phillips New Testament (PHI) (London: G. Bles, NT, 1958; rev. edn, 1972).

Jerusalem Bible (JB) (London: Darton, Longman and Todd, 1966).

King James Version (KJV) (originally London: Robert Barker, 1611).

Knox Bible (KNOX) (London: Burns, Oates and Washbourne, NT, 1944; full Bible, 1955; rev. edn, 1956, 1961).

Living Bible (LB) (Wheaton, IL: Tyndale House, NT, 1967; full Bible, 1971).

The Message (MSG) (Colorado Springs, CO: NavPress (NT, 1993; full Bible, 2002).

New American Standard Bible (NASB) (originally Carol Stream, IL: Creation House, NT, 1963; full Bible 1971; updated 1997).

New Century Version (NCV) (formerly A New Easy-to-Read Version and the International Children's Version) (originally Grand Rapids, MI: Baker, NT, 1978; full Bible 1986; Revised 1991).

New English Bible (NEB) (Oxford and Cambridge: OUP and CUP, NT, 1961; full Bible, 1970).

New International Version (NIV) (Grand Rapids, MI: Zondervan, NT, 1973; full Bible, 1978; rev. edn, 1984, 2011).

New Jerusalem Bible (NJB) (London: Darton, Longman and Todd, 1985).

New King James Version (NKJV) (Nashville, TN: Thomas Nelson, NT, 1979; full Bible, 1982).

New Living Translation (NLT) (Wheaton, IL: Tyndale House, 1996; rev. edn, 2004).

New Revised Standard Version (NRSV) (Nashville, TN: Thomas Nelson, 1989).

New World Translation (NWT) (New York: Watchtower Bible and Tract Society, NT, 1950; full Bible, 1961; rev. edn, 1971, 1981, 1984).

Revised English Bible (REB) (Oxford and Cambridge: OUP and CUP, 1989).

Revised Standard Version (RSV) (New York: Thomas Nelson, NT, 1946; full Bible, 1952; rev. edn, 1971).

Revised Version (RV) (Oxford and Cambridge: OUP and CUP, NT, 1881; full Bible, 1885).

The Voice (VOI) (Nashville, TN: Thomas Nelson, 2012).

Weymouth New Testament in Modern Speech (WEY) (London: James Clarke 1900; rev. edn, 1903, 1909, 1924, 1929).

Young's Literal Translation (YLT) (originally Edinburgh, Dublin and London: A. Fullarton & Co., 1863; rev. edn, 1898).

Sixteen key verses in thirty different Bible versions

	KJV	YLT	RV	DBY	WEY	ASV	KNOX	RSV	NWT	PHI	AMP	NEB	NASB	JB	GNB
Ps. 45.6	✓	✓	✓	✓	–	✓	✓	X	X	–	✓	X	✓	✓	X
Isa. 9.6	✓	✓	✓	✓	–	✓	✓	✓	✓	–	✓	X	✓	✓	✓
Mt. 1.23	✓	✓	✓	✓	✓	✓	✓	✓	X	✓	✓	X	✓	X	X
Jn. 1.1	✓	✓	✓	✓	✓	✓	✓	✓	X	✓	✓	?	✓	✓	✓
Jn. 1.18	X	X	X	X	X	X	X	X	X	X	✓	X	✓	X	✓
Jn. 10.33	✓	✓	✓	✓	✓	✓	✓	✓	X	✓	✓	X	✓	✓	✓
Jn. 20.28	✓	✓	✓	✓	✓	✓	✓	✓	✓	✓	✓	✓	✓	✓	✓
Acts 20.28	✓	✓	✓	?	✓	X	✓	X	X	✓	(✓)	X	✓	✓	
Rm. 9.5	?	?	?	?	?	?	✓	X	X	✓	✓	X	?	?	X
Phl. 2.6	?	?	?	?	✓	X	X	X	X	✓	?	X	X	?	?
2 Th. 1.12	X	✓	X	X	X	X	X	X	X	X	X	X	X	X	X
1 Tm. 3.16	✓	✓	X	✓	X	X	X	X	X	X	(✓)	X	X	X	X
Tit. 2.13	X	✓	✓	✓	✓	X	?	✓	X	X	✓	X	✓	✓	✓
Hb. 1.8-9	✓	✓	✓	✓	✓	✓	✓	✓	X	✓	✓	✓	✓	✓	✓
2 Pt. 1.1	X	✓	✓	✓	X	X	✓	✓	X	X	✓	✓	✓	✓	✓
1 Jn. 5.20	?	✓	?	✓	✓	?	(?)	?	?	?	✓	?	?	X	?
Total	9	13	10	11	9	7	11	8	2	8	14	4	11	9	8

	VOI	CEB	ESV	HCSB	NLT	MSG	CEV	CJB	REB	NRSV	NJB	NCV	NKJV	NIV	LB
Ps. 45.6	✓		✓	✓	✓	X	✓	✓	X	✓	X	✓	✓	✓	✓
Is. 9.6	✓	✓	✓	✓	✓	✓	✓	✓	X	✓	✓	✓	✓	✓	✓
Mt. 1.23	✓	✓	✓	X	X	X	X	X	X	X	X	X	✓	✓	X
Jn. 1.1	✓	✓	✓	✓	✓	✓	✓	✓	?	✓	✓	✓	✓	✓	✓
Jn. 1.18	X	✓	✓	X	✓	?	X	X	X	✓	X	✓	X	✓	X
Jn. 10.33	✓	✓	✓	✓	✓	✓	✓	✓	✓	✓	✓	✓	✓	✓	✓
Jn. 20.28	✓	✓	✓	✓	✓	✓	✓	✓	✓	✓	✓	✓	✓	✓	✓
Acts 20.28	X	X	✓	✓	✓	?	X	X	X	X	X	X	✓	✓	✓
Rm. 9.5	?	✓	✓	✓	✓	✓	X	X	X	?	✓	✓	✓	✓	X
Phl. 2.6	?	?	X	?	✓	?	✓	X	X	?	X	?	?	✓	✓
2 Th. 1.12	X	X	X	X	X	X	X	X	X	X	X	X	X	X	X
1 Tm. 3.16	X	X	X	X	X	X	X	X	X	X	X	X	✓	X	X
Tit. 2.13	✓	✓	✓	✓	✓	✓	✓	X	✓	✓	✓	✓	✓	✓	✓
Hb. 1.8-9	✓	✓	✓	✓	✓	✓	✓	✓	✓	✓	✓	✓	✓	✓	✓
2 Pt. 1.1	✓	✓	✓	✓	✓	✓	✓	X	✓	✓	✓	✓	✓	✓	✓
1 Jn. 5.20	✓	?	✓	✓	✓	✓	✓	X	✓(?)	?	✓	✓(?)	?	✓	✓
Total	10	10	13	11	14	9	9	7	5	10	9	11	12	14	11

Endnotes

1. Jesus: More Than a Messiah?

[1] Pinchas Lapide, *Jewish Monotheism and Christian Trinitarian Doctrine: A Dialogue* (trans. Leonard Swidler; Philadelphia: Fortress, 1981), p. 68. For a markedly different view, see E.P. Sanders, *The Historical Figure of Jesus* (London: Penguin, 1993), pp. 28–30.

[2] Calculating either in lunar years from the decree given by Artaxerxes to rebuild Jerusalem in 445 BC, or in solar years from the earlier decree to rebuild the temple in 457 BC, sixty-nine 'weeks' of seven years each would take us to around AD 30, exactly the time of Jesus' ministry. The former viewpoint was popularized in recent times by Sir Robert Anderson in *The Coming Prince* (London: James Nisbet, 10th edn, 1915), pp. 67–75, while the second is explained by R.J.M. Gurney in 'The Seventy Weeks of Daniel 9:24–27', *Evangelical Quarterly* 53.1 (January–March 1981): pp. 29–36. The exact working out of such timings depended on different calendars used by different groups, with results which varied considerably. See Roger T. Beckwith, 'Daniel 9 and the Date of Messiah's Coming in Essene, Hellenistic, Pharisaic, Zealot and Early Christian Computation', *Revue de Qumran* 40 (1981): pp. 521–42.

[3] Emphasis, both italic and bold, in quotations from different Bible translations is mine throughout.

[4] It seems likely that Josephus applied the calculation in Daniel 9 to the years running up to the siege of Jerusalem in AD 70 (there are possible references in *Ant.* 10.11.7 and *J.W.* 6.5.4).

[5] Suetonius, *Vesp.* 4; Tacitus, *Hist.* 5.13.

[6] Potential candidates (depending on exactly what we mean by the word 'Messiah') might include, in order of mention, Theudas (Acts 5.36), Judas the Galilean (Acts 5.37), Simon the Sorcerer (Acts 8.9) and the unnamed Egyptian (Acts 21.38). A useful overview of these figures

can be found in Geza Vermes, *Who's Who in the Age of Jesus* (London: Penguin, 2005).

7　The principal source of this idea is Mal. 4.5. Further allusions can be found in Sir. 48.10; Matt. 16.14; Mark 8.28; Luke 7.16; 9.19; John 6.14.

8　*Jub.* 1.25,27.

9　*1 En.* 1.9 (cf. Jude 14–15). It is interesting to note that both *Jubilees* and *1 Enoch* form part of the Bible used by the Ethiopian Orthodox Church.

10　See Isa. 28.29; 10.21; 63.16. It is instructive, also, to compare such passages as Isa. 2.2–4; 25.6–8; 30.19–26; 35.1–10 with 11.1–12; 32.1–4; 42.1–4.

11　See, e.g., Josephus, *Ant.* 20.8.6.

12　Here the reference to a 'firstborn son' recalls the description of the messianic ruler in Ps. 89.26–27.

13　*Lam. Rab.* 1.51.

14　R.T. France, *Jesus and the Old Testament* (London: Tyndale, 1971), p. 157.

15　N.T. Wright, *Jesus and the Victory of God* (London: SPCK, 1996), p. 615. Curiously, Wright seems (p. 653) to sidestep the obvious conclusions of his own argument.

16　The fourth-century church historian Eusebius concluded from this passage that both Father and Son are called 'Almighty': 'Here, then, you have clearly two Persons using one Name, the Almighty Lord that sent, and Him that is sent having the same Name as the Sender' (*Dem. ev.* 6.16).

17　In keeping with standard Jewish practice at the time, Jesus would probably have spoken the word *'ǎ·dō·nāy* ('Lord') here in place of Yahweh ('LORD') which appears in the written text of Ps. 110.1. As Larry Hurtado points out, *'ǎ·dō·nāy* was 'widely used as a reverential oral substitute for Yahweh by Hebrew-speaking readers of the Bible' (in his book *Lord Jesus Christ: Devotion to Jesus in Earliest Christianity* [Grand Rapids, MI: Eerdmans, 2003], p. 183).

2. Jesus and the Divine Paradox

1　See also Jer. 50.34 and 51.36 (RSV).

2　Literally, 'the angel of the face [of God]'.

3　Philo, *QG* 2.62. The same argument, concerning the very similar verse in Genesis 1.27, was later put forward by the Christian writer Tertullian in *Prax.* 12.

4　See for example, *Barn.* 5.5; 6.12; Justin Martyr, *Dial.* 62.1–3; Theophilus, *Autol.* 2.18; Irenaeus, *Haer.* 4.20.1; Tertullian, *Prax.* 12.

⁵ This usage, though unusual in the Bible, is, ironically, relatively common in the Qur'an. The closest equivalent here is probably Sura 15.26: 'We created man from sounding clay, from mud moulded into shape.'

⁶ Philo, *Conf.* 169. Later some Jewish commentators attempted to explain the 'us' by suggesting that God was talking to the angels. However, at least one Jewish authority, the third-century rabbi Ammi bar Nathan, concedes the idea of a dialogue *within* God's nature when he suggests that in Gen. 1.26 God was talking to his own heart (*Gen. Rab.* 8.3). It is interesting to note in this regard that the Hebrew words for 'creator' at Eccl. 12.1 and 'maker' at Job 35.10, Ps. 149.2 and Isa. 54.5 all appear in the *plural*.

⁷ The reference here seems to be to passages such as Exod. 34.10–13; Deut. 7.2; 12.2–3.

⁸ This verse really knocks on the head the idea, frequently encountered in Jewish rabbinical literature, that the angel is merely God's *agent*: clearly here he is none other than Yahweh himself.

⁹ In *structure* it is remarkably similar to the threefold blessing at the end of 2 Cor.: 'May the grace of the *Lord Jesus Christ*, and the love of *God*, and the fellowship of the *Holy Spirit* be with you all' (13.14).

¹⁰ Compare John 4.5–6 with Gen. 48.22.

¹¹ The rejection of the community is obvious in that she is collecting water *on her own* at the hottest time of the day.

¹² Gen. 16.13; John 4.29.

¹³ The account in Luke refers to the couple as 'two of them' (24.13), apparently referring to those men and women described in vv. 9 and 10. One of these Luke specifically tells us was Cleopas (v. 18). Other names have been canvassed for his unidentified companion, including Luke himself. However, if this 'Cleopas' was the same as the 'Clopas' mentioned in John 19.25, whose wife Mary was standing at the foot of the cross (and a similar spelling variation occurs between 'Simeon' and 'Simon' in 2 Pet. 1.1 [RSV] and Mark 1.16), then it is entirely possible that he and his wife were returning home together. The church historian Eusebius of Caesarea tells us that Clopas was the brother of Joseph the carpenter of Nazareth, and therefore Jesus' uncle, and that his son succeeded James, the brother of Jesus, as head of the Jerusalem church (Eusebius, *Hist. eccl.* 3.11, 32).

¹⁴ See Gen. 32.29; Judg. 13.18.

¹⁵ Broadcast talk on the BBC, 1 October 1939.

¹⁶ Lynne Truss, *Eats, Shoots & Leaves: The Zero Tolerance Approach to Punctuation* (London: Profile, 2003), p. 10.

[17] The closest match here occurs between the New Jerusalem Bible (1985) and *The Message* (2002), but even here we fall short of a total agreement between the two.

3. Jesus as the Image of God

[1] Bruce Metzger, *A Textual Commentary on the Greek New Testament* (Stuttgart: United Bible Societies, 2nd edn, 1994), p. 657. The same reading also appears in the Alexandrinus manuscript, the Vulgate, and citations in Jerome and Cyril, all from around the fifth century AD. In one even earlier manuscript, p[72], we actually find the words 'God Christ'.

[2] Young Kyu Kim, 'Palaeographical Dating of p[46] to the Later First Century', in *Biblica* 69.2 (1988): pp. 248–57.

[3] The same reading of this verse appears in the Syriac *Peshitta*, the Latin Vulgate, and citations by Irenaeus, Clement of Alexandria, and Origen.

[4] Writing in *Dial.* 127, Justin comments that 'neither Abraham, nor Isaac, nor Jacob, nor any other man, saw the Father and ineffable Lord of all, and also of Christ, but [saw] Him who was according to His will His Son, being God, and the Angel because He ministered to His will, whom also it pleased Him to be born man by the Virgin; who also was fire when He conversed with Moses from the bush.'

[5] Whichever location one chooses for the crucifixion of Jesus, I am assuming that 'Mount Moriah' (Gen. 22.2; 2 Chr. 3.1) refers to a wider range of upland than merely the Temple Mount itself.

[6] See Gal. 4.13–15.

[7] In Paul's case, the change of name does not become apparent until Acts 13.9, but must surely be rooted in his experience on the Damascus road.

[8] I will seek to demonstrate the latter point more clearly in chapter seven.

[9] See b. *Hag.* 14b.

[10] See b. *Hag.* 15a. A similar account appears in *3 En.* 16.1–5. Samson H. Levey, in 'The Best Kept Secret of the Rabbinic Tradition', in *Judaism* 21.4 (Fall 1972): pp. 454–69, argues that the account is a retelling of a deliberate attempt by the sages to explore Christian belief, and that Rabbi ben Zoma also became a Christian as a result, with even Akiba himself being influenced by some Christian ideas.

[11] The saying runs as follows: 'One in whom there are good works, who has studied much Torah, to what may he be likened? To a person who builds first with stones and afterward with brick; even when much water comes and collects by their side, it does not dislodge them. But

one in whom there are no good works, though he studied Torah, to what may he be likened? To a person who builds first with bricks and afterward with stones: even when a little water gathers, it overthrows them immediately' ('*Abot R. Nat.* 24a 1). The resemblance to Jesus' words in Matt. 7.24–27 should be obvious.

[12] See b. *Hag.* 15b.

[13] In *T. Ab.* 1 – 4 and *2 En.* 22.6; 33.11, he is referred to as Michael, the Lord's commander-in-chief, while in *Apoc. Ab.* 10.7 he is described as Yahoel, in whom God's inexpressible name dwells.

[14] For example, b. *Sanh.* 38b. The name may come from the Greek *meta thronon*, meaning 'next to the divine throne'.

[15] See *3 En.* 12.5.

[16] A more detailed discussion of this question appears in Daniel Abrams, 'The Boundaries of Divine Ontology: The Inclusion and Exclusion of Metatron in the Godhead', in *HTR* 87.3 (1994): pp. 291–321. The article covers some fascinating later attempts, both Jewish and Christian, to compare or equate Metatron with Jesus himself.

[17] The figure who is referred to as 'an angel of the Lord' in the nativity stories in the gospels (for example, Luke 2.9), and at various points in Acts, is clearly a created being distinguished from Christ. He is always introduced *without* the definite article ('*an* angel of the Lord'); the definite article is only used to refer *back* to the angel already described. But the fact that Matt. and Luke use the *same* description as the Old Testament writers only raises further questions here.

[18] For example, Justin Martyr writes that 'he who has but the smallest intelligence will not venture to assert that the Maker and Father of all things, having left all supercelestial matters, was visible on a little portion of the earth' (*Dial.* 60). See also Theophilus, *Autol.* 2.22.

[19] Both Justin Martyr (*Dial.* 127) and Clement of Alexandria (*Paed.* 1.7) state their clear belief that it is Christ who is being described as 'Lᴏʀᴅ' in Gen. 17.

[20] Evidence for a belief that the angel of the Lᴏʀᴅ is involved in these direct exchanges can be found in Acts 7.38, where the 'angel' which Stephen describes in his speech to the Sanhedrin as talking with Moses on the mountain is clearly none other than God himself (see also Gal. 3.19–20; Heb. 2.2).

[21] Christopher Rowland, *The Open Heaven: A Study of Apocalyptic in Judaism and Early Christianity* (New York: Crossroad, 1982), pp. 96–7. Rowland writes of the figure as 'deity himself described in human form' (p. 98).

[22] There is no space here to defend the apostolic authorship of this or any other disputed New Testament book. The case for 2 Pet. has already

been admirably made by Michael Green in *The Second Epistle General of Peter and the General Epistle of Jude: An Introduction and Commentary* (Leicester: IVP, 2nd edn, 1987), pp. 13–39.

[23] Robert Reymond, *Jesus, Divine Messiah: The New and Old Testament Witness* (Tain: Christian Focus, 2003), p. 323.

[24] See, e.g., 12.41; 17.5,22,24.

[25] Larry Hurtado, *Lord Jesus Christ: Devotion to Jesus in Earliest Christianity* (Grand Rapids, MI: Eerdmans, 2003), p. 379.

[26] The name of Jesus is not mentioned in the original Greek here, but the context clearly implies it.

[27] As a form of address the doubling up of names is not uncommon in Hebrew (see, e.g., Gen. 22.11; 46.2; Exod. 3.4; 1 Sam. 3.10; cf. Matt. 7.21, Luke 22.31). As a form of self-description, however, it is much more unusual. In the Talmud the repeated divine name is explained here as 'I am he before one sins, and I am he after one sins and repents' (b. *Roš Haš.* 17b).

[28] Report on research conducted by Professor Yuan Yin and a team at the University of Science and Technology of China in Shanghai, posted online on 6 March 2013 in *MIT Technology Review*.

4. Jesus as the Son of Man

[1] In John 15.1–8 Jesus uses the same image of the vine with a similar 'double meaning' to describe both himself individually, and the total sum of believers who belong to him.

[2] There is a fascinating parallel here with the appearance of the angel of the LORD in the flames of the bush in Exod. 3.2. Moses saw that 'though the bush was on fire *it did not burn up*'. It is intriguing in this connection that the 'river of fire' flowing from the throne of the 'Ancient of Days' in Dan. 7.10 seems to be equivalent to the 'river of the water of life' flowing from the throne of God and the Lamb in Rev. 22.1. A later Jewish tradition records that angels are made up of both water and fire in equal proportions and that God creates peace between the opposing elements (j. *Roš Haš.* 2.58a).

[3] Seyoon Kim, *The 'Son of Man' as the Son of God* (Tübingen: Mohr Siebeck, 1983), p. 208.

[4] There is possibly a further parallel here with Ps. 2, where once more the nations conspire together *against* God, but a figure described as God's *Son* is said to 'break them with an iron rod' and 'shatter them in pieces like a clay pot' (Ps. 2.7,9 GNB). Connecting this passage to Dan. 2 and 7 would inevitably imply that the 'Son' and the 'son of man'

are the same figure, suggesting that the *Son of Man* is also the *Son of God*. The reference to *the Son* is unique in this absolute form in the Old Testament, but is used repeatedly in John's gospel to describe Christ's divine nature, as we will argue in chapter ten.

5   *b. Sanh.* 38b (see also *b. Hag.* 14a).

6   Christopher Rowland, *The Open Heaven: A Study of Apocalyptic in Judaism and Early Christianity* (New York: Crossroad, 1982), p. 98.

7   David Capes, 'Preexistence', in *Dictionary of the Later New Testament and Its Developments* (Downers Grove, IL: IVP, 1997), p. 959.

8   Joseph Kreitzer points out that the same sort of 'blurring' of the boundaries between God and the 'Son of Man' that we see in Dan. 7 appears in both *1 En.* and other apocryphal Jewish books such as *4 Ezra*. See L. Joseph Kreitzer, *Jesus and God in Paul's Eschatology* (Sheffield: JSOT Press, 1987), pp. 29, 62, 90, 157. Although no one can be sure of the dates of the relevant sections of these documents (which may, particularly in the case of *4 Ez.*, belong to the late first century AD), they do suggest that the 'Son of Man' in Dan. 7 was widely understood to represent both a human and a divine figure.

9   Matt. 25.31–33. The first two verses bear a fascinating similarity to a passage in *1 En.* 62.5,8: 'When they see that Son of Man sitting on the throne of his glory . . . all the elect shall stand before him on that day.'

10 But even here we should notice that Yahweh claims the same relationship with his people in Joel 3.3–4, from which the third quotation above is taken ('They cast lots for my people . . . Are you repaying *me* for something *I* have done?'). A similar idea appears in Num. 5.6 and Isa. 63.9.

11 Robert Reymond, *Jesus, Divine Messiah: The New and Old Testament Witness* (Tain: Christian Focus, 2003), p. 253.

12 A later Jewish tradition describes this as a characteristic of Adam before he disobeyed God (*b. Sanh.* 38b).

13 The only exceptions, apart from Stephen's use of the term in Acts 7.56, are Heb. 2.6; Rev. 1.13; 14.14, and these all seem to be referring back to 'son of man' passages in the Old Testament.

14 Joseph Ratzinger (Pope Benedict XVI), *Jesus of Nazareth from the Baptism in the Jordan to the Transfiguration* (trans. Adrian J. Walker; London: Catholic Truth Society, 2008), p. 322.

15 Ratzinger, *Jesus*, pp. 333–4.

5. Jesus as the Wisdom of God

1   The closest matches are probably between Sir. 4.10 and Luke 6.35; Sir. 11.18–19 and Luke 12.17–21; and Sir. 28.2–3 and Matt. 6.14–15.

But there are some statements that also run counter to those of Jesus (notably 25.25–26).

2 Try comparing, for example, Wis. 5.17–20 with Eph. 6.13–17; Wis. 13.1–5; 14.22–31 with Rom. 1.18–32; Wis. 13.6 with Acts 17.27; or Wis. 15.7 with Rom. 9.21.

3 The same is true of Matt. 11.19, where Jesus, in justifying his daily lifestyle, says, 'wisdom is proved right by *her deeds*'.

4 It is noticeable that the Septuagint translation of Prov. 8.23 includes the same Greek words *ēn arche* ['in the beginning'] with which John 1.1 begins.

5 A similar thought is expressed in Sir. 43.26, which says that 'by his word all things hold together' (RSV); cf. Paul's descriptions of Christ in Col. 1.17.

6 One example appears in Ps. 147.15, where the Word is likened to a swift runner.

7 Many later manuscripts add here the words '*who is in heaven*'. If these words can rightfully be traced back to the original (and a number of modern translations include them), they would leave one of two options: either John added them subsequently as a comment on what Jesus has said, or that Jesus himself was declaring a cosmic omnipresence!

8 An example of this appears in *Gen. Rab.* 44.11, where the 'word of the LORD' which came to Abraham in a vision is presented as the visit of an angel.

9 Later Jewish tradition comments on the immense height of certain angels (e.g. *b. Hag.* 13b), as does the apocryphal *Gospel of Peter* (10.30).

10 There is also a striking similarity here with several passages about Yahweh in the Dead Sea Scrolls, including this one from the concluding hymn of the *Community Rule*: '*All things come to pass* by His knowledge; He establishes all things by His design and *without Him nothing is done*' (1QS 11.10).

11 Examples appear, for instance, in *Tg. Ps.-J.* at Gen. 16.3 and Isa. 63.8–9.

12 See also *Tg. Ps.-J.* to Hos. 1.7 and Zech. 10.12.

13 Joseph J. Gurney, *Biblical Notes and Dissertations: Chiefly Intended to Confirm and Illustrate the Doctrine of the Deity of Christ: With Some Remarks on the Practical Importance of that Doctrine* (London: Rivington, 2nd edn, 1833), p. 141.

14 James D.G. Dunn, *Christology in the Making: A New Testament Inquiry into the Origins of the Doctrine of the Incarnation* (London: SCM, 1980), p. 226–7.

15 Philo, *Deus* 176. Philo's understanding of 'democracy' would, of course, have been somewhat different from our own.

16 Examples of each of these ideas appear in *Deus* 182; *Conf.* 146; *Leg.* 1.43.

17 See, e.g., Thomas Henshaw, *New Testament Literature in the Light of Modern Scholarship* (London: Allen and Unwin, 1952), p. 344 and R.C.H. Lenski, *The Interpretation of the Epistle to the Hebrews and of the Epistle of James* (Columbus, OH: Wartburg, 1946), p. 24.

18 Philo headed a delegation representing Alexandrian Jews to the Roman emperor Caligula in AD 39/40.

19 It is interesting, for example, to compare Philo's *Fug.* 117 ('As long, therefore, as this most sacred word lives and survives in the soul, it is impossible for any involuntary error to enter into it; for it is by nature so framed as to have no participation in, and to be incapable of admitting any kind of error') with 1 John 3.9 ('No one who is born of God will continue to sin, because God's seed remains in them; they cannot go on sinning, because they have been born of God').

20 See J. Edgar Bruns, 'Philo Christianus: The Debris of a Legend', *HTR* 66.1 (Jan. 1973): pp. 141–5.

21 Eusebius, *Hist. eccl.* 2.17.1.

22 The word for 'breath' here in Hebrew is the same as that for 'spirit'.

23 We find a whole range of personal characteristics attributed to the Spirit throughout Scripture such as creating (Job 33.4; Ps. 33.6), searching (1 Cor. 2.10), contending (Gen. 6.3; Acts 16.6–7), teaching (John 14.26), sending (Ezek. 2.2–4; Acts 10.19–20), and so on. The Spirit can be grieved (Isa. 63.10; Eph. 4.30), blasphemed against (Matt. 12.31), lied to (Acts 5.3), tested (Acts 5.9), resisted (Acts 7.51) and insulted (Heb. 10.29). Frequently he gives instructions (Neh. 9.20; Ezek. 2.2ff.; Acts 8.29; 10.19–20 etc.) or tells of future events (John 16.13; Acts 21.11; 1 Tim. 4.1; 1 Pet. 1.11). Moreover, if the Holy Spirit were merely an 'active force', those occasions where his activity is directly *contrasted* with that of an evil spirit (as in 1 Sam. 16.14 and Mark 3.29–30 RSV) could only make sense if *both* were impersonal forces.

24 In chs 15 and 16 of his gospel, John goes out of his way to emphasize the personality of the Spirit by using masculine singular pronouns where the Greek word *pneuma* would normally take neuter pronouns – in effect, he is deliberately breaking a grammatical rule to get the point across. Moreover, Jesus is careful here to liken the Spirit both to the Father and himself: he describes him as 'another counsellor' with the Greek word *allos* used here implying 'another of the same kind' (rather than *heteros*, which would imply another of a different kind).

25 The same Hebrew word, *rū·aḥ*, means 'breath', 'wind' and 'spirit'.

26 *Gen. Rab.* 2.4.

27 See, e.g., Luke 12.10; Rom. 15.30; 1 Cor. 6.11; Phil. 3.3; Heb. 10.29.

[28] Further examples appearing to identify Christ and the Spirit can also be found in certain second-century Christian writings, including *Herm. Sim.* 5.6; 9.1; *2 Clem.* 14.4; Justin Martyr, *1 Apol.* 33.6; Theophilus, *Autol.* 2.10.

[29] For example, we are in God (Col. 3.3) but God is also in us (1 John 4.16); we are in Christ (1 Cor. 1.30) but Christ is also in us (Col. 1.27); we are in the Spirit (Rom. 14.17) but the Spirit is also in us (1 Cor. 3.16). Likewise, we find such parallels as:

- the God of glory (Acts 7.2); the Lord of glory (1 Cor. 2.8); and the Spirit of glory (1 Pet. 4.14)
- the living Father (John 6.57); the living bread of the Son (John 6.51); and the living water of the Spirit (John 7.38–39)
- the Holy Father (John 17.11); the Holy One [Jesus] (John 6.69); and the Holy Spirit (Matt. 1.18)
- the eternal Father (Rom. 16.26); the eternal Son (Heb. 13.8); and the eternal Spirit (Heb. 9.14)
- the life-giving Father (1 Tim. 6.13); the life-giving Son (John 10.10); and the life-giving Spirit (John 6.63)

[30] Justin Martyr later ties many of these concepts together when he writes that 'God begat . . . a certain rational power [proceeding] from Himself, who is called by the Holy Spirit, now the Glory of the Lord, now the Son, again Wisdom, again an Angel, then God, and then Lord and Logos' (*Dial.* 61).

[31] Alan Segal, *Two Powers in Heaven: Early Rabbinic Reports about Christianity and Gnosticism* (Leiden: Brill, 1977), p. 42.

6. Jesus as Immanuel

[1] *Ign. Eph.* 19.3, in *The Epistles of St. Ignatius, Bishop of Antioch* (trans. J.H. Strawley; London: SPCK, 1900), p. 51.

[2] Tatian, *Orat. ad Graecos* 21.

[3] Tertullian, *Marc.* 5.5.

[4] Tertullian, *Carn. Chr.* 4.

[5] Melito of Sardis, *Fragments* 7.

[6] Irenaeus, *Haer.* 4.6.7.

[7] The one exception here is the tongue-in-cheek remark he directs at Caligula's description of himself as a 'god': 'it would have been easier to change God into man, than a man into God' (Philo, *Legat.* 118).

[8] Rabbi Leslie Edgar, *A Jewish View of Jesus* (London: The Liberal Jewish Synagogue, 1940), p. 4.

[9] *b. Ber.* 7a; *b. Avodah Zarah* 3b; *b. Baba Metzi'a* 86a. See Jacob Neusner, *The Incarnation of God: The Character of Divinity in Formative Judaism* (Philadelphia: Fortress, 1988), pp. 172, 190, 194.

[10] See, e.g., Ps. 75.1; Isa. 30.27 for the 'name' of Yahweh, and Exod. 33.18–23; Ezek. 1.26–28 for his 'glory'.

[11] The word is spelt differently by various writers, according to different methods of representing Hebrew letters in English. I have adopted one standard spelling for the different quotations in this chapter.

[12] In some Targum passages, the 'Word' of Yahweh and his 'Shekinah' are used side by side, suggesting that they are broadly similar ideas (see, e.g., *Tg. Ps.-J.* to Gen. 16.13 and Num. 10.36).

[13] *Exod. Rab.* 34.1.

[14] *Gen. Rab.* 4.4.

[15] Stephen seems to make the same point in Acts 7.44–53. After describing David's request to 'provide a dwelling-place for the God of Jacob', he points out that 'the Most High does not live in houses made by human hands' but seems instead to see David's true motive as being fulfilled in 'the coming of the Righteous One'.

[16] *m. 'Abot.* 3.2.

[17] *Lam. Rab.* 25.

[18] This issue has been a hot topic of debate for almost 2,000 years. In *Dialogue with Trypho*, written around AD 150 (ch. 67), Justin Martyr contends that the word means 'virgin' and the child described is Christ, while his Jewish debating colleague Trypho argues that it means 'young woman' and the child described is Hezekiah.

[19] The principal points of contact here (which also have parallels with Gen. 3) are these:

- The shame that Isaiah and Joshua, as representatives of Yahweh's people, feel in the presence of a holy God (Isa. 6.5; Zech. 3.3)
- God's 'covering over' of that sin through a symbolic action, leading to a commissioning for service (Isa. 6.6–10; Zech. 3.4–7)
- An emblem of hope for the future: a 'Branch' in Zech. 3.8–9 who will remove sin from the land, and the 'holy seed' (Isa. 6.13) that later becomes a 'Branch' establishing universal righteousness (11.1–9)

[20] cf. Matt. 22.41–46 and Rev. 22.16.

[21] Alec Motyer, 'Messiah', in *The Illustrated Bible Dictionary* (Leicester: IVP 1980), p. 991.

[22] There are occasional, less obvious, exceptions: see Isa. 16.6; Jer. 30.5 (RSV).

[23] Jürgen Moltmann, *The Crucified God: The Cross of Christ as the Foundation and Criticism of Christian Theology* (London: SCM, 1974), p. 86.

[24] In Isa. 43.10 the word 'servant' is specified as referring to the entire nation of Israel. However, the term 'Israel' can itself possess an individual *as well as* collective meaning (cf. Gen. 32.28), just as we saw earlier with the 'seed' (Gal. 3.16 / Gen. 13.15–16 KJV), the 'vine' (John 15.1/Ps. 80.8) and the 'son of man' (Heb. 2.6–9/Ps. 8.4 RSV). In Isa. 49 the servant is again called 'Israel' (v. 3) but is sent to *redeem* Israel (vv. 5–6). It is significant that, after this point, the nation of Israel is described only as 'servants' in the plural (54.17; 63.17; 65.8–15; 66.14).

[25] Richard Bauckham, *Jesus and the God of Israel: God Crucified and Other Studies on the New Testament's Christology of Divine Identity* (Milton Keynes: Paternoster, 2008), p. 35.

[26] Bauckham, *Jesus*, pp. 48–50.

[27] Bauckham, *Jesus*, p. 50.

[28] Most modern translations of the Bible attempt to allocate the last line of this statement to another speaker. However, there is absolutely no warrant in the original Hebrew for doing so.

[29] See, e.g., Lev. 6.2; 18.20; 19.15.

[30] The Hebrew verb used here for 'making' a covenant is precisely the one translated as 'cut off' to describe the sacrificial death of 'Messiah the Prince' in Dan. 9.25–26 (NASB).

[31] This surely is the meaning of the much-disputed verse at Gal. 3.20: a mediator does not represent just one party, but God in Christ *represents both*.

[32] Franz Rosenzweig, *The Star of Redemption* (trans. William W. Hallo; London: Routledge & Kegan Paul, 1971), pp. 409–10, quoted by Jürgen Moltmann in *Jewish Monotheism and Christian Trinitarian Doctrine: A Dialogue* (trans. Leonard Swidler; Philadelphia: Fortress, 1981), pp. 50–51. A more concise expression of this total solidity between God and his people appears in *Exod. Rab.* 2.5, which declares, 'Just as in the case of twins, if one has a pain in his head the other feels it also, so God said, as it were "I will be with him in trouble"' [Ps. 91.15].

[33] Although no surviving manuscripts of the Septuagint have this reading, it is mentioned by Justin Martyr (*Dial.* 73) and Augustine (*Exposition on Psalm 96.2*).

[34] One of the verses runs as follows:

> Fulfilled is all that David told
>
> In true prophetic song, of old:
>
> Unto the nations, lo! saith he,
>
> Our God hath reignèd from the Tree.

From *Vexilla Regis* by Venantius Fortunatus (530–609), translated in *The Psalter, or Seven Ordinary Hours of Prayer according to the Use of* the *Illustrious and Excellent Church of Sarum* (London: Joseph Masters, 1852), p. 346.

[35] Karl Barth, *Dogmatics in Outline* (trans. G.T. Thomson; London: SCM, 1949), p. 84.

7. Jesus as Yahweh

[1] Henry J. Liddon, *The Divinity of Our Lord and Saviour Jesus Christ* (London: Rivington, 12th edn, 1888), p. 350.

[2] Millard J. Erickson, *The Word Became Flesh: A Contemporary Incarnational Christology* (Grand Rapids, MI: Baker, 1991), p. 439.

[3] Charles E.B. Cranfield, *I and II Peter and Jude: Introduction and Commentary* (London: SCM, 1960), p. 35.

[4] The Jewish Tosefta tells us that the priests stopped pronouncing the divine name after the death of the high priest Simon the Just around 200 BC, with a single exception on the Day of Atonement (*t. Sotah* 13.8). Evidence from Philo (*Mos.* 2.206), Josephus (*Ant.* 2.12.4) and the Dead Sea Scrolls (1QS 6.27b – 7.2a) shows that it was considered too sacred to be pronounced in the first century AD across a wide spectrum of Judaism.

[5] Josephus, *J.W.* 7.10.1.

[6] Alan F. Segal, *Paul the Convert: The Apostolate and Apostasy of Saul the Pharisee* (New Haven, CT: Yale University Press, 1990), p. 62.

[7] Richard Bauckham, *Jesus and the God of Israel: God Crucified and Other Studies on the New Testament's Christology of Divine Identity* (Milton Keynes: Paternoster, 2008), p. 199.

[8] Robert Bowman and Ed Komoszewski, *Putting Jesus in His Place: The Case for the Deity of Christ* (Grand Rapids, MI: Kregel, 2007), p. 170.

[9] Significantly enough for the later use of *egō eimi* by Jesus, this statement is actually made by the angel of the LORD (v. 11).

[10] This, again, is an emphatic expression of being – both *'ă·nî* ('I') and *hū* ('he') are used in rabbinical literature as substitute titles for God. For further background see Ethelbert Stauffer, *Jesus and His Story* (trans. Dorothea M. Barton; London: SCM, 1960), pp. 145–9, and Philip. B. Harner, *The 'I am' of the Fourth Gospel: A Study in Johannine Usage and Thought* (Philadelphia: Fortress, 1970), pp. 18–25.

[11] Hebrew *'ā·nō·ḵî 'ā·nō·ḵî hū.*

[12] Hebrew *'eh·yeh 'ă·šer 'eh·yeh.*

[13] Stauffer, *Jesus*, p. 174.

[14] The apocryphal *Gospel of Thomas*, which may contain some authentic sayings of Jesus, includes the declaration 'I am the light that is above them all' (Logion 77).

15 Peter Lewis, *The Glory of Christ* (London: Hodder & Stoughton, 1992), p. 92.

16 In the Septuagint version of Isa. 47.8, Babylon attempts to steal the divine name *egō eimi* for herself.

17 An early Christian document called *Ascension of Isaiah* seems to underline this when it states that the Antichrist 'will do and speak like the Beloved and he will say: "*I am God* and before me there has been none." And all the people in the world will believe in him. And they will sacrifice to him and they will serve him saying: "*This is God* and beside him there is no other"' (*Mart. Ascen. Isa.* [trans. R.H. Charles] 4.6–8).

18 In the Mishnah, *Sanh.* 7.5 says that '"the blasphemer" is not culpable unless he pronounces the Name itself' (Herbert Danby, *The Mishnah* (London: OUP, 1933), p. 392). Clearly this position dates back to an earlier period: we should note, e.g., that the Septuagint translation of Lev. 24.16 states, 'Let him who pronounces the name of the Lord be punished with death.'

19 Examples of each of these substitutes for the divine name can be found in the New Testament at Luke 15.18; Acts 5.41; 1 John 2.20.

20 Josephus, *Ant.* 4.8.6.

21 Most commentators disagree here, but support for this view can be found in Stauffer, *Jesus*, pp. 149–59, and Sherman E. Johnson, *Commentary on the Gospel According to St. Mark* (London: A&C Black, 1960), pp. 127, 245. It is clear, however, that Matthew and possibly Luke place a different interpretation on Jesus' reply (Matt. 26.64; Luke 22.70).

22 Liddon, *Divinity*, p. 190.

23 Eusebius, *Praep. ev.* 9.27.

24 *Exod. Rab.* 1.29.

25 *m. Yoma* 6.2. See also Sir. 50.20–21.

26 Greg G. Stafford, *Jehovah's Witnesses Defended: An Answer to Scholars and Critics* (Huntington Beach, CA: Elihu, 2000), pp. 113–61.

27 Deut. 32.39; Isa. 41.4; 43.10; 43.13; 46.4; 48.12; 52.6.

28 John 6.35/41; 8.12; 10.7/9; 10.11/14; 11.25; 14.6; 15.1/5.

29 John 4.26; 6.20; 8.24; 8.28; 8.58; 13.19; 18.5/6/8.

30 Matt. 14.27; Mark 6.50; 13.6; 14.62; Luke 21.8; 22.70; 24.36. (The last of these is, technically, 'I am he'.)

31 Ethelbert Stauffer, 'EGO', in *Theological Dictionary of the New Testament*, vol. 2 (ed. G. Kittel; Grand Rapids, MI: Eerdmans, 1964), p. 353.

8. Jesus the Miracle Worker

[1] There are apparent references, e.g., in Josephus, *Ant.* 18.3.3 (though this passage is much disputed); *b. Sanh.* 43a, 107b; and *t. Hul.* 2.22–23. We also find further evidence of Jewish attitudes to Jesus' miracles reported in Justin Martyr, *Dial.* 69; Origen, *Cels.* 1.38,68; and Eusebius, *Dem. ev.* 3.6.

[2] *b. Ber.* 22–25; *Gen. Rab.* 11.10; *Exod. Rab.* 30.6.

[3] Philo, *Leg.* 1.3.

[4] Tertullian, *Marc.* 4.9.

[5] Tertullian, *Marc.* 4.20, trans. Ernest Evans in *Tertullian: Adversus Marcionem* (Oxford: Clarendon, 1972), p. 369.

[6] See E.P. Sanders, *The Historical Figure of Jesus* (London: Penguin, 1993), p. 138, and Geza Vermes, *The Changing Faces of Jesus* (London: Penguin, 2000), p. 238ff.

[7] Although similar miracles are reported in the ministries of Elijah and Elisha (see 1 Kgs 17.10–16; 2 Kgs 4.1–7,42–44), this one easily eclipses them in sheer scale. As Matthew tells us that the figure of five thousand fed does *not* include women and children, the total figure may run into tens of thousands of people. Such a spectacle gives a broad indication of the kinds of numbers that were following Jesus during his Galilean ministry.

[8] It should be noted that the 'greenness' of the grass here backs up the detail in John's gospel that the Passover festival was near, furnishing further evidence for the fundamental authenticity of the different accounts.

[9] Robert Reymond, *Jesus, Divine Messiah: The New and Old Testament Witness* (Tain: Christian Focus, 2003), p. 410.

[10] It is not beyond the bounds of possibility, however, that Paul is referring to New Testament scriptures (i.e., early prototypes of our present gospels) in Rom. 16.26. Certainly 1 Tim. 5.18, written (if Paul is definitely the author) within a decade of 1 Cor., cites the words of Christ as 'scripture'.

9. Jesus Through the Eyes of Others

[1] See Matt. 14.33; 28.9,17.

[2] Richard Bauckham, 'The Worship of Jesus', in *Anchor Bible Dictionary*, vol. 3 (ed. David N. Freedman; New York: Doubleday, 1992), p. 813.

[3] Ethelbert Stauffer, *Jesus and His Story* (trans. Dorothea M. Barton; London: SCM, 1960), p. 113.

4 Arthur W. Wainwright, *The Trinity in the New Testament* (London: SPCK, 1962), p. 69. Such a possibility might help us to make sense of why, for example, in Rom. 9.5, Paul suddenly appears to describe Jesus as 'God over all, for ever praised'. Like Thomas in John 20.28, or like his own stunned exclamation 'Who are you, Lord?' on the Damascus road, Paul may suddenly have felt compelled in his spirit to express something that at that stage he could not fully explain in his mind.

5 Ralph P. Martin, 'The New Testament Hymns: Background and Development', *Expository Times* 94 (1982–3): p. 136.

6 Larry Hurtado, *Lord Jesus Christ: Devotion to Jesus in Earliest Christianity* (Grand Rapids, MI: Eerdmans, 2003), p. 650.

7 Hurtado, *Lord Jesus Christ*, p. 391.

8 Robert Bowman and Ed Komoszewski, *Putting Jesus in His Place: The Case for the Deity of Christ* (Grand Rapids, MI: Kregel, 2007), p. 49.

9 Bowman and Komoszewski, *Putting Jesus*, p. 50.

10 See also Gal. 6.18; Phil. 4.23; 1 Thess. 3.12–13; 5.28; 2 Thess. 3.5,16,18; 2 Tim. 1.16,18; 4.22; Phlm. 25.

11 Henry Liddon, *The Divinity of Our Lord and Saviour Jesus Christ* (London: Rivington, 12th edn, 1888), p. 375.

12 Tertullian, *Pat.* 13.

13 Murray Harris, *Three Crucial Questions about Jesus* (Carlisle: OM, 1994), p. 64.

14 Pliny, *Ep.* 10.96.7.

15 Hurtado, *Lord Jesus Christ*, p. 73.

16 Bowman and Komoszewski, *Putting Jesus*, p. 167.

17 Robert Reymond, *Jesus, Divine Messiah: The New and Old Testament Witness* (Tain: Christian Focus, 2003), p. 449.

18 Hurtado, *Lord Jesus Christ*, pp. 592–3.

19 Carey Newman, 'God', in *Dictionary of the Later New Testament and Its Developments* (Downers Grove, IL: IVP, 1997), p. 428.

20 *Mart. Ascens. Isa.* 9.27–36.

21 Justin Martyr, *Dial.* 68.

22 Melito of Sardis, fragment from the *Apology to Marcus Aurelius Antoninus*, quoted in the anonymous 'Chronicon Paschale' (c. AD 630).

23 Irenaeus, *Haer.* 1.10.1.

24 Clement of Alexandria, *Paed.* 3.12 (concluding hymn).

25 Tertullian, *Adv. Jud.* 7. In this passage, Tertullian has just reported the impact of the gospel on those parts of Britain beyond the Roman Empire.

26 Origen, *Cels.* 8.13.

27 *Martyrdom of Polycarp* 17.2.

[28] Translation from *The Book of Common Prayer according to the Use of the Episcopal Church* (New York: Church Hymnal Corporation, 1979), p. 111.

[29] *Odes of Sol.* 17, in Rendel Harris and Alphonse Mingana, *The Odes and Psalms of Solomon*, vol. 2 (London: Longmans, Green & Co., 1920), p. 290.

[30] Eusebius, *Hist. eccl.* 5.28.1–6.

[31] Cited in Robert E. Van Voorst, *Jesus outside the New Testament: An Introduction to the Ancient Evidence* (Grand Rapids, MI: Eerdmans, 2000), p. 59.

[32] Celsus, 'On the True Doctrine: A Discourse against the Christians', reproduced by Origen in *Cels.* 8.12.

[33] Cited by Minucius Felix in *Octavius* 29.2.

[34] Cited by Edward Burton in *Testimonies of the Ante-Nicene Fathers to the Divinity of Christ* (Oxford: Clarendon, 1826), p. 147.

[35] Arnobius, *Adversus Gentes* 1.36, in *The Seven Books of Arnobius Adversus Gentes* (trans. Archibald H. Bryce and Hugh Campbell (Edinburgh: T&T Clark, 1871), p. 27.

[36] Lactantius, *Inst.* 4.16.

[37] Tacitus, *Annals* 15.44.5.

[38] Pliny, *Ep.* 10.96.7.

[39] Tertullian, *Apol.* 37. 4.

[40] *Did.* 10.12.

[41] There are definite references in *Eph.* – introduction; 1.1; 7.2; 18.2; 19.3; *Trall.* 7.1; *Rom.* – introduction (twice); 3.3; 6.3; *Smyr.* 1.1; *Poly.* 8.3; and probable mentions in *Eph.* 15.3 and 17.2.

[42] Polycarp, *Letter to the Philippians* 12.2 (not present in all manuscripts).

[43] *2 Clem.* 12.1 and 13.4.

[44] *Diogn.* 7.4.

[45] Bauckham, 'The Worship of Jesus', p. 817.

[46] Quoted in Liddon, *Divinity*, p. 407.

[47] Liddon, *Divinity*, p. 418.

[48] Gerald Bray, 'The Deity of Christ in Church History', in Christopher W. Morgan and Robert A. Peterson, *The Deity of Christ* (Wheaton, IL: Crossway, 2011), p 175.

[49] *b. Git.* 56a.

[50] *t. Sanh.* 9.7. There are probably other ways to interpret this slightly obscure passage; the view here is the one expressed by R. Travers Herford in *Christianity in Talmud and Midrash* (London: Williams & Norgate, 1903), p. 87.

[51] *Yal.* 766 on Num. 23.7. The passage was subsequently removed from the *Yalqut* for fear of provoking retaliation from Christians.

[52] *j. Ta'an.* 65b.

[53] *Pesiq. Rab.* 21 100b.

[54] Apart from Cerinthus and some Gnostic groups who believed in a distinction between the man Jesus and the 'Christ' who descended upon him at his baptism, the main exceptions here are the Ebionites, a group of Jewish Christians who for the most part regarded Jesus purely as a man, chosen and anointed by God. Hans Küng in *Christianity: Essence, History and Future* (London: Continuum 1995), pp. 105–6, cites various writers from Harnack onwards who discussed the influence of this movement on the rise of Islam.

10. Jesus and the Father

[1] See, e.g., Deut. 4.35; 32.39; 1 Kgs 8.60; Isa. 43.10; 44.6 etc.; John 17.3; 1 Cor. 8.4–6; 1 Tim. 1.17; 2.5; Jas 2.19; Jude 25.

[2] See, for instance, Rom. 8.9,35/39 and 1 Cor. 2.16.

[3] Different theories of the attributes associated with the divine names are advanced by Philo (*Somn.* 1.163; *Abr.* 121; *QG* 1.57; 2.16; *QE* 2.68) and later Jewish commentators (e.g. *b. Hag.* 14a; *b. Sanh.* 38b and *Exod. Rab.* 3.6).

[4] Charles F.D. Moule, *The Origin of Christology* (Cambridge: CUP, 1977), p. 7.

[5] Extraordinarily enough, the previous verse, translated in the NIV (and similarly in most other Bibles), 'I have not learned wisdom, nor I have I attained to the knowledge of the Holy One' actually ends in a plural. In *Young's Literal Translation* it appears as 'Nor have I learned wisdom, Yet the knowledge of the Holy Ones I know'. Is this implying that the pairing of the heavenly creator and his 'son' in verse 4 is a reflection of the relationship between Yahweh and Wisdom at the beginning of Proverbs, where see the *same* concealed plural in the reference to the 'Holy One[s]' (Prov. 9.10)?

[6] Robert Bowman and Ed Komoszewski, *Putting Jesus in His Place: The Case for the Deity of Christ* (Grand Rapids, MI: Kregel, 2007), p. 240.

[7] Robert Reymond, *Jesus, Divine Messiah: The New and Old Testament Witness* (Tain: Christian Focus, 2003), p. 390.

[8] Tertullian, *Prax.* 17.

[9] *b. Ber.* 61b. The exact date of his death is disputed.

[10] It is worth noting that the Hebrew word for 'one' (*'e·ḥāḏ*) in the *Shema'* of Deut. 6.4, like the Greek word *hen* in John 10.30, is capable of pointing to a composite unity. The same word, for instance, is used in Gen. 2.24: 'That is why a man leaves his father and mother and is united to his wife, and they become *one* flesh.'

[11] Geza Vermes, *The Changing Faces of Jesus* (London: Penguin, 2000), p. 47.

[12] Peter Lewis, *The Glory of Christ* (London: Hodder & Stoughton, 1992), p. 79.

[13] Reymond, *Jesus*, p. 208.

[14] Stanley J. Grenz and Denise Muir Kjesbo, *Women in the Church: A Biblical Theology of Women in Ministry* (Downers Grove, IL: IVP, 1995), pp. 153–4. Richard Bauckham, *Jesus and the God of Israel: God Crucified and Other Studies on the New Testament's Christology of Divine Identity* (Milton Keynes: Paternoster, 2008), p. 106, makes a similar point with respect to John 10.30.

[15] John Milton, 'Ode on the Morning of Christ's Nativity' (1629), first published in his *Poems of 1645* (London: Ruth Raworth, 1645), p. 1.

[16] See, e.g., *Ign. Rom.* 6.3 and Tertullian, *Marc.* 5.5.

[17] David F. Wells, *The Person of Christ: A Biblical and Historical Analysis of the Incarnation* (Westchester, IL: Crossway, 1984), p. 64.

[18] Edmund L. Strong, *Lectures on the Incarnation of God* (London: Longmans, 1920), p. 68. (We should guard, here, however, against any idea of Christ somehow being two persons in one, a view that was later proposed by Nestorius, but ultimately condemned by the wider church.)

[19] Many theologians, following the example of Rudolf Bultmann, have even suggested on this basis that Jesus actually considered the 'Son of Man' to be someone other than himself (see, e.g., Wolfhart Pannenberg, *Jesus, God and Man* [trans. Lewis L. Wilkins and Duane A. Priebe; London: SCM, 1968], p. 327).

[20] Examples include Matt. 5.35; Mark 2.19; 12.35–37; Luke 24.26–27; John 4.10; 6.46; 10.2–4.

[21] cf., e.g., Gen. 4.23–24; 1 Cor. 1.13; 3.5; 2 Cor. 12.1–5, and perhaps the references to 'the beloved disciple' in John's gospel.

11. Jesus and Eternity

[1] Eusebius, *Vit. Const.* 3.4.

[2] Eusebius, *Vit. Const.* 2.72.

[3] Ammianus Marcellinus, *Res Gestae* 21.16.18.

[4] Gregory of Nyssa, *Deit.* (PG 46:557–9).

[5] Gregory of Nazianzus, *Or. Bas.* 27.2.

[6] Quoted from Charles T. Cullen, *Jefferson's Extracts from the Gospels: The Papers of Thomas Jefferson, Second Series* (Princeton, NJ: Princeton University Press, 1983), p 409. Although his prediction was never

fulfilled, Harvard University maintained a continuous succession of Unitarian presidents for 123 years from 1810 onwards.

7 More accurately, Newton was an Anglican with Arian beliefs. Unitarianism was not officially tolerated in England until almost a century after his death.

8 The achievements of the Unitarian minister Joseph Priestley (1733–1804) range from the discovery of oxygen on the one hand to the invention of soda water on the other. He was also the first person to work out (in 1770) that pencil marks could be removed with a rubber!

9 Darwin's mother was a Unitarian and a year of his education was spent at a Unitarian school. The Unitarian church in Shrewsbury contains a memorial tablet declaring that he was 'a member of and a constant worshipper in this church'.

10 Unitarianism denies the fall of humankind and is therefore characterized by an enormous optimism about human nature. Chamberlain and Obama came from strong Unitarian family backgrounds and both regularly attended Unitarian churches during their childhood. Whether there is possible any connection here with their domestic or foreign policies while in power is, of course, an entirely open question!

11 This process was accelerated in 1961 when the American Unitarian Association amalgamated with the Universalist Church of America. There are a number of other sects, however, notably the Christadelphians and The Way International, that preserve earlier Unitarian views about the nature of Christ.

12 Derek Kidner, *The Proverbs: An Introduction and Commentary* (London: Tyndale, 1964), p. 79.

13 Symmachus, who rejected the deity of Christ, translated the passage as 'the Lord possesses me, the beginning of his ways'.

14 Strictly speaking, the phrase 'before the mountains' also appears in many English translations at Mic. 6.1, but the context and meaning are different (as is the Hebrew).

15 Athanasius, *Decr.* 15. The same thought appears in the *Encyclical Letter of Alexander*, section 4 (ad 321), very possibly written by Athanasius, which is translated by John Henry Newman in *Select Treatises of St. Athanasius in Controversy with the Arians* (London: Pickering, 1881), pp. 5–6.

16 Larry. W. Hurtado, *One God, One Lord: Early Christian Devotion and Ancient Jewish Monotheism* (Philadelphia: Fortress, 1988), p. 47.

17 In chapter 24 of the apocryphal book Sirach (Ecclesiasticus), Wisdom is quite definitely described as 'created', but the book, for all its beauty and quiet humour, contains several doctrines which directly contradict those of the New Testament. Moreover its conclusions run

counter to those in Wisdom of Solomon, where Wisdom is clearly portrayed as an extension of God's own being.

[18] See, e.g., Gen. 48.13–14; 49.3–4; 1 Chr. 5.1–2; 26.10.

[19] Robert Bowman and Ed Komoszewski, *Putting Jesus in His Place: The Case for the Deity of Christ* (Grand Rapids, MI: Kregel, 2007), p. 104.

[20] Robert Reymond, *Jesus, Divine Messiah: The New and Old Testament Witness* (Tain: Christian Focus, 2003), p. 437.

[21] See Bowman and Komoszewski, *Putting Jesus*, pp. 108, 317 (n. 13).

[22] Martin Hengel, *Studies in Early Christology* (Edinburgh: T&T Clark, 1995), p. 225.

[23] *C. Ap.* 2.23.

[24] The use of *agapētos* in the New Testament is coloured by the strong overtones of sacrifice and loss with which it appears in the Septuagint. Thus it appears in connection with Abraham's planned sacrifice of Isaac in Gen. 22.2; Jephthah's sacrifice of his daughter in Judg. 11.34–40, and in passages such as Amos 8.10 and Zech. 12.10, which were understood by later Christian writers as prophecies of the crucifixion.

[25] Henry Liddon, *The Divinity of Our Lord and Saviour Jesus Christ* (London: Rivington, 12th edn, 1888), p. 253.

[26] Bowman and Komoszewski, *Putting Jesus*, pp. 79–80.

[27] Liddon, *Divinity*, p. 314.

[28] Irenaeus, *Haer.* 1.8.5.

[29] Athanasius, *Letters to Serapion* 1.10, in C.R.B. Shapland, *The Letters of Saint Athanasius Concerning the Holy Spirit* (London: Epworth, 1951), p. 85.

[30] Robert C. Gregg and Dennis E. Groh, *Early Arianism: A View of Salvation* (London: SCM, 1981), p. 8.

[31] Although we are discussing groups here that *deny* the deity of Christ, the same can be said of sects (such as the Mormons or various Oneness Pentecostal groups) which *distort* the doctrine. In the case of Mormonism, it is worth noting Gregg and Groh's later observation that the Arians considered Jesus, as a created being, one who 'advanced by moral excellence to God' as an example for our own salvation (p. 65). To a degree, Mormonism applies an Arian view of Christ, as a created being with a definite beginning in time, to all three members of the Trinity.

[32] Joseph J. Gurney, *Biblical Notes and Dissertations: Chiefly Intended to Confirm and Illustrate the Doctrine of the Deity of Christ: With Some Remarks on the Practical Importance of that Doctrine* (London: Rivington, 2nd edn, 1833), p. 480.

[33] Alan Gomes, 'The Deity of Christ and the Cults', in *The Deity of Christ* (ed. Christopher W. Morgan and Robert A. Peterson; Wheaton, IL: Crossway, 2011), p. 246.

[34] Unitarian Universalist Association, *Report of the Committee on Goals* (Boston: UUA, 1967), p. 26.

[35] James Casebolt and T. Nieko, 'Some UUs are more U. than U. Theological Self-Descriptors Chosen by Unitarian Universalists', in *Review of Religious Research* 46.3 (2005): pp. 235–42.

[36] Alan Gomes, 'Deity of Christ and the Cults', p. 250.

12. Who Do You Say I Am?

[1] The church historian Eusebius quotes Papias, the bishop of Hierapolis in the early second century, as saying that 'Mark having become the interpreter of Peter, wrote down accurately whatsoever he remembered' (Eusebius, *Hist. eccl.* 3.39).

[2] 2 Pet. 1.1. (For a defence of his authorship of this disputed letter see ch. 3, n. 22.)

[3] *Mek.* on Exod. 21.2.

[4] Joseph Ratzinger (Pope Benedict XVI), *Jesus of Nazareth: Holy Week, from the Entrance into Jerusalem to the Resurrection* (trans. Adrian J. Walker; London, Catholic Truth Society, 2008), p. 277.

Through My Enemy's Eyes

Envisioning Reconciliation in Israel–Palestine

Salim Munayer and Lisa Loden

This unique book addresses reconciliation in the context of the Israeli Messianic Jewish and Palestinian Christian divide. This remarkable work, written in collaboration by a local Palestinian Christian and an Israeli Messianic Jew addresses head-on divisive theological issues (and their political implications); land, covenant, prophecy, eschatology. The struggle for reconciliation is painful and often extremely difficult for all of us. This work seeks to show a way forward.

'This is a unique conversation in which each partner gives full expression to all that they are and think and feel about themelves and the conflict in their land. Above all we come to share the hope and courage that shines through the pain and struggle.' *Christopher Wright, Langham Paternership.*

'Given the divides between their communities, this book is a remarkable achievement, a cry of hope from the land where Jesus walked.' *Chris Rice Duke Divinity School, US.*

Salim Munayer is on the faculty of Bethlehem Bible College, Bethlehem, Palestine and director of Musalaha Ministry of Reconciliation, Jerusalem, Israel. Lisa Loden is on the faculty of Nazareth Evangelical Theological Seminary, Nazareth, Israel, and Director of Advancing Professional Excellence, Israel.

978-1-84227-748-5 (e-book 978-1-84227-859-8)